UPROOTED

ALSO BY ALBERT MARRIN

Black Gold: The Story of Oil in Our Lives

FDR and the American Crisis

Flesh and Blood So Cheap: The Triangle Fire and Its Legacy

Thomas Paine: Crusader for Liberty

A Volcano Beneath the Snow: John Brown's War Against Slavery

THE JAPANESE AMERICAN EXPERIENCE DURING WORLD WAR II

UPROOTED

ALBERT MARRIN

ALFRED A. KNOPF  NEW YORK

THIS IS A BORZOI BOOK PUBLISHED BY ALFRED A. KNOPF

Text copyright © 2016 by Albert Marrin
Jacket photographs copyright © by U.S. National Archives

For picture credits, see page 240.

Visit us on the Web! randomhouseteens.com

Educators and librarians, for a variety of teaching tools, visit us at RHTeachersLibrarians.com

Library of Congress Cataloging-in-Publication Data
Names: Marrin, Albert.
Title: Uprooted : the Japanese American experience during World War II / Albert Marrin.
Description: New York : Alfred A. Knopf, 2016. | Audience: 12-up.
Identifiers: LCCN 2015025406 | ISBN 978-0-553-50936-6 (trade) | ISBN 978-0-553-50937-3 (lib. bdg.) |
    ISBN 978-0-553-50938-0 (ebook)
Subjects: LCSH: Japanese Americans—Evacuation and relocation, 1942–1945—Juvenile literature. | World War,
    1939–1945—Japanese Americans—Juvenile literature.
Classification: LCC D769.8.A6 M329 2016 | DDC 940.53/170973—dc23

The text of this book is set in 12-point Granjon.

MANUFACTURED IN MALAYSIA
October 2016
10 9 8 7 6 5 4 3 2 1

First Edition

For those who seek *denshō,* "to pass on to future generations"

We were suddenly uprooted. . . . We were in shock. You'd be in shock. You'd be bewildered. You'd be humiliated. You can't believe this is happening to you. To think this could happen in the United States. We were citizens. We did nothing. It was only because of our race.

—Miné Okubo, artist

CONTENTS

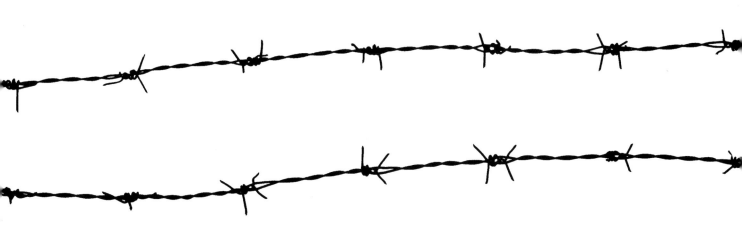

DAY OF INFAMY

Yesterday, December 7, 1941—a date which will live in infamy—
the United States of America was suddenly and deliberately attacked
by naval and air forces of the Empire of Japan.
—PRESIDENT FRANKLIN D. ROOSEVELT (DECEMBER 8, 1941)

On this bright Sunday morning, deck crews scurried about, hurrying to make final preparations. A huge flag bearing the red rays of the Rising Sun fluttered from the tall radio mast of each ship. These ships had graceful, poetic names: *Misty Island, Shimmering Mist, Haze, Daybreak Cloud,* and *Wind on the Beach.* Such names, however, belied the terrific firepower of the thirteen battleships, cruisers, and destroyers of the task force. At its heart were the six aircraft carriers they protected. The flagship, the 36,500-ton carrier *Red Castle,* steamed ahead, followed by the *Flying Dragon, Green Dragon, Increased Joy, Crane Flying in Heaven,* and *Lucky Crane.* Their objective was a shallow harbor on the western coast of Oahu in the Hawaiian

Islands, the U.S. Navy's chief Pacific Ocean base. Native people called it Wai Momi (Pearl Waters) for the pearl-bearing oysters that once were plentiful there—Pearl Harbor.

The coming attack was part of a grand scheme to make Japan the ruler of Asia. To that end, the country's forces had invaded China four years earlier, in 1937. However, to succeed, Japan's military rulers decided they had to destroy the American fleet at Pearl Harbor. They knew their action would ignite global war—a Second World War—for the armies of German tyrant Adolf Hitler were already rampaging across Europe. What they could not know was that the conflict would be the greatest war of all time, claiming the lives of over seventy million, mostly civilians. This number, however, is far from the war's total cost, which can never be known. Because for each person killed, we must add countless others wounded and crippled, widowed and orphaned.[1]

At 6:00 a.m., the carriers turned into the wind to launch their planes from a position 270 miles north of Pearl Harbor. At a signal from the *Red Castle,* pilots raced their motors. As the planes sped forward, deckhands shouted *"Banzai!,"* meaning "Long life!," "Hurrah!," and "Forward!" Hours earlier, on the other side of the globe, in Washington, D.C.,

A Japanese navy carrier attack plane takes off for Pearl Harbor as its crewmen shout *"Banzai!"* (December 7, 1941)

Operation Magic, a top-secret program for decoding Japanese radio signals, had told President Franklin D. Roosevelt that an attack was coming, but not where. So the War Department sent an alert to bases throughout the Pacific. Yet communication foul-ups prevented the message from reaching Pearl Harbor until *after* the attack.

It was a normal peacetime Sunday morning at Pearl Harbor. The navy ships were at anchor and tied up at their docks. No bugle calls woke their crews. Sunday was a day of rest, and captains ordered "late hammocks," so the sailors could get up whenever they liked. That was good, since many nursed hangovers from Saturday night in Honolulu's saloons, dance halls, and "social clubs."

At 7:55 a.m., early risers heard the drone of motors overhead. Moments later, 360 Japanese raiders—fighters, dive-bombers, torpedo planes—swooped

The USS *Shaw* explodes during the Japanese raid on Pearl Harbor. (December 7, 1941)

down, each heading for its assigned target. Meeting little organized resistance, within a half hour they sank, ran aground, or severely damaged 18 warships. Three battleships became total wrecks, and 177 planes that had been parked on airfield runways were blown to bits, with a loss of only 29 Japanese planes and pilots. The enemy killed 2,403 Americans and injured 1,178 others. The next day, President Roosevelt asked Congress to declare war on Japan.

Americans often idealize the "good war." It surely was a just war, and, in that sense, good. The United States did not fire the first shots; it fought in self-defense, but also to rid the world of Asian and European tyrannies. Americans fought, said President Roosevelt, for every person's right to enjoy the Four Freedoms: freedom of speech, freedom of religion, freedom from want, and freedom from fear.

But as Civil War general William Tecumseh Sherman famously said: "War is all hell." A man I knew, a former infantryman, recently joined his long-gone friends from the Pacific campaigns. "We were always at the spear-point," he would say, always risking their lives at the front. Glib talk of the "good war" infuriated him. Those who experienced it at the sharp end often called it the "dirty war," a crusher of minds and bodies. "Combat is torture," wrote one who knew, "and it will reduce you, sooner or later, to a quivering wreck."[2]

The war brought out the worst in people who in peacetime would never have dreamed of harming another live being. Marine corporal Eugene B. Sledge—"Sledgehammer" to his friends—described how combat in the Pacific changed him from a gentle eighteen-year-old who loved birds into a killer. "To me the war was insanity,"

FDR signs the declaration of war against Japan at the White House. (December 8, 1941)

Sledge recalled bitterly. "We had all become hardened. We were out there, human beings, the most highly developed form of life on earth, fighting each other like animals." It was a living nightmare. "The war I knew was totally savage," Sledge continued. "It was savage. We were savages." Some Japanese soldiers used the same words to describe what the war made of them. Nobody had a monopoly on virtue, and each side committed atrocities. Whether they did so to the same degree is still a matter of debate.[3]

On a deeper level, the Second World War was about racism. Racism is more than bias, an opinion formed without judging fairly. The term *racism* as used in this book refers to an ideology, a set of beliefs, fervently held, about others and how the world works. At its core, it insists that God, gods, or Mother Nature has divided humanity into distinct groups—races—with shared qualities. Racists, or those who believe in racism, hold that these groups are arranged pyramid-like, with the "best" or "superior" at the top, and the "worst" or "inferior" at the bottom.

Rightly called humanity's most dangerous myth, racism has no scientific basis. Modern genetics, neuroscience,

and physiology have proved there are no basic differences between races. Apart from skin color, hair texture, and facial features, all human beings are essentially alike. We inherit physical traits from our parents, but social traits—morality, manners, ideas, religious beliefs, work habits—are not, and cannot be, inherited. We acquire these from our upbringing, education, and life experiences.

Those who regard themselves as "superior" have claimed rights and privileges, wealth and opportunities, denied to their "inferiors." Though unsupported by science, racism has been a potent force for evil in modern history. Racist ideas have been used to uphold political, social, and economic systems aimed at exploiting those deemed worthy of no better. Racists have justified slavery, discrimination, oppression, and conquest. By the same token, racism "explains" that when things go wrong, the outcomes are the fault of the "Other," not of oneself or real-life conditions.

At its worst, racism has led to, and justified, mass murder. During the Second World War, Adolf Hitler aimed at world conquest and at exterminating the Jewish people, whom he declared an "evil" race, the enemy of humanity doing the devil's work. While acting on this notion, he had six million European Jews, including as many as one and a half million children, starved, shot, or smothered by poison gas. We also should keep in mind that other forms of racism—Japanese, British, and American—made the war in Asia and the Pacific all the more horrific.

Calling someone a racist in today's America is no small thing. It is a serious charge, with the power to bring public shame and end careers. Yet it has not always been so. Long before Pearl Harbor, Asian and African Americans were a focus of racial hatred. Against this background, the attack created such hysteria that President Roosevelt, citing "military necessity," approved the uprooting of all people of Japanese ancestry, citizens and non-citizens alike, living on the West Coast. Most spent the next two to three years in what officials delicately called "relocation centers," in some of the nation's most unpleasant places.

How could this have happened in a nation dedicated to the Four Freedoms? The short answer: Our government failed in its duty to protect the rights of everyone living in the United States. Dangerous times call for cool heads and balanced judgment, for clear thinking based on facts. Sadly, these qualities were scarce in the chaotic early days of the Second World War. "Japanese aggression," historian John W. Dower writes, "provoked a response bordering on the apocalyptic," whereby countless Americans dreaded the victory of Satan unless they won the war. Thus, the fear and insecurity produced by the Pearl Harbor disaster became emotional rocket fuel, energizing long-held hatreds.[4]

A proverb says, "Time heals all wounds." But the experiences of Japanese Americans in the last century still evoke strong feelings because of lingering memories of injustice but also because those events pose vital questions.

In wartime, the price of defeat may be the loss of territory, even an end to national existence. Given such high stakes, must liberty be sacrificed to security? Or is it possible to balance liberty and security in some way? Is it true that "the end justifies the means" and "necessity knows no law"? May the government, led by the president, do as it thinks best in the name of "military necessity" and "national security"? If so, what are the limits, if any? At what cost in lives, safety, and property must the government follow every detail of the law? Was the uprooting and confinement of Japanese Americans justified in the context of wartime? These questions have no easy answers.

The historian's job is to explain the behavior of human beings in the past. Yet to explain is not to explain away, much less excuse. It is to see how people saw themselves and their world, made choices, and acted according to their beliefs and interests as they understood them at the time. Even so, the story we tell here is not pretty—far from it. On the side of the Imperial Japanese enemy, it shows how racism and militarism can affect a sensitive and creative people. On the American side, with its own brand of racism, the story reveals a shameful chapter in our nation's history. For it shows that freedom is not free and that democracies do not automatically live up to their declared ideals. Democracies, unhappily, are also vulnerable to hysteria and racial hatred.

CHAPTER I

THE PACIFIC AGE

*The age of the Pacific Ocean begins, mysterious and unfathomable
in its meaning for our own future.*
—FREDERICK JACKSON TURNER, "THE WEST AND AMERICAN IDEALS" (1914)

OLD JAPAN

At first, there was only heaven and a salty, jelly-like slime shimmering below it. Two divine beings, Izanagi (Male Who Invites) and Izanami (Female Who Invites), stood above the slime on the Floating Bridge of Heaven. Slowly, Izanagi dipped his jeweled spear into the formless mass. As he withdrew it, droplets slid off the point and hardened to form the islands of Japan, the first land on our planet. The couple then came down to Earth and married. Being divine, both could bear children. From his left eye, Izanagi produced the sun goddess Amaterasu Omikami (She Who Illuminates the World). Eventually, her grandson, Jimmu Tenno, became Japan's first emperor. His descendants have reigned ever since, for more than 2,600 years, history's longest unbroken royal line. The sun's disk and the rays of the Rising Sun depicted on Japanese flags symbolize the nation's divine origins.

This charming story is just that, an ancient way of explaining the unknown. For Japan's origins are hidden in the mists of time. What is certain is that Japan is a chain of four main islands and 4,072 smaller ones, some little more than large rocks. The island chain extends southwest to northeast for 1,200 miles, roughly the length of the east coast of the United States. Japan's four largest islands—Kyushu, Shikoku, Honshu, and Hokkaido—have a combined land area of 145,000 square miles, about the size of the state of Montana.

Geologists, scientists who study the earth's crust, believe that powerful forces created the islands. A zone of active volcanoes and violent earthquakes called the Ring of Fire surrounds the Pacific Ocean. Over millions of years, eruptions and upheavals formed new land, and they continue to do so. Japan is famous for earthquakes and has, on average, twenty a day! Though these

A painting of Izanami and Izanagi creating Japan. (c. 1885)

are usually minor and hardly noticed, severe tremors have caused frightful destruction and loss of life. In 1923, Japan's worst earthquake all but erased the port city of Yokohama and nearby Tokyo, the capital. Within an hour, the tremors, and the fires they ignited, left 115,000 dead, 363,000 injured, and two million homeless.[1]

Nobody knows precisely where the Japanese people came from. Scientists, however, think they did not originate in the islands that eventually became their home. It is likely that in prehistoric times, before written history began, settlers came in small groups from the mainland of Asia, particularly Korea, barely a hundred miles away. Apparently, others made their way from distant Pacific islands: Borneo, Java, and the Philippines. The Japanese, then, are a nation of migrants from various places who intermarried over many generations to form one people.

In the sixth century, with Europe slipping into the Dark Ages after the collapse of the Roman Empire, Chinese traders visited what they called Jihpen (Land of Sunrise). Japanese people referred to it as Nippon (Land of the Rising Sun). The Chinese name reached the West as Japun—Japan. Chinese scholars also brought Buddhism, a religion that teaches happiness is achieved by freeing oneself from attachment to worldly things, and arts such as making fine pottery, ceramic tiles, and scroll paintings. Above all, Chinese scribes introduced writing. The Japanese then adapted Chinese character script to their language.[2]

Though descended from the sun goddess, the emperor was a figurehead with little power to influence events. Power lay in the hands of several hundred *daimyo*, or the headmen of large extended families called clans. Accountable only to themselves, these great lords lived in stone castles and ruled their local districts, even entire provinces. Poor farm families worked their lord's personal lands and their own small plots from sunrise to sunset. Besides paying him taxes in rice, the basic food crop, these peasants did whatever else he demanded, such as stonework, woodcutting, and well digging. In return, the daimyo gave protection.

Lacking a strong central government, Japan was a chaotic land. The daimyo fought incessantly to gain land and power and to keep what they already had. In doing so, they depended on a unique social class: the *samurai,* or "one who serves." Samurai looked and acted differently from Japan's three other classes: farmers, merchants, and priests. They shaved the top of their heads in front, leaving the hair at the back and sides gathered, tied, and doubled over to form a topknot. Between wars, they practiced calligraphy, or elegant script, painted delicate pictures on rice paper or silk, and wrote poetry. Samurai saw poetry as a manly art, a reflection of an individual's soul. One wrote, "A military man without poetry is a savage, not a samurai." A tenth-century author further explained: "It is poetry which, without effort, moves heaven and earth . . . smooths the relations of men and women, and calms the hearts of fierce warriors." Writing and reciting poetry is an ancient tradition that is very much a part of the modern Japanese culture.[3]

The samurai was, above all, a warrior. Starting around the age of five, he underwent physical and mental toughening. He learned to walk barefoot in snow, and to master fear, he spent nights alone in haunted graveyards. Complaining was for sissies. "It is a disgrace to feel hungry," he was told when his empty belly growled. Crying showed weakness. "Does a little booby cry for any ache?" parents scolded. "What a coward to cry for a trifling pain! What will you do when your arm is cut off in battle? What when you are called upon to commit *hara-kiri* [suicide]?"[4]

Known as a "two-sword man," the samurai carried a long sword for fighting and a shorter one for committing

A two-sword samurai in armor. (c. 1860)

suicide, each made by a master craftsman who devoted his life to creating fine blades. Considered major works of art today, worthy of display in museums, genuine samurai swords are as deadly as they are beautiful. More than a weapon, the sword represented its owner's soul forged in gleaming steel.

Wielded with a strong arm, it could slice through armor "as easily as a sharp knife cuts a tender [slab of meat]."[5]

A sword's master lived by the code of *Bushido,* the "way of the warrior," which originated in China, though the name itself came into use in Japan in the early 1600s. Bushido taught honesty, mercy, sincerity, refinement (good manners), courage, duty, loyalty, and self-control, the most important virtue. Lack of self-control made a man into a beast. One showed self-control by avoiding needless violence. "To be incited by mere impetuosity to violent action cannot be called valor," samurai learned. "If you affect valor and act with violence, the world will in the end detest you and look upon you as wild beasts." Dying for an unjust cause was unworthy of an honorable man, merely a "dog's death."[6]

Violating the code of Bushido brought "loss of face"—disgrace and shame. Only by committing hara-kiri could a samurai cleanse his "face"— his honor. Hara-kiri called for the offender, clad in a white robe to show his pure intention, to kneel before witnesses, bow his head, and slowly cut open his abdomen. The Japanese considered the abdomen the seat of human emotions, so exposing the intestines by belly cutting was believed to free the samurai's spirit while redeeming his honor. When the pain became unbearable, as it always did, a friend beheaded him with a fighting sword.

SOUTHERN BARBARIANS

In 1192, a powerful lord named Yorimoto Minamoto declared the emperor to be so holy that it was a grave insult to expect him to govern. So he forced the emperor to declare him *shogun,* or "supreme military leader." For almost seven centuries, Japan's emperors remained virtual prisoners in their palace at Kyoto, Japan's first capital, where they lived in luxury, powerless while generations of shoguns governed the country.

Things began to change when the Japanese encountered people they called the "southern barbarians." During the sixteenth century, Europeans sailed across the Indian Ocean in search of Asian spices, silks, and jewels. In time, the Dutch took over the Spice Islands (now called the Moluccas, an archipelago within Indonesia). Portuguese merchants set up shop in Goa, on the west coast of India. The English built "factories," or trading posts, in India and ultimately conquered the entire subcontinent, except Goa.

In 1549, Francis Xavier, a Jesuit missionary, arrived in Japan from India. The future Roman Catholic saint found the Japanese very different from the Indians he had converted to Christianity. "They prize and honor all that has to do with war, and there is nothing of which they are so proud as of weapons adorned with gold and silver," he wrote. "They always wear swords . . . both in and out of the house, and when they go to sleep they hang them at the bed's head. In short, they value arms more than any people I have ever seen."[7]

Catholic and Protestant missionaries and merchants—English, Dutch, Portuguese, Spanish—settled in the port city of Nagasaki, on the southern island of Kyushu. Japanese and Europeans found each other strange, even repulsive. Japanese saw the outsiders as fairy-tale monsters come to life, "hobgoblins" with "sickly white coloring," like that of a dead squid. Europeans, reeking of dirt and sweat, squeezed their nostrils between their fingers, blew their snot on the ground, and wiped their noses on their sleeves.[8]

Japanese people prized cleanliness. In the seventeenth century, English traveler Peter Mundy described what sounds like an early version of Kleenex. "They blow their Noses with a certaine sofft and tough kind of paper which they carry aboutt them in small peeces," Mundy wrote, "which having used, they Fling away as a Fillthy thing." Humble laborers bathed several times a week, nude men and women together in high-sided wooden tubs filled with hot water. Europeans thought such a display of bare flesh immoral.[9]

The missionaries' conversion of thousands of Japanese worried the Imperial authorities, who thought Christianity promoted disloyalty. Therefore, Iemitsu Tokugawa, the shogun, ordered Japan's 280,000 Christians to abandon their faith and pledge loyalty to Buddhism. To prove their sincerity, they had to stamp on images of Jesus Christ and the Virgin Mary. Those who refused died publicly under torture, often by crucifixion, as a warning to others.

In 1635, Iemitsu Tokugawa declared Japan a "closed country." Except for a few Dutch traders, forced to live on a tiny island in Nagasaki's harbor, all foreigners had to leave on pain of death.

The shogun banned the building of oceangoing ships, and Japanese caught trying to leave went to the executioner. He went further yet, banning foreign devices such as firearms. This policy made sense to the samurai. Guns were ugly, clumsy, and noisy, unfit for honorable men, especially since they made it possible for humble folk to shoot the best swordsmen from a distance. The banning of firearms, however, froze Japanese military technology. For the next two centuries, it did not advance beyond the sword, spear, and bow.

Yet Japan's isolation would not last forever. Events in China forced the closed country to reopen its gates.

CHINA IN TURMOIL

The Chinese saw themselves as superior to all other people, and certainly to Europeans. They called their land Zhongguo, or the "Middle Kingdom." They believed that heaven was round and cast a circular shadow on the flat, square earth and that China lay at the center of the circle, a position indicating that China was most favored by the gods. China's emperors believed they had the "Mandate of Heaven," ruling because the gods chose them above all

others. With a civilization going back 3,500 years, China was the wealthiest country on the planet. Its many inventions included silk cloth, gunpowder, rockets, paper, printing with movable type, suspension bridges, canal locks, matches, the umbrella, and a method of drilling for oil. Until the twentieth century, China produced more iron than did all of Europe combined. Chinese painting, architecture, and literature set the standard of excellence throughout Asia.

The Chinese believed that surrounding their Middle Kingdom were the lands of the "outer barbarians," whose inhabitants were loud, vulgar, and ugly. Westerners, for example, had big noses, in Chinese folklore a mark of evil—thus the popular nickname *fan-kuei,* "foreign devils." An imperial official explained: "At bottom, they belong to the class of brutes"—wild animals. An official history of China described in gory detail the brutes' method of boiling and eating babies. Another account told how some European towns had only women, who became pregnant by staring at their own shadows. So the less China had to do with the outer barbarians, the better.[10]

Orders came from the Forbidden

City, the red-walled palace in Peking (now Beijing), barring Western traders from China. However, the emperors graciously allowed them to have a trading post on a sliver of land outside the seaport of Canton (now known as Guangzhou). There, merchants bought Chinese silk, porcelain, and tea for resale in their home markets. In the 1700s, tea came only from China, which is why we still say a very valuable object is worth "all the tea in China." Dried tea leaves, steeped in boiling water, were a necessity of life, particularly in England, where the average family spent 5 percent of its yearly income on tea. "A nice cup of tea" lifted one's spirits, calmed jittery nerves, and took the edge off hunger.[11]

Yet there was a catch. Foreigners had to pay for their purchases in Chinese money—that is, in silver. This requirement benefited China, because the increasing amounts of silver kept prices there stable and taxes low. For England, the West's largest consumer of tea, paying in silver had the opposite effect. It drained away the precious metal, causing prices to rise, while forcing the British government to raise taxes to pay its bills. Even windowpanes in a house, legal documents such as wills, and the

wheels on carts were taxed. Higher taxes caused unrest, leading to riots in which British soldiers fired into mobs, killing hundreds at a time.

In 1793, King George III sent an ambassador to Beijing to ask Emperor Qianlong to accept manufactured goods instead of silver in payment for tea. The "Son of Heaven" refused. "I set no value on objects strange or ingenious, and have no use for your country's manufactures," he replied indignantly. "Our Celestial Empire possesses all things in prolific abundance and lacks no product within its own borders. There [is] therefore no need to import the manufactures of outside barbarians

An advertisement showcasing the uses of laudanum, a medicine prepared from opium and morphine. (Date unknown)

in exchange for our own produce." Obviously, the English had to find something the Chinese could not resist, and make them pay for it in silver. And that something was opium.[12]

Opium is made from the dried sap of a type of poppy first cultivated in ancient Turkey, Egypt, and Iraq. Gradually, its use spread to Europe, where it became a panacea, a cure-all for nearly every illness. Eaten or drunk occasionally, and in tiny doses, the drug seemed magical. Doctors gave it as a painkiller; they still prescribe morphine and codeine, chemicals derived from raw opium. Opium stopped severe diarrhea, which can cause death by dehydrating the body. Women relied on opium to relieve their "monthly troubles" and the pain of childbirth. Into the twentieth century, opium was the "babysitter in a bottle." Mothers gave teaspoons of opium-laced "calming syrups" to soothe cranky infants and relieve teething pains. Syrups were sold in all drugstores, without a doctor's prescription or government control. However, larger doses, or small doses taken frequently, caused addiction. Addicts became physically dependent on the drug. Without taking it in ever greater amounts, they suffered the agonies of withdrawal: fever, chills, trembling, nausea, vomiting, cramps, constipation, sweating.

Around the year 500, Arab traders brought opium and poppy seeds to China. Though opium from the variety of poppies grown in China was mild, and its medical use spread slowly, the emperors banned it as a health hazard. Addiction remained a low-level problem in China until the early 1800s. By then, farmers in British-ruled India were growing a far more potent variety of the opium poppy. The government had a monopoly on the production and sale of the drug. After each harvest, the authorities purified the raw opium in special state-owned facilities and then auctioned it, at a huge profit, to merchants. These later sold it for silver to Chinese smugglers, who in turn sold it to opium dens, shops where users came to take the drug. As if that were not bad enough, the Chinese preferred to smoke opium in pipes. This method sent the vapor directly into smokers' lungs, causing rapid addiction.

By 1839, an imperial official noted, opium had become "a life-destroying drug threatening to degrade the entire Chinese people to a level with reptiles, dogs and swine." To enforce the

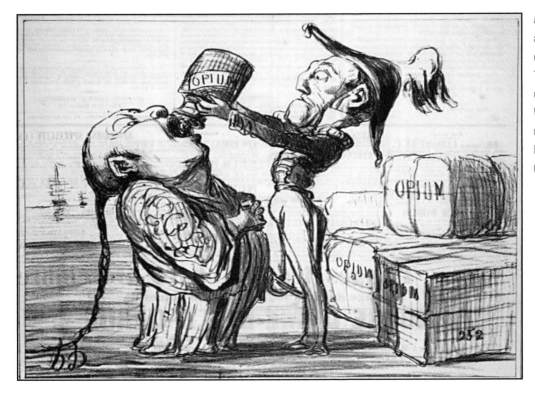

A French cartoon showing a Western soldier forcing opium on a Chinese man. The cartoon was published during the Second Opium War, which was a joint military operation by England and France. (December 29, 1858)

ban, police destroyed tons of smuggled "black mud" in Canton. Great Britain responded by declaring war in the name of "free trade": every nation's "God-given" right to sell its goods wherever and to whomever it pleased.[13]

Britain easily defeated China in two Opium Wars (1839–1842 and 1856–1860). The Middle Kingdom may have been at the center of the world, but its military was no match for Britain's "devil ships"—steam-powered warships—and troops armed with modern guns. After both defeats, China had to pay a heavy fine and open more

A French cartoon depicting China being divided among other nations for their own consumption. From left to right, Queen Victoria of the United Kingdom, William II of Germany, Nicholas II of Russia, the French Marianne, and a samurai representing Japan slice up the pie while a Chinese official looks on, outraged but powerless. (January 16, 1898)

seaports to foreign trade. Chief among these were Hong Kong and Shanghai.

By 1900, eighteen countries had gained trading rights in China. In each treaty port, their nationals settled in "concessions," areas reserved for foreigners. In effect, concessions were foreign land embedded within Chinese cities. Concession residents shopped in exclusive stores, ate in European-style restaurants, attended Europeans-only theaters, and had Chinese servants to cater to their every wish. Of equal importance, they enjoyed extraterritoriality, immunity from Chinese law. If a Chinese person accused a foreigner of a crime, the trial took place in a foreign court, before a foreign judge, and in accordance with foreign laws. Foreign officials ran a concession's government and collected its taxes. Foreign police and troops kept order in the streets. Foreign warships patrolled China's rivers.[14]

To make matters worse, the treaty ending the Second Opium War legalized the sale of opium. Now the poison flooded into China unchecked, spreading even to members of the imperial court in the Forbidden City. By one estimate, 25 percent of all Chinese men were addicted. "There is no slavery on earth to be compared with the bondage into which opium casts its victim," declared the *Chinese Observer,* an English-language magazine published in Hong Kong.[15]

Since addicts needed to get opium at any cost, they had little money left for food. Addicts became listless and pale, merely living skeletons. Samuel Merwin, an English traveler in the early 1900s, reported:

It is just at this period, when the smoker is so enslaved by the drug that he has lost his earning power, that his opium expenditure increases most rapidly. He is buying opium now, not so much to gratify his selfish vice, as to keep himself alive. A diseased, decrepit, insane being, he forgets even his family.... He sells his daughters, even his wife, if she has attractions, as slaves to rich men.... And at last he crawls out on the highway, digs himself a cave in the [dirt]... and prostrates himself before the camel and donkey drivers, whining, chattering, praying that a few copper cash [small coins] be thrown to him.[16]

Opium ate into Chinese society like an acid. As the nation's silver supply dwindled, the government raised taxes, and food prices skyrocketed. Unrest took the form of local peasant uprisings and nationwide rebellions, which were harshly put down by imperial troops. Yet none of this mattered to the opium sellers or the British colonial authorities. They became as addicted to opium profits as users were to the drug itself. With profits ranging as high as 2,000 percent, a fantastic sum, opium became the lifeblood of the British Empire in Asia. Britain used this gushing income stream to finance its rule in India, Burma, and Malaya (now Malaysia). In building roads and railroads, harbors and palaces, it paid "coolies"— the poorest class of manual laborers— partially in opium, thus enslaving them to their employers.[17]

Other nations followed Britain's lead. In Indochina (today's Vietnam, Laos, and Cambodia) France held the monopoly on imported Indian opium, which officials auctioned to the highest bidders. By the end of the First World War (1914–1918), Vietnam had 1,512 licensed opium dens and 3,098 opium shops, where addicts could buy the drug for home use. In most years, the French earned more from opium than they spent on all of Indochina's schools, hospitals, and libraries. The Netherlands' record in the Dutch East Indies was equally shameful.[18]

Westerners justified the opium trade in the name of profit and racism. Asia, they declared, was God-created for exploitation by the "superior" white race. Englishmen, for instance, boasted of "British China" as if it were a suburb of London. Many Englishmen saw the inhabitants as "wogs," the "lowest form of animal life," "worthless yellow-skinned reptiles," who "should only be treated as the animals they are." Chinese men were demeaned as "boys," just as plantation owners in the American South thought of their enslaved blacks as "property."[19]

It seemed best to keep as much distance as possible between "superior" whites and "inferior" Asians. Chinese people were humiliated in their own country. In Shanghai, park signs warned: DOGS AND CHINESE NOT ADMITTED. Normally, in India, an English bishop reported, "we shut out the natives from our society, and a bullying, insolent manner is continually assumed in speaking to them." So as not to touch the "filthy wretches," employers threw workers' wages on the ground. A low-ranking British army officer could afford to have several Indian servants to bathe him, dress him, fan him, and cut his toenails as he relaxed. The wives of low-grade colonial officials expected to be treated like royalty.[20]

Americans, too, profited from opium. The "flowery-flag devils," as Chinese called Americans, saw opium as a business opportunity, not a moral issue, insisting that if they did not sell it, others would. American traders, mostly New Englanders, bought opium in India and sold it to Chinese smugglers. Upon returning to the United States, traders invested in various business ventures, thus increasing their fortunes. From a sense of duty or a troubled conscience, the wealthiest poured money into "social uplift" causes. In doing so, they followed the example of the dealers in "black ivory"—African slaves—who helped fund Ivy League colleges, hospitals, and charities.[21]

"OPENING" JAPAN

The Japanese watched and worried. Though they were isolated, news of the outside world seeped into their country, mainly through the Dutch merchants at Nagasaki. Japanese people knew the opium trade and the aggression it incited were destroying China. By the mid-1800s, they feared the West would turn its attention to their islands.

In 1848, the United States defeated Mexico and seized what is today the American Southwest, an area extending from Texas to California. Now, with a coast bordering the Pacific Ocean, American businessmen and politicians envisioned regular, large-scale trade in manufactured goods with Asia. The means were already available. The port of San Francisco, in California, was ideal for ships crossing the Pacific. Increasingly powered by steam engines, more and more ships could make the voyage faster than anything with sails, including the famous China clippers, designed to move "at a fast clip."[22]

The only drawback was coal. Steamships burned coal to boil water to make the steam that drove their engines. Economic success, then, required coaling stations along the ocean route to Asia. Japan had plenty of coal. However, it wanted nothing to do with outsiders, so it had to be made to end its isolation.

To achieve this objective, trade and religion joined forces. Yankee clergymen, in their ignorance, preached that

A photograph of Commodore Perry, left, and a Japanese depiction of him, below. (left c. 1856–58, below c. 1854)

bear. A hero of the Mexican War, Perry was strict, ordering crewmen whipped for the slightest breach of his rules.

On November 24, 1852, Perry sailed from Norfolk, Virginia. In his baggage, he had a letter from President Millard Fillmore to the emperor of Japan. Addressed to Fillmore's "Great and Good Friend," it demanded a treaty of "friendship and commerce." To stress

Buddhism was the "grossest paganism" and that Japan's isolation was at odds with "God's plan of mercy." Buddhist Japan, they scolded, had a "*Christian* obligation to join the family of Christendom." As for all that coal, Secretary of State Daniel Webster declared it "a gift of Providence, deposited by the Creator of all things in the depths of the Japanese Islands, for the benefit of the human family." Therefore, it was "time the Yankee schoolmaster was sent" to teach Japan its duty to humanity![23]

That schoolmaster was Commodore Matthew Calbraith Perry of the U.S. Navy. Sailors called the burly, sour-faced officer "Old Bruin" because he had the temper of an angry grizzly

JAPAN EXPEDITION PRESS.

U. S. STEAM-FRIGATE "POWHATAN," SIMODA, JAPAN, MAY 1st, 1854.

LETTER FROM THE PRESIDENT OF THE UNITED STATES.

MILLARD FILLMORE,
PRESIDENT OF THE UNITED STATES OF AMERICA,
To his IMPERIAL MAJESTY,
THE EMPEROR OF JAPAN.
Great and Good Friend!

I send you this public letter by Commodore Matthew C. Perry, an officer of the highest rank in the Navy of the United States, and commander of the squadron now visiting your Imperial Majesty's dominions.

I have directed Commodore Perry to assure your Imperial Majesty that I entertain the kindest feelings towards your Majesty's person and government; and that I have no other object in sending him to Japan, but to propose to your Imperial Majesty that the United States and Japan should live in friendship, and have commercial intercourse with each other.

The constitution and laws of the United States forbid all interference with the religious or political concerns of other nations. I have particularly charged Commodore Perry to abstain from every act which could possibly disturb the tranquillity of your Imperial Majesty's dominions.

The United States of America reach from ocean to ocean, and our territory of Oregon and state of California lie directly opposite to the dominions of your Imperial Majesty. Our steam-ships can go from California to Japan in eighteen days.

Our great state of California produces about sixty millions of dollars in gold, every year, besides silver, quicksilver, precious stones, and many other valuable articles. Japan is also a rich and fertile country, and produces many very valuable articles. Your Imperial Majesty's subjects are skilled in many of the arts. I am desirous that our two countries should trade with each other, for the benefit both of Japan and the United States.

We know that the ancient laws of your Imperial Majesty's government do not allow of foreign trade except with the Dutch. But as the state of the world changes, and new governments are formed, it seems to be wise from time to time to make new laws. There was a time when the ancient laws of your Imperial Majesty's government were first made.

About the same time, America, which is sometimes called the New World, was first discovered and settled by the Europeans. For a long time there were but a few people, and they were poor. They have now become quite numerous; their commerce is very extensive; and they think that if your Imperial Majesty were so far to change the ancient laws as to allow a free trade between the two countries, it would be extremely beneficial to both.

If your Imperial Majesty is not satisfied that it would be safe, altogether, to abrogate the ancient laws which forbid foreign trade, they might be suspended for five or ten years, so as to try the experiment. If it does not prove as beneficial as was hoped, the ancient laws can be restored. The United States often limit their treaties with foreign states to a few years, and then renew them or not, as they please.

I have directed Commodore Perry to mention another thing to your Imperial Majesty. Many of our ships pass every year from California to China; and great numbers of our people pursue the whale fishery near the shores of Japan. It sometimes happens, in stormy weather, that one of our ships is wrecked on your Imperial Majesty's shores. In all such cases we ask and expect, that our unfortunate people should be treated with kindness, and that their property should be protected, till we can send a vessel and bring them away. We are very much in earnest in this.

Commodore Perry is also directed by me to represent to your Imperial Majesty that we understand there is a great abundance of coal and provisions in the empire of Japan. Our steam-ships, in crossing the great ocean, burn a great deal of coal, and it is not convenient to bring it all the way from America. We wish that our steam-ships and other vessels should be allowed to stop in Japan and supply themselves with coal, provisions and water. They will pay for them, in money, or anything else your Imperial Majesty's subjects may prefer; and we request your Imperial Majesty to appoint a convenient port in the southern part of the empire, where our vessels may stop for this purpose. We are very desirous of this.

These are the only objects for which I have sent Commodore Perry with a powerful squadron to pay a visit to your Imperial Majesty's renowned city of Yedo: friendship, commerce, a supply of coal, and provisions and protection for our shipwrecked people.

We have directed Commodore Perry to beg your Imperial Majesty's acceptance of a few presents. They are of no great value in themselves; but some of them may serve as specimens of the articles manufactured in the United States, and they are intended as tokens of our sincere and respectful friendship.

May the Almighty have your Imperial Majesty in his great and holy keeping!

In witness whereof I have caused the great seal of the United States to be hereunto affixed, and have subscribed the same with my name, at the city of Washington in America, the seat of my government, on the thirteenth day of the month of November, in the year one thousand eight hundred and fifty-two.

Your Good Friend,
MILLARD FILLMORE.

By the President,
EDWARD EVERETT,
Secretary of State.

The letter that Commodore Perry delivered to the emperor of Japan on behalf of President Fillmore explaining why the two nations should have a friendly relationship. (c. 1852)

hulls were painted jet-black, and they moved under clouds of black smoke, *against* the wind. Immediately, riders sped inland with an urgent call to arms. Within hours, 20,000 samurai lined the shore, armed with swords, spears, bows, and antique cannons that had not been fired in decades (if not centuries). Commodore Perry rolled out *his* guns and ordered crewmen to prepare for a battle. Since nobody wanted that, the shogun accepted President Fillmore's letter on behalf of the emperor. After six days, Perry sailed to Hong Kong, promising to return for an answer, but with a larger fleet.[24]

Perry reappeared on February 13, 1854, with ten ships. He did not come empty-handed, though, bringing gifts intended to impress his hosts with the marvels of American technology: clocks, iron stoves, hand-pumped fire engines, rifles, Colt six-shooters, and a mile-long telegraph line. But the highlight was a miniature railroad with a steam locomotive, a tender and passenger car, and 350 feet of track, which sailors laid out in a circle. As the train sped along at a dizzying twenty miles an hour, gleeful samurai took turns sitting on the roof of the passenger car, their kimonos flapping in the breeze. Perry's

the letter's importance, Perry led a squadron of four steam-powered warships bristling with friendly cannons.

The sight of Perry's "black ships" led by his flagship, the *Powhatan,* arriving on July 8, 1853, stunned Japanese onlookers ashore, who were "too alarmed to open their mouths." They had never seen such monsters. Their

A Japanese depiction of the American "black ships" led by Commodore Perry. (c. 1854)

gifts, backed by the threat of force, did the trick. He sailed away with a treaty opening three ports for American ships to take on coal and provisions. Four years later, Japan was forced to sign a treaty with the United States opening it to American trade.[25]

Other Western powers wanted the same trading rights—or else. After a series of nasty incidents, such as the killing of drunken sailors by samurai, the powers acted. In 1863, a fleet of British, French, Dutch, and American ships bombarded several coastal towns. Nothing the defenders had could withstand the solid iron cannonballs and exploding shells. Like China after each Opium War, Japan was forced to repay the cost of its own defeat. A diplomat explained, probably with a straight face, "All [we] English wanted was the good of the Japanese as a nation!"[26]

RISE OF MODERN JAPAN

Clearly, Yoshinobu Tokugawa, the shogun, could not protect his country from the southern barbarians. Since 1854, the government had time and again "lost face," been humiliated by foreigners.

Emperor Meiji as a young man, five years after taking the throne at the age of fifteen. (c. 1872)

adopt Western technology. The group's chance came in 1867, when Emperor Komei died and was succeeded by Mutsuhito, his fifteen-year-old son. Early the next year, the group staged a bloodless rebellion, politely described as "restoring" power to the emperor. Mutsuhito called his reign Meiji (Enlightened) and moved the capital from Kyoto to Edo, which was renamed Tokyo (Eastern Capital). He later took the name Meiji.

That the emperor Meiji had been "restored" hid the reality of his being only the symbolic head of state, as the emperor had been during the time of Yorimoto Minamoto in the twelfth century. The leading daimyo, determined and very competent men, made the key decisions, which His Majesty approved, and they issued them in his name. Those decisions changed Japan as nothing had ever done, astonishing everyone, not least the Japanese themselves.

No nation had ever taken such a great leap forward, and done it so quickly. Within a generation, Japan catapulted into the modern age. Change was in the air. The position of shogun, outmoded and ineffective, vanished. All daimyo gave up their lands. The most important became governors of prov-

The handwriting was on the wall. For Japan to avoid China's fate, it needed to modernize, impossible without a change in leadership.

A group of daimyo took as their motto "Rich Country, Strong Army." In other words, to defend itself against pushy Westerners, Japan would have to

inces under control of Tokyo; the lesser ones received pensions. Abolished as a social class, the samurai took commands in the army and navy, became civil servants, or went into business. Yet their ideals persisted as standards of honor and courage for the nation at large. A written constitution provided for a compulsory educational system, a postal system, courts, police, taxation, and government departments run by officials called ministers. Most important, it provided for a parliament, or Diet, to make the laws.

Japan learned much from the West. Its people developed a taste for Western foods, such as McIntosh apples and Concord grapes. Along with the traditional *sake*—rice wine—they drank beer and whiskey. "Modern" city people favored Western-style clothing. Men sported suits, ties, and top hats; women wore dresses and high-buttoned shoes. Baseball became the rage. Each year, Tokyo sent the brightest high school graduates, male and female, to Western universities to study economics, mathematics, the sciences, and engineering. Japan's ancient traditions of craftsmanship were easily adapted to modern technology. By the 1880s, *Scientific American* magazine reported: "The inhabitants of Japan are already supplied with microscopes, telescopes, clocks, watches, knives, spoons, etc., made by themselves from European models." Often, too, they improved on the foreign models, making them better and more cheaply.[27]

Japan's military expanded. Westerners saw political and economic advantages in modernizing its armed forces. For a price, the British designed and built warships for Japan, then taught the Japanese to build their own. The United States, too, helped develop Japanese naval power. New England shipyards sent parts for five submarines to American mechanics in Nagasaki to assemble. Japanese students learned modern sea warfare at the U.S. Naval Academy. German and French officers taught the Japanese army the latest battlefield tactics.

Not everyone thought such assistance wise. An American journalist sourly observed: "We can only hope that we may not find ourselves among the earliest victims of our overzealous and mistaken benevolence." He had a point. For Japan might use its newfound expertise not only to defend itself but also to press its demands on others.[28]

The lesson Japan's leaders took from the example of Westerners in Asia was clear. In foreign affairs, the law of the

A cartoon depicting the small-statured Japan standing in victory over the massive China after the 1894 conflict. (c. 1894)

jungle ruled: You eat or you are eaten. Powerful nations, leaders came to believe, had the right to dominate the weak. It followed that, to gain respect, Japan needed colonies. In 1894, it quarreled with China over the control of Korea. During the war that followed, the Japanese navy made mincemeat of the outdated Chinese fleet. Defeated, China surrendered the island of Formosa (Taiwan) and recognized Japan's right to "paramount influence" in Korea.

Next Japan challenged Russia. For more than two centuries, Russia had expanded eastward, across Siberia and into Manchuria, a region nearly three times the size of Texas. Located in northeast China, Manchuria was rich in coal and iron and had virgin grasslands ideal for farming. When Russian troops marched into northern Korea, the "Land of the Morning Calm" became "a dagger pointing at the heart of Japan." So began the Russo-Japanese War (1904–1905). At first, it seemed foolish to think that a small Asian country could defeat a major European power. "A Japanese?" a Russian general sneered. "Pooh! He's a mosquito. Why, I'll stick a pin through him and send him home in a letter."[29]

Some mosquito! Without bothering to declare war, Japan launched a surprise attack, crippling Russia's Far Eastern Fleet anchored at Port Arthur in Manchuria, then won a series of ferocious land battles. The resulting peace treaty forced Russia out of Manchuria, allowing Japan to base troops to guard the railroads that carried the territory's minimal wealth to the seaport and the Japanese cargo ships waiting there.

Despite these victories, Japan had severe problems. The nation was resource-poor and people-rich. Although it had plenty of coal, it lacked the raw materials vital to modern industry: oil, rubber, tin, aluminum, zinc, copper, nickel. These Japan had to buy abroad and turn into finished goods for export, using the earnings to buy more raw materials, pay wages, and give investors profits. Its exports were inexpensive consumer goods like silk and cotton cloth, pottery, glassware, toys, and brushes. Because of the limited amount of farmland, Japan could barely feed itself. The numbers reveal a grim picture. From 33 million in 1868,

the population went to 73 million in 1940, a rise of 121 percent, the largest increase of any nation on earth. Japan therefore faced a double bind. It did not control the sources of key raw materials, and it had to find living space for millions of "surplus" people.

Beginning in 1929, the Great Depression, a worldwide economic downturn, struck Japan. To resist competition and protect jobs, Europe and America taxed foreign imports heavily. By 1931, Japan's overseas trade had fallen by nearly half. Prices of silk and cotton cloth, the chief moneymakers, collapsed. Unemployment soared. Millions went hungry. In the countryside, desperate parents sold daughters into prostitution to buy food for the rest of the family. A farmer remembered how neighbors sold "seven or eight" girls, his classmates. "Because that family was poor, well, they went. I felt very sorry."[30]

Despite recent gains in Korea and Manchuria, further overseas expansion seemed the only way to avert disaster. According to a Japanese army study, China had "a limitless treasure trove" of natural resources and was getting steadily weaker. Cooped up in the Forbidden City, the Son of Heaven was powerless to defend his opium-ridden country. As a result, millions of Chinese no longer believed their ruler had the Mandate of Heaven, the gods' favor. In 1911, revolutionaries overthrew the emperor and declared China a republic. But the republic could not halt the downward slide. Torn by political feuds, the central government lost control of many provinces. By the early 1920s, generals had made themselves warlords, each ruling a province with his troops. Civilians dreaded the soldiers, who acted more like violent bandits than protectors. Making matters worse, warlords raised taxes and seized crops, forcing peasants in certain areas to eat grass and tree bark. Viewed from Tokyo, China seemed ripe for conquest.[31]

MILITARISM AND RACISM

By the mid-1920s, military leaders had become Japan's rulers in all but name. A power unto themselves, they moved on three fronts at once. On the political front, uniformed assassins killed members of the Diet before stunned onlookers as an example to other members. No civilian official was too high to die by bullet or dagger, the fate of two prime ministers. Juries, too frightened of retribution to convict assassins, set them free.[32]

The second front involved tightening the military's hold on society. Officers of the Kempeitai, the Japanese secret military police, eavesdropped on private conversations, arresting anyone who might pose a threat. The military's

Japanese schoolboys
practice rifle drills.
(January 13, 1916)

aim, however, was not merely to silence opposition but to control the minds of the Japanese people. Under the slogan "One People, One Mind," the military forced the Diet to pass the Peace Preservation Act of 1925. This law made it a crime to spread "information that confuses public sentiment"—that is, that questioned the actions of the military.[33]

A new organization, the Tokko (Thought Police), enforced the Peace Preservation Act. Like a gigantic octopus, it wrapped its tentacles around every form of expression: newspapers, magazines, books, films, theater, and music. Jazz was banned because it promoted American-style "decadence," as did guitars and banjos, also banned. Accused "thought criminals" faced trial by "thought prosecutors." Conviction brought a filthy jail cell or, in many cases, an unmarked grave.[34]

The third front was education. Schools served as the military's training camps for youth. Elementary school textbooks extolled a fighting spirit and self-sacrifice. A first-grade reader, used in every school, pictured toy soldiers under the caption "Advance! Advance! Advance!" Another book had a lesson titled "Takeo Joins the Service." In it, a father tells his son: "Don't be afraid

to die. Don't worry about us here." It was common to see on the Ginza, Tokyo's main shopping street, little boys dressed in army uniforms, complete with wooden swords.[35]

Active-duty officers and reservists staffed Japan's middle and high schools. A woman's first responsibility, they taught, was to bear children, preferably sons for the military. Boys learned to use weapons and drilled constantly. To promote physical fitness, instructors ordered a routine of wrestling, running, and fighting with bamboo poles as swords. For war was glorious, and dying for the emperor a passport to heaven. "The emperor at that time was called a 'living god,'" recalled a former schoolboy. "We were taught that the emperor was a god in the form of a human being." Another added, "The Japanese people belonged to the emperor. We were his children." Teachers had to read his public announcements to their classes with utmost care. When one teacher stumbled over a phrase, he committed suicide for "insulting" His Imperial Majesty.[36]

Japan's schools, mass media, and official propaganda preached racism. The people learned that as children of the god-emperor, they were superior to all others, regardless of wealth or social position. Even the lowliest citizen belonged to the "Yamato race," the "most superior race in the world." Japanese were the "Chosen People" and thus the "sole superior race," a "superhuman" race of "supermen." There was nothing this "master race" could not do or was not entitled to have.[37]

Not surprisingly, feelings of superiority bred contempt for others, including Koreans and Chinese. In racist eyes, Koreans were trash. Korea's seven major products, racists insisted, were "shit, tobacco, lice, prostitutes, tigers, pigs, and flies." Whenever Koreans appeared on Tokyo streets, children jeered: "Ugh, a Korean! A Korean!" Chinese fared even worse. Once respected for its contributions to Japanese culture, China had, supposedly, fallen into "sin and decay, and dishonor." Racist jargon dehumanized Chinese people. They were *chancorro,* "chinks," "sub-humans," and "vermin." Youngsters chanted: "Chinka, Chinka, Chinka, Chinka, so stupid and they stinka."[38]

Logically, it followed that Japan had the right to drive the white barbarians from Asia and "guide" Asia's peoples for their own good, whether they liked it or not. Yet even that was not enough for extremists. The "Asiatic Chosen People," they declared, had a greater mission. Their notion of *Hakko Ichiu,* literally "the whole world under one roof," was a fancy term for world domination. For only firm Japanese rule could "prevent the human race from becoming devilish . . . and lead it to the world of light." This threat included America, "which belongs to Japan because it was originally owned by the Indians, who are Asiatics," said a prominent Japanese university professor.[39]

A huge war machine, inspired by a corrupted version of Bushido, would be the instrument of conquest. The traditional "way of the warrior" taught sympathy for the weak, loyalty, self-control, and the dishonor of dying for an unworthy cause. Yet, as genuine samurai officers retired after the war with Russia in 1905, the sons of small landowners and shopkeepers took their places. At the age of twelve or thirteen, they were enrolled by their parents in military academies, where they were further brainwashed with racism and the concept of war as "the father of creation and the mother of culture." The Bushido ideal of loyalty morphed into total, unquestioning obedience. If a superior gave an order, however cruel and idiotic, it carried the same weight as if it had come from the god-emperor himself.[40]

Most of the enlisted men were "hicks," the sons of poor country folk. Seen as mindless robots, they, too, learned obedience. To ensure they learned well, the military created what social scientists call a "ladder of oppression." If, let us say, a major displeased his colonel, the colonel would slap his face in front of the entire unit. The major, in turn, would slap any captain who rubbed him the wrong way—and so on down the line. Privates stood on the lowest rung of the ladder; officers called them "less than a penny," the price of a postcard draft notice. Dubbed "consumable goods," they were to be used, and used up, without regard to their humanity.[41]

Officers struck recruits with their fists and canes. Even something so trivial as wearing a shirt with a button missing brought a slap in the face and punishment for the entire barracks. The officer in charge lined the men up and struck each in turn until blood flowed. "Beaten like a dog! Beaten like a bag of flour!" a recruit wrote home.

"Once the instructors got tired of beating you up," another wrote, "they would have recruits face each other and slap each other. . . . Gradually I felt that I'd missed something if by night-time I hadn't been beaten up at least once." In such a way were the brutalized men taught to take out their suffering on others. And now they were being sent to conquer China.[42]

THE CHINA WAR

In 1931, Japanese forces moved out of their bases along the railroads and seized all of Manchuria. Over the next decade, nearly two million Japanese poured into the territory. Manchuria was a place to better yourself, if you were Japanese. As in the Western colonies in Asia, a separate society arose in the cities of Manchuria: banks, trading companies, hotels, schools, movie houses—each run by Japanese for Japanese. Eager to enrich themselves, firms with famous names like Nissan, Mitsubishi, and Mitsui built factories. In the countryside, troops evicted the Chinese to make room for land-hungry Japanese farmers.

In 1937, Japan invaded China itself, igniting a war that eventually claimed ten million Chinese lives. Advancing against light resistance, troops seized Beijing in July and the following month attacked Shanghai, the nation's commercial capital, known as the "New York of China." After Beijing, Japan's military high command did not expect Shanghai's defenders to put up much of a fight. But they did. Chinese politicians and generals patched up their differences and rushed troops to the beleaguered city. In response, the Japanese cut loose with everything they had. Battleships anchored in the Whangpoo River pounded the city's Chinese sections with their cannons, taking care to avoid the foreign concessions. For the first time in history, bombers deliberately targeted civilians.

Images of baby Ping-Mei, the only survivor of the Japanese bombing of Shanghai's South Station, rallied the world against Japan. (August 28, 1937)

An air raid left the Shanghai railroad station a mass of twisted steel and charred rubble. The only survivor was an infant named Ping-Mei. Rescuers found the diapered boy sitting between the tracks, crying. A Chinese newsreel photographer recorded the scene, then promptly released the footage. Images of Ping-Mei appeared in newspapers and magazines, shocking the world. President Roosevelt was horrified. In a radio address, he condemned "the slaughter of civilian populations from the air" as "barbarous." A U.S. Senate resolution branded the Shanghai bombing a "crime against humanity." But worse was to come.[43]

Shanghai fell in November after a three-month battle. The Japanese sustained 40,000 men killed or wounded, the Chinese 270,000. Infuriated at their losses, the invaders drove inland, determined to break Chinese resistance at all costs. They looted, burned, or killed anybody and anything they pleased. In some places, they handed out opium, still a major problem in China, to destroy the people's will to fight; the remains of those broken people who died of overdoses ended up in town garbage dumps. Japanese newspapers also reported that two officers held a "friendly

新聞日日京東

〔日曜月〕

昭和十二年十二月十三日

百人斬り"超記録"

向井106─105野田

両少尉さらに延長戦

"百人斬り競争"の両將校

（右）野田巖少尉

（左）向井敏明少尉

An article in a Japanese newspaper about the contest between the two soldiers shown to be the first to behead 100 Chinese people. (December 12, 1937)

contest" (their term) to see who would be first to behead 100 Chinese. The loser's sword had bent while slicing a captive in half.[44]

On December 13, 1937, Japanese forces stormed Nanking, a walled city of one million on the south bank of the Yangtze River. Imperial Japanese Army commanders, among them the emperor's uncle, General Prince Asaka, gave written orders to commit wholesale murder. History records the result as the "Rape of Nanking." This term is no exaggeration.

For three weeks, Japanese troops committed horrible atrocities. Some soldiers, however, regretted what they had done. Nagatomi Hakudo, later a respected doctor, was tormented by his actions in Nanking. Fifty years afterward, they still gave him nightmares. He recalled:

> I remember being driven in a truck along a path that had been cleared through piles of thousands and thousands of slaughtered bodies. . . . Few know that soldiers impaled babies on bayonets and tossed them still alive into pots of boiling water. They gang-raped women from the ages of twelve to eighty and then killed them when they could no longer satisfy sexual requirements. I beheaded people, starved them to death, burned them, and buried them alive, over two hundred in all. It is terrible that I could turn into an animal and do these things. There are really no words to explain what I was doing. I was truly a devil.[45]

An unnamed veteran wrote in his diary: "The innocence I possessed at the time of leaving the homeland has long since disappeared. Now I am a hardened sinner and my sword is always stained with blood. . . . May God forgive me. May my mother forgive me."[46]

Racism fueled the insanity at Nanking, dehumanizing victims, making them seem vile creatures unworthy of sympathy. "I felt like I was just killing animals, like pigs," explained a former soldier. Said others: "The Chinese didn't belong to the human race," and "[we] did not see Chinese people as human beings," but "of rather less value than a dog or a cat." Nobody will ever know the exact human cost of this atrocity. The best estimate is that 300,000 Chinese died before commanders called a halt. By then, however, the world knew the worst—from members of the Imperial Army themselves.[47]

Some Japanese soldiers had cameras and snapped souvenir photos. In the era before digital photography, special shops developed the film and made prints. Most Chinese photo shops were in Shanghai. So when soldiers went on leave, they handed in their rolls of film to be developed. Chinese shop owners made extra prints, which they gave to Europeans in the concessions, who then released them to the world. Those photos still make us cringe. They show dreadful scenes of Japanese about to behead Chinese with their swords, holding severed heads, burying prisoners alive, and killing captives in live bayonet practice. When *Life* and *Look,*

A photograph of the aftermath of the Rape of Nanking taken by Itou Kaneo, a soldier in the Kisarazu Air Unit of the Japanese navy. (c. 1937)

America's leading picture magazines, published these photos, public opinion turned sharply against the Japanese.[48]

After the Rape of Nanking, the Japanese army made sex slaves of some 200,000 Chinese and Korean women, 80 percent of them between fourteen and eighteen years of age. Imprisoned in brothels with lyrical names like New Buds, Cherry Blossom, and House of Restful Consolation, the women were considered not human beings but objects to be used. Soldiers dubbed them "military supplies," "war supplies," and "public toilets." One woman said what others surely felt in their hearts: "To me it was worse than dying. . . . They had ruined my young life. They had stripped me of everything, my self-esteem, my dignity, my freedom, my possessions, my family." The Japanese government has refused to apologize or pay damages for the abuse of these "comfort women," sparking protests that continue to this day.[49]

The Japanese army even formed a secret unit in Manchuria—Unit 731—to research bubonic plague, cholera, and other diseases. Researchers tested their findings on living people, mostly Chinese but also, after Pearl Harbor, a few American prisoners. Afterward, they dropped millions of plague-infected fleas on Chinese cities in sealed clay pots suspended from small parachutes. Researchers called their human subjects "experimental animals," "monkeys," and "lumps of meat on a chopping block." Asked how people could think this way, researcher Tamura Yoshio

later admitted: "We were all implanted with a narrow form of racism, in the form of a belief in the superiority of the so-called 'Yamato Race.' We disparaged all other races. . . . If we didn't have a feeling of racial superiority, we couldn't have done it." After the war, the United States quietly pardoned the chief of Unit 731, General Shiro Ishi, in return for his records of the unit's experiments. By then, the Soviet Union was fast becoming an enemy, and the U.S. military feared it might use biological weapons if the nations went to war. Unit 731's information, U.S. authorities hoped, would further their own research into biological weapons.[50]

Despite its conquests, Japan learned the truth of the saying "It is easier to start a war than to end it." China lacked many things—modern aircraft, warships, and artillery—but it had advantages Tokyo's war planners had not considered. China was a vast country with a population (511 million in 1937) seven times Japan's. Thus, the invader could capture cities but lacked the manpower to control the countryside. It hardly took a genius to understand what this disparity meant. "Fighting and death everywhere," a wounded Japanese soldier scrawled on a wall.

"China is limitless and we are like drops of water in an ocean."[51]

Japan felt the effects of its Chinese adventure in countless ways. Its economy got worse. "The length of a match stick and the skin of a rat represent important economic factors in continuing the war in China," the *New York Times* reported. Workers tanned rat skins as a leather substitute. By shortening matchsticks by exactly 0.029 inches, Japan saved enough money in a year to support the war for an hour and five minutes. Most everyday items, from gasoline to iron frying pans and children's rubber balloons, were scarce or unobtainable. Yet the underlying problem remained. The war in China became a struggle Japan could not win but did not know how to end.[52]

What to do?

THE ROAD TO PEARL HARBOR

Adolf Hitler seemed to give the answer. In September 1939, the German tyrant attacked neighboring Poland. After a quick victory, his armies turned west. In the spring of 1940, they conquered Norway, Denmark, France, Belgium, and the Netherlands. Britain fought on, alone, protected by the English

A Japanese postcard celebrating the alliance between Germany, Japan, and Italy, with children waving the flags of each country. (c. 1938)

Channel and the Royal Air Force. Hitler became a hero in Japan. His picture appeared in all the newspapers, and, noted a Japanese American student in Tokyo, "all the women are crazy about him." But he was not crazy about the Japanese, privately describing them as "racially inferior," though useful in fighting the Western democracies.[53]

Hitler's victories left the defeated nations' Asian and Pacific colonies "orphaned," unable to defend themselves with the tiny forces on the scene. Here was an opportunity Tokyo felt it dared not miss. Plundered tin and rubber from British Malaya, rice from French Indochina, and oil from the Dutch East Indies promised to solve Japan's economic problems.

In late September 1940, Tokyo pressured French colonial officials into allowing Japan to build naval and air bases in Vietnam. The following July, as the French garrison watched helplessly, Japanese forces overran all of Indochina without firing a shot. The Vietnamese cities of Hanoi in the north and Saigon (today's Ho Chi Minh City) in the south became likely jumping-off points for attacking the Dutch East Indies, the Philippines, and Australia.

President Roosevelt watched these events with growing anxiety. He had long distrusted Japanese people because of their race. Now Japanese aggression threatened the Philippines, where America had major military bases, and the Hawaiian Islands, our future fiftieth state. To signal his displeasure, in late 1940 the State Department barred the sale to Japan of scrap iron, a key ingredient for turning iron into steel. When Japan refused demands to withdraw from China, the president ordered full-scale economic sanctions. The State Department froze Japanese assets, preventing Japan from using its money deposited in American banks to pay for goods already purchased. To drive the message home, oil sales were also banned. Oil has been called the lifeblood of modern war. Without the slippery black stuff and its by-product gasoline, planes cannot fly, tanks cannot roll, and ships cannot sail. The Japanese navy alone burned 12,000 tons of oil a day in *peacetime*. Because 85 percent of Japan's oil came from Texas, Oklahoma, and California, it faced national paralysis.[54]

Economic pressure, however, is not a surefire way to discourage an aggressor. It may even have the opposite effect. American sanctions forced Tokyo to make hard choices. Japan could pull out of China. But if it did so, all the blood, money, and effort it had spent would count for nothing, and the problems that had prompted it to invade in the first place would remain unsolved. Or Japan could launch an all-out attack while it still had fuel reserves. Crippling the U.S. Pacific Fleet at Pearl Harbor would buy time, perhaps two or three years. And while America struggled to rebuild its fleet, Japan could set up a defense zone on the Gilbert, Caroline, and Marshall Islands, taken from Germany after the First World War. These would serve as fortresses from which to strike and defeat the enemy before he came within range of the Japanese homeland. In the meantime, Japan could conquer Europe's orphaned colonies, seize their natural resources, and finish the war in China.

One officer, however, scorned these rosy predictions. A military genius, Admiral Isoroku Yamamoto was commander in chief of the Combined Fleet of the Imperial Japanese Navy. Yamamoto had hated America since boyhood, when his father told him stories about Commodore Perry and the "black ships." But the admiral saw things as they were, not as he wished them to be. A former student at Harvard University, he spoke English fluently. Yamamoto knew Americans had no interest in another war; they had spilled enough blood in the First World War. He may well have recalled the proverb "A rat who gnaws at a tiger's tail invites destruction." America was a sleeping tiger. If Japan bit its tail, Japan, too, invited destruction.[55]

Yamamoto's superiors overruled him, ordering him to plan a devastating attack on Pearl Harbor. He obeyed, but warned: "If you insist on my going

A portrait of Admiral Yamamoto. (c. 1943)

ahead, I can promise to give them hell for a year or a year and a half, but can guarantee nothing as to what will happen after that." In other words, be sensible. Do all you can to avoid war, and realize that the fate of the Empire of Japan is in your hands.[56]

The high command knew little about America and Americans. Worse yet, Japanese officers believed their own racist myths. Americans, they sneered, were physically inferior to Japanese. Though generally taller, they were weaker, especially around the hips, because they sat on chairs instead of, Japanese-style, on floor mats.

America was "a barbaric nation" of "hairy, twisted-nosed savages," of "animals who have lost the human spirit." Americans were "inwardly corrupt" and bloated money-grubbers. Years of soft living had made America a "paper tiger," a nation of cowards who loved life more than honor. Surely, such people were no match for *Yamato damashii,* and this Japanese spirit was, according to official propaganda, "worth all the money and factories in the world."[57]

Westerners clung to their own racial myths. The British considered the Japanese simply shorter, creepier versions of the Chinese. One British "authority" railed against the "Jap" as a "stunted . . . yellow-faced heathen, with a mouthful of teeth three sizes too big for him, bulging slits where his eyes ought to be, blacking-brush hair, a foolish giggle, and the conceit of the devil."[58]

White Americans were equally race-proud. Many military men, who should have known better, considered the Japanese unworthy foes. Evidently, "they could not build good warplanes." And even if they could, they were awful pilots because Mother Nature had made them nearsighted and given them poor balance. What is more, they could not fire machine guns "because they were very bad shots." Americans also scorned the Japanese common soldier. A short, skinny creature in an oversize uniform that made him look like a hobo, he could never outfight a red-blooded American! And Japanese "weak minds" worked "as a woman's is supposed to do"—by emotion rather than logic.[59]

This was nonsense bred of racism and a willful refusal to face reality. Japan's navy was large and capable, its fighting spirit high. It had the mightiest battleship ever built, the *Yamato* (*Japan*), and the Long Lance torpedo, larger and more accurate than anything in the American arsenal. Japan's air force used the Zero, the best fighter plane in Asia, flown by top-notch pilots. The Japanese soldier, as time would tell, was brave, tough, and dedicated.

The Pearl Harbor attack was like a pebble tossed into a still pond. Its ripples spread in all directions. Within days, what had been separate European and Asian wars became a global war, as Adolf Hitler and his Italian crony, Benito Mussolini, sided with Japan and declared war on the United States.

War unified Americans against the common enemy, yet also aggravated long-held racial prejudices. Our focus will be on the Japanese Americans caught up in wartime hysteria. But before we can see how this happened, we must explore racial attitudes in the United States toward immigrants from across the Pacific Ocean.

CHAPTER 2

DREAMS OF FORTUNE

Huge dreams of fortune
Go with me to foreign lands,
Across the ocean.
—Anonymous

A WHITE MAN'S COUNTRY

Ships entering New York Harbor pass within sight of Liberty Island and the Statue of Liberty towering over it. In 1883, Emma Lazarus wrote a sonnet later engraved on a bronze plaque set into an inner wall of the statue's pedestal. Titled "The New Colossus," the poem describes a "mighty woman" raising her torch as a beacon of welcome to all seeking new lives in the land of liberty. She cries "with silent lips":

Give me your tired, your poor
Your huddled masses yearning to breathe free,

*The wretched refuse of your teeming
   shore.
Send these, the homeless, tempest-tost
   to me,
I lift my lamp beside the golden door!*

Generations of schoolchildren have learned that Lady Liberty symbolizes the world's great refuge, its "melting pot" of peoples. In our country, supposedly, newcomers' differences are burned away, blending them into something new: Americans. The truth, however, is not so simple. For until the mid-twentieth century, the ingredients allowed to go into the "pot" were carefully selected according to race. Even as Emma Lazarus wrote her welcome, another poet hailed the statue quite differently: "O Liberty, white Goddess!"[1]

The idea of whiteness as basic to Americanism is older than the nation by nearly two centuries. New England's Puritan settlers believed the Almighty had sent them on a sacred "errand into the wilderness." In his 1630 sermon aboard the *Arbella,* Governor John Winthrop preached that they would be a model of holiness and liberty: "We shall be as a City upon a Hill." In Puritan minds, America was truly a God-given country, reserved for His

Jewish refugee children wave at the Statue of Liberty as they arrive in New York Harbor from Europe. (c. 1939)

"Chosen People" (their term) as a refuge for white Protestant Englishmen.[2]

America's Founders thought so, too. Benjamin Franklin saw the white-skinned English as the highest branch on the human family tree. The English, he wrote with pride, were the "principal Body of white People on the Face of the Earth." So why "darken" America with Spaniards, Italians, and Germans of "a swarthy Complexion"? Franklin asked. "Why increase the Sons of

The future President Lincoln in a photograph taken by one of his law students. (c. 1846)

Africa, by Planting them in *America,* where we have so fair an Opportunity, by excluding all Blacks and Tawneys, of increasing the lovely White?"[3]

The Founders recognized "the lovely White" in the law. The Naturalization Act of 1790 was among the first laws passed by Congress after the adoption of the Constitution. Naturalization is the process by which an "alien"—a foreigner living in the country—may become a citizen. The 1790 law, however, said that the rights of citizenship could be granted only to "any Alien being a free white person," and it denied citizenship not only to nonwhite immigrants but also to Indians, America's original inhabitants.[4]

By "Sons of *Africa,*" Franklin meant enslaved black people. Since colonial times, most educated whites regarded people of African ancestry as inferior. In Franklin's day, prominent European and American thinkers justified slavery chiefly in racial terms. British philosopher and historian David Hume declared, "The Negroes, and in general all other species of men, [are] naturally inferior to the whites." Germany's leading philosopher, Immanuel Kant, claimed, "The Negroes of Africa have received from nature no intelligence that rises above the foolish." After all, Kant wrote, blacks were black, the "color of Satan," naturally empty-headed simpletons lacking self-control and prone to "mindless" violence.[5]

Racists viewed black people as animals, base and inferior creatures, to the point of denying their humanity. They imagined blacks as creatures of wild lust. It followed that whites should avoid "amalgamation," an evil-sounding term for interracial mating. Racists called "blood-mixing" an "unnatural act" that weakened the white race by creating "mongrels." Such mixing, Thomas Jefferson wrote, "produces a degradation to which no lover of his country, no lover of the excellence of the human character can innocently consent." Yet this assertion did not prevent the author of the Declaration of Independence and the third president of the United States from amalgamating with his teenage slave Sally Hemings and fathering all six of her children. Whether they loved each other or not is a question no one can now answer.[6]

The idea that America was only for white people moved westward as the nation grew. In 1803, President Jefferson bought a vast stretch of territory from France. The Louisiana Purchase doubled the nation's size, pushing its boundaries from the Mississippi River to the Rocky Mountains. The war with Mexico forty-three years later advanced the border to the Pacific shore. People called Free-Soilers opposed the spread of slavery into the new lands. These, they vowed, should forever be "free lands for free people"—that is, white people.

An ambitious Illinois politician, one Abraham Lincoln, could not have agreed more. Lincoln was a white supremacist, a believer in the superiority of the white race, and laced his early speeches with this idea. The Declaration of Independence, he insisted, was "the white man's charter of freedom."

The Founders had made the United States government "for the white people and not for the Negroes." The future sixteenth president called blacks members of "the inferior races" and Mexicans "a race of mongrels." He also saw the West as the "happy home of teeming millions of free, white, prosperous people," insisting that it "should be kept open for the homes of free white people." Blacks, Lincoln argued, could never assimilate—never become Americans in their ideals, customs, and lifestyle—for the physical differences between the races would "probably forever forbid [blacks and whites] living together upon the footing of perfect equality."[7]

The idea of America as a country made by God exclusively for whites persisted despite the abolition of slavery as a result of the Civil War. By the mid-1920s, most western and all southern states had enacted laws banning interracial marriage, especially between blacks and whites. Virginia's Racial Integrity Act of 1924 was a classic example of racism embodied in law. It forbade the marriage of "any white person" to someone of another race, defining a "white person" as someone having "no trace whatsoever of blood other than Caucasian." Such a marriage was automatically illegal, a criminal offense punishable by up to five years in prison. A popular newspaper, the *Richmond Times-Dispatch,* left no doubt about where the majority of the all-white Virginia legislature stood: "amalgamation" between black and white meant race suicide. "Once a drop of inferior blood gets into [the white man's] veins, he descends lower and lower in the mongrel scale." In 1927, the U.S. Supreme Court upheld all anti-amalgamation laws.[8]

This doctrine of white supremacy and black inferiority is key to understanding what follows. For such ideas were enormously flexible, easily adapted to fit other peoples and situations.

CALIFORNIA

Writing in 1884, a historian listed "rude race-hatred" among "the darkest threads in the fabric" of Western history. And no Western state had a darker history of race hatred than California, the Golden State.[9]

In 1848, just days before U.S. and Mexican diplomats signed the treaty ending the Mexican War, a workman found gold nuggets at John A. Sutter's sawmill in the Sacramento Valley. News of the discovery produced an epidemic of "gold fever," a nationwide frenzy. "California or Bust!" became the motto of all who wanted to get rich quick. By February 1849, thousands of "forty-niners" had set out to make their fortunes. By 1850, California had over 100,000 white people, enough for admission to the nation as the thirty-first state.

From the outset, gold seekers and Native Americans quarreled. Miners needed land to explore, timber to shore up mine shafts, and streams to drive waterwheels. For centuries, bands of Maidu, Miwok, Pomo, and other tribes had lived in areas destined to become goldfields. The strangers, they realized, would do anything to get the yellow "crazy-making metal." To justify their actions, miners animalized these peaceful people, calling them "beasts," "swine," "snakes," "pigs," "baboons," "apes," and "gorillas." The common name, however, was "Diggers," because they dug up edible roots.[10]

If hungry Diggers, driven from their lands, stole a cow or a sack of flour, miners attacked their villages. California's first governor, Peter H. Burnett, encouraged the violence, promising that "a war of extermination will continue to be waged between the races until the Indian race becomes extinct." Without saying it in so many words, Burnett had issued a death warrant for an entire people.[11]

Groups of volunteers set out to exterminate the pesky "brutes." To encourage "the white man, to whom time is money," Burnett had the state treasury pay generous bounties: twenty-five cents per Digger scalp and five dollars for each Digger head. Some settlements hired professional huntsmen to track down and shoot Diggers "like beasts of prey." An estimated 150,000 Diggers lived in California when the Gold Rush began. By 1870, fewer than 30,000 remained. Those the killers spared, mostly children, became slaves in a state whose constitution banned black slavery. Huntsmen, an official report noted, "auctioned [them] off to the highest bidder" in Los Angeles, Sacramento, and San Francisco. Southern whites who moved to California thought Diggers made "as obedient and humble slaves as the negroes in the south." Even so, there were too few of them to satisfy the demand for workers because so many had been killed. Only immigrants from China could fill that need.[12]

GOLD MOUNTAIN

In the 1850s, the Middle Kingdom suffered from soaring opium addiction, crippling taxes, droughts, floods, crop failures, and famines. So when news of the Gold Rush reached China, people imagined California as a paradise. Rumors about Gam Saan (Gold Mountain) spread like dust in a high wind, growing more fabulous with each telling. "Money is in great plenty and to spare in America," people told each other. Why, dollar bills grew on trees, and gold nuggets lay in the streets![13]

A one-way ticket on a sailing ship cost a great deal. Few people could afford the fifty-dollar fare, but labor contractors willingly advanced them the money, to be deducted from their future wages.

It was hard for a man—most Chinese migrants were men—to leave the only home he'd ever known. A folk song caught the mood:

In [1852], a trip to Gold Mountain
was made.

With a pillow on my shoulder,
  I began my perilous journey:
Sailing a boat . . . across the sea,
Leaving behind wife and sisters
  in search of money,
No longer lingering with the woman
  in the bedroom,
No longer paying respect to parents
  at home.

The typical migrant saw himself not as a settler in a new country but as a "bird of passage." He expected to work hard, live frugally, save as much as possible, and return wealthy to his native village after a few years. There, he would enjoy the rest of his life amid an adoring family and respectful neigh-bors. The reality, however, proved quite different. Hard as they worked, few of these men were able to save enough to return to China.[14]

Migrant ships usually sailed from Canton, China's opium capital. The voyage lasted from six to ten weeks, depending on the weather. Many ships sank in storms, drowning everyone aboard. Disease, bad food, and foul water also took a heavy toll. Some ship captains reported sailing through patches of floating corpses, Chinese thrown overboard when they died.

Upon landing in San Francisco, newcomers headed for the goldfields, easily getting work as miners. By the 1860s, as gold production fell and new

Chinese immigrants mining
for gold in California.
(Date unknown)

mines became harder to find, laborers were taking jobs elsewhere. An estimated 10,000 Chinese were hired by the Central Pacific Railroad to build the western section of the first transcontinental rail line, which, when completed in 1869, linked California to the eastern United States.

Employers valued their Chinese workers. Central Pacific president Leland Stanford, who later founded Stanford University, praised them for being "quiet, peaceable, industrious, economical—ready and apt to learn all the different kinds of work" needed in railroad building. After all, their ancestors had built the Great Wall of China. All-Chinese crews laid tracks, built bridges across wide valleys, and tunneled through mountains in the dead of winter. An astonished observer wrote: "The rugged mountains looked like stupendous ant-hills. They swarmed with [Chinese], shoveling, wheeling, carting, drilling and blasting rocks and earth." Opium addiction does not seem to have been a problem among construction crews, though police reported opium dens in several West Coast cities, notably San Francisco. Originating in India, the raw opium was usually refined in the town of Victoria, on Van-

THE YELLOW TERROR IN ALL HIS GLORY

A fear-mongering cartoon warning of "the yellow terror" and the grave danger posed to white women. (c. 1899)

couver Island, off Canada's west coast, dubbed the "opium capital of the New World."[15]

After completion of the transcontinental line in 1869, the workers sought other occupations. Ranches employed Chinese as cowboys and cooks on cattle drives. Nearly every western town had a Chinese community—a little Chinatown. Some Chinese opened small businesses of their own: laundries, restaurants, and bakeries. Those who worked for wages, a report noted, sought the same jobs "performed by white men at higher wages." And that spelled trouble.[16]

In California, the trouble began in the goldfields, then spread to the towns. Police officers might look the other way as white mobs went on a "tear." In the best-known outrage, a Los Angeles mob shot and hung twenty Chinese in one night in 1871. "Chinese treated worse than dog," a survivor recalled years later. "We were simply terrified; we kept indoors after dark for fear of being shot in the back." The justice system gave no justice, for the law barred Chinese, blacks, and Indians from testifying against whites.[17]

The belief in white supremacy intensified economic rivalries. The racist slogan "California for Americans" became commonplace. By definition, racists insisted, whites alone could be Americans. "We desire only a white population in California," announced San Francisco's *Californian* newspaper. The *Shasta Courier* went further, recycling the anti-black fable of race mixing. "If the Chinese are to live amongst us as our equals," an editorial writer asked, "are we willing that they should marry our sons and daughters and people our country with a motley race of

half-breeds?" A farmers' convention drew the logical conclusion. It resolved: "This State should be a State for white men. We want no other race here. . . . All other races shall be excluded."[18]

An organized movement to keep the Chinese out of the United States began in California. One group's very name embodied its program: the Order of Caucasians for the Extermination of the Chinaman. California's state legislature, however, was unwilling to go that far. So, in 1879, it asked the U.S. Congress to bar "Chinamen." Support for the measure grew steadily; members of the U.S. House of Representatives from western and southern states favored it unanimously. In May 1882, Congress easily passed the Chinese Exclusion Act. According to this law, Chinese laborers already in the United States could stay but, as nonwhites, could never become U.S. citizens. An updated version of the act, passed in 1888, forbade entry to "all persons of Chinese race" except teachers, students, and merchants.

The banning of Chinese laborers had an unexpected result. It served as a magnet, drawing Japanese immigrants to American shores.[19]

SONS OF THE RISING SUN

Japan changed rapidly under Emperor Meiji, but modernization did not benefit everyone. After 1868, land was scarce and farms were as small as ever. To ensure that a farm could support a family, by custom the eldest son inherited the entire property when his father died. The heir's sisters might hope to marry farmers with land of their own. But his brothers had little to look forward to in their home village or in the cities, where factory jobs paid low wages in order to hold down the prices of exports the economy relied upon. Going into the army was a possibility, though it offered almost no chance of advancement for the common soldier.

America's lure was plentiful work at good pay, compared to the sixteen cents a day offered by Japanese factories. From 1885 to 1908, some 72,000 Japanese came to the West Coast directly or by way of Hawaii, which became a U.S. territory in 1898. About the same number stayed in Hawaii, mostly working as field hands on sugar and pineapple plantations. Emigrants were a select group of young men with an eighth-grade education who had been screened by Tokyo, Imperial officials said, to "maintain Japan's national honor." The largest number came from the Hiroshima district, where farm conditions were awful. Like the Chinese, they intended to work, save, return to their native country, marry, and buy farms or start small businesses. As it did for the Chinese, that dream faded with the passing years. Those immigrants were called *Issei,* the "first generation" of Japanese in America.[20]

Issei (pronounced *EE-say*) usually landed in California, where they found jobs in lumbering, mining, and fishing. Others worked on the Northern Pacific Railway, which ran from St. Paul, Minnesota, to Seattle, Washington, and Portland, Oregon. Sweltering in summer and freezing in winter, they laid tracks, built bridges, and cleared the right-of-way of snow and fallen rocks. The men sang:

A railroad worker—
That's me!
I am great.
Yes, I am a railroad worker.

Complaining:
"It is too hot!"
"It is too cold!"
"It rains too often!"
"It snows too much!" . . .
I am a railroad worker![21]

Hard work paid off. Before long, Issei began to leave entry-level jobs, using their savings to strike out on their own. A survey taken in 1906 lists some of their occupations: barbers, shoemakers, tailors, restaurant and grocery store owners, and operators of laundries, watch-repair shops, shooting galleries, and bathhouses. A few owned rooming houses and small hotels.[22]

Coming as they did from rural Japan, many Issei hoped to become farmers. When they had saved enough money, they leased or bought plots of land. Though they could not afford the best-quality land, which was owned by whites, they knew how to get the most from what they had. Carefully, lovingly, they turned marginal lands into productive fields and orchards. Those with land near cities became truck farmers, growing food to sell at local markets in San Francisco, Los Angeles, and Sacramento. By 1910, Issei were growing 70 percent of California's strawberries and nearly half its citrus fruits, celery, cucumbers, tomatoes, onions, peppers, green peas, and spinach. The growing and selling of flowers in nurseries became a virtual Issei monopoly, with Mother's Day their most profitable day of the year.[23]

While the Issei prospered, white California's resentments against them escalated. In 1900, labor unions and farm groups joined forces to protest "unfair" competition. The frugal Issei, opponents declared, "can underlive us"—that is, could live more cheaply. Pressure built for Congress to revise the Chinese Exclusion Act to apply to the Japanese. Otherwise, they "would wipe out American standards of living . . . and implant an alien and half-breed race on our soil which might make the Negro problem look white."[24]

Openly racist organizations formed, taking names like the Japanese Exclusion League of California, the Japanese and Korean Exclusion League, and the Asiatic Expulsion League. The largest organization, the Native Sons of the Golden West, still exists, though it has turned away from racism. The members of these organizations believed California was the whites' promised land. The Golden State, they said,

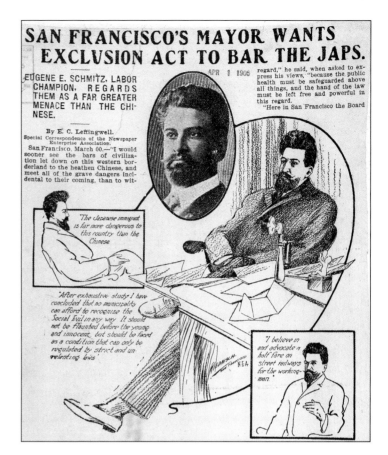

A newspaper article about the need for the Chinese Exclusion Act to be expanded to include Japanese immigrants, citing recognition of the "social evil." (April 1, 1905)

should be what "it has always been and God Himself intended it shall always be—the White Man's Paradise." The slogan "Keep California White" appeared on billboards and signs in store windows across the state.[25]

The charge of sexual aggressiveness was foul as ever. "Driven by a beastly sexual urge, the Jap would endanger the white female and the purity of the Anglo-American stock," racists shrieked. "Would you like your daughter to marry a Japanese?" No "decent"

Newspaper mogul William Randolph Hearst. (c. 1906)

person could condone such an "unnatural act," because "American womanhood is too sacred to be subjected to such degeneracy."[26]

Newspapers fanned the flames of hatred. The Founders believed that democracy required a free press to inform voters about key issues and expose corruption, inevitable in any political system. Since colonial times, newspapers had been written for the educated reader. Dull and expensive, they appeared in small type, without illustrations. Their aim was not to excite readers but to present facts and let readers judge for themselves.

By the time the first Issei arrived in the 1880s, a new kind of newspaper was available in America. To increase sales and profits, owners sought to attract a larger, less educated audience, not just upper-class readers. Owners redesigned their papers, using bold, eye-catching headlines, line drawings, and comic strips. Each issue sold for a penny and featured articles about secret plots, murders, and scandals written in simple words and short paragraphs. Articles with titles like "Why Young Girls Kill Themselves," "How It Feels to Be a Murderer," and "Strange Things Women Do for Love" appeared regularly.

A San Francisco native, William Randolph Hearst, presided over what one historian has called the "sewer system of American journalism." For Hearst and his kind, "truth" was anything that boosted sales, even if reporters had to make up a "story." Eventually, his publishing empire had twenty major newspapers and five leading magazines, including *Cosmopolitan* and *Harper's Bazaar.* In 1905, Hearst began a campaign against Japan and Japanese immigrants that lasted through the Second World War.[27]

Hearst's *San Francisco Examiner* ran anti-Japanese stories under scary headlines:

JAPAN MAY SEIZE THE PACIFIC SLOPE

THE YELLOW PERIL IS HERE

BROWN MEN HAVE MAPS AND COULD

SEIZE LAND EASILY

JAPAN PLANS TO INVADE AND

CONQUER THE UNITED STATES

It also charged the Issei with being Japanese soldiers in disguise, an outright lie.

The *Examiner*'s competitor, the *San Francisco Chronicle,* ran a series of equally fantastic stories:

JAPANESE A MENACE TO AMERICAN

WOMEN

BROWN MEN AN EVIL IN THE PUBLIC

SCHOOLS

THE YELLOW PERIL — HOW JAPANESE

CROWD OUT THE WHITE RACE

BROWN ARTISANS STEAL BRAINS OF

WHITES[28]

It took a natural disaster to still the drumbeat of hatred, at least temporarily. In April 1906, an earthquake struck San Francisco, killing more than 4,000 and leaving the city in ruins. Japanese people knew about earthquakes, which occur frequently in Japan, and they sympathized with the victims. Issei in California, Canada, and Hawaii contributed to the relief effort, as did people in Japan itself. Of the 30,000 destitute San Franciscans who applied for public relief, not one was an Issei. The Issei cared for their own.[29]

If they were expecting thanks, they were in for a shock. In October 1906, the San Francisco Board of Education ordered Japanese children to attend a segregated "Oriental School" in Chinatown. Why? Those youngsters—93 out of the city's 25,000 public school pupils—were said to be crowding whites out of classrooms! Tokyo's ambassador to Washington protested. "It seems too bad," he said, "that the poor, innocent Japanese school children should be subjected to such indignities. Such action . . . is resented very bitterly by all Japanese." Japan erupted with indignation. Anti-American riots swept the country. In Tokyo, members of the Diet demanded war.[30]

President Theodore Roosevelt—called "TR" by his friends—was astonished. Though he considered the Chinese a "race-foe" and believed God had reserved America "as a heritage for the white people," he admired the Japanese. He loved to traipse around the White House in samurai armor and practice *jujitsu,* the Japanese art of fighting without weapons. He read about Bushido and bought sixty copies of a book on the subject to give as gifts.[31]

But now the "infernal fools in California," TR complained, had created a crisis. "With so proud and sensitive a people [as the Japanese], neither lack of money nor future complications will prevent a war if once they get sufficiently hurt and angry," he wrote a senator. To avoid a Pacific war, he vowed to use federal power to protect Japanese immigrants. If mobs threatened them with violence, he would send troops to keep order, with bullets if necessary. At a White House meeting, he persuaded San Francisco's school board to cancel its segregation order in return for his promise to bar Japanese from entering the United States from Hawaii, Canada, and Mexico.[32]

Problem: How to "save face" for Tokyo? TR knew the Japanese government could not publicly agree to anything that appeared to yield to Yankee pressure. So he secretly negotiated the so-called Gentlemen's Agreement of 1907. Under its terms, Japan "voluntarily" agreed to stop issuing passports to laborers. The president then promised to persuade congressional leaders to kill any proposal to limit emigration from Japan itself. There would be no Japanese Exclusion Act.

The deal did not satisfy certain Japanese generals and admirals. Rumors reached the White House that they favored a surprise attack on the United States, like the one recently launched on Russian forces in Manchuria. Though the Imperial high command firmly rejected this idea, the president decided to play it safe. When the Gentlemen's Agreement went into effect, he asked Congress for money to develop Pearl Harbor as a naval base.

PICTURE BRIDES

President Roosevelt either ignored or failed to see the importance of a clause in the Gentlemen's Agreement that allowed Tokyo to issue passports to the wives, children, and parents of Japanese citizens already living in the United States.

Most of those Issei were male, young, and single. In 1900, only 410 married Japanese women were living in America, nearly all in California. Only 25 of the 93 children ordered to attend San Francisco's segregated school were American-born. The Gentlemen's

Picture brides from Japan arriving at Angel Island, California, for processing. (c. 1910)

Agreement came at a time when many Issei men no longer earned a living as common laborers, but as farmers and businessmen. Obviously, their economic future lay in America.[33]

Married men who had left wives and children in Japan, and could afford the expense, sent for them. Other men went to Japan seeking mates in person and then brought them to America. A third group could not afford to take the time to travel or lacked the funds to pay for two return steamship tickets. The Gentlemen's Agreement gave them the chance to marry *and* to save money.

When a bachelor decided to marry, he wrote his parents, asking them to find him a wife. Normally, they went to a matchmaker, a person who arranged marriages for a fee. When the matchmaker found a likely young woman, the fathers met to discuss their families' backgrounds, education, and money matters. By Japanese custom, marriage was not a private affair, the result of a couple meeting and "falling in love." Parents "knew best" and had the final say in questions of marriage. Their children simply obeyed. A refusal showed disrespect for parents, an unforgivable offense. Love probably would follow later, as the couple came to know each other.

If both sets of parents approved the match, the couple exchanged photographs. The would-be groom also wrote about his life in America: his work, his home, even his bank account. A few weeks later, with her parents' blessing, the "picture bride" appeared at the wedding ceremony. Because the groom was thousands of miles away, a male relative or friend stood in his place. After the ceremony, the newly-wed went to live with her in-laws until it was time to leave for America.

Picture brides knew they had little chance of seeing Japan again. One expressed in a haiku what so many must have felt:

> *With tears in my eyes*
> *I turn back to my homeland,*
> *Taking one last look.*[34]

The women became anxious as Japan faded behind the waves.

Many from the interior of the country had never gone beyond the boundaries of their villages, much less seen the ocean or a steamship. Only a privileged few could afford a cabin on an upper deck. Most traveled in steerage, the lowest deck, which housed the cables that controlled the ship's rudder. They slept on bunk beds, arranged three-high in double rows. "We were packed into the ship in one big room," one woman recalled. "There was no privacy, no comforts, no nothing. We were like silkworms on a tray, eating and sleeping." Ship's food was awful: "The soup served every morning contained only two or three small pieces of dried tofu and was watery and tasteless." Rice, the staple of the Japanese diet, "was so hard it wouldn't go down the throat." Thumping, clanging, vibrating engines made restful sleep impossible. The ship's endless rocking caused seasickness and vomiting. Steerage stank to high heaven.[35]

After two or three weeks at sea, the ship docked at the Angel Island Immigration Station in San Francisco Bay. "I had never seen such a prison-like place," recalled Kamechiyo Takahashi. "There were threefold wire nets on the wall, and a thick wire net outside" the wooden barracks. Immigration agents checked passports and asked a series of questions, as required by U.S. law: Have you ever been a prostitute? Did you work in Japan? At what? Will someone meet you? Who? Since American law barred immigrants with serious illnesses, agents were especially alert to signs of trachoma and hookworm infection. Trachoma is a contagious eye disease caused by bacteria; hookworms are tiny bloodsucking worms that live in the intestines. After several days of "processing," an agent led the newcomers to the ferry to the mainland.[36]

Picture brides walked down the gangplank onto the dock with their hair piled high and their faces heavily powdered. To make a good impression on their waiting husbands, they had saved their best outfit for this moment. Many wore brightly colored traditional *kimonos,* ankle-length silk robes embroidered with intricate patterns. On their feet, they wore white split-toe socks that fit around the fabric thongs attached to their *geta,* which resembled today's flip-flops. A wooden board formed the sole of this sandal, and two wooden blocks, called "teeth," were affixed underneath to raise the foot several inches above the ground.

Their "welcoming committees" were not always what the women had expected. Gangs of waterfront toughs had a field day with them. Nisuke Mitsumori never forgot the experience.

"As we went along," she recalled, "we were bombarded with abuses such as 'Japs.' . . . They even picked horse dung off the street and threw it at us. I was baptized with horse dung. This was my very first impression of America."[37]

Any number of picture brides found that pictures could lie. Husbands might not be as youthful as they'd appeared. Some photos had been doctored to hide warts, pimples, and pockmarks. Nor were the men as well-off as they had claimed, having posed for photos with someone else's fine house in the background. Farm laborers presented themselves as farm owners, and shopkeepers as big-time merchants. Brides might be so disappointed that they took the next ship back to Japan, if they had enough money. The vast majority, however, resolved to adjust to their new lives.

Upon leaving the dock, husbands usually took their wives to a store that sold Western-style clothes. Sakiko Suyama, married in 1913, recalled the experience. Off with your kimono and geta! Afterward, she hardly recognized herself in the mirror: "I, in a big hat and high laced shoes, wearing a high-necked blouse and trailing skirt belted and buckled at the waist—and of course for the first time in my life a brassiere."

The outfit was strange enough, but "the trouble was the underwear! Japanese women were only accustomed to use petticoats. Wearing Western panties for the first time, I frequently forgot to pull them down when I went to the toilet so I often got them wet."[38]

Between 1908 and 1924, some 67,000 picture brides landed on Hawaii and the U.S. mainland. Nearly all had to work beside their husbands. Farmers' wives toiled especially hard in the fields, from daybreak to sundown. One described the numbing fatigue:

> *Vexed beyond my strength,*
> *I wept. And then the wind came*
> *Drying up all tears.*

For these women and their sisters, work never really ended, because they had three jobs: field work, housekeeping, and child care.[39]

NISEI

Picture brides were usually in their late teens or early twenties; Issei husbands were usually ten to fifteen years older. Because these women were in their peak childbearing years, nature took its course. Babies arrived, lots of them, in the two decades after the Gentlemen's Agreement. They were called *Nisei,* the "second generation."

Nisei (pronounced *NEE-say*) were special. American law defined their Japanese-born parents as "resident aliens" ineligible for citizenship because they were not "white persons." Members of the second generation, however, were automatically citizens, because they were born in the States. Their arrival had a profound effect, convincing their Issei parents to stay in the new land. For despite all the prejudice, America was "a good place to live," a land of opportunity. An Issei quoted a Chinese poem:

> *Ancestors' land is not the only*
> *place where you should bury your*
> *bones.*
> *Man can be buried in any mountain*
> *of the world.*[40]

The first generation, like all immigrants who arrived as adults, could never completely shed their Japaneseness. Nor did they wish to, because Japanese culture had shaped them in many positive ways, such as devotion to family and work. Also, adjusting to America was not easy. The English language was hard to learn and to speak correctly. Even those who became proficient in it had a Japanese accent. This is not unusual with immigrants. When I was a boy, my parents and their friends could read English perfectly. But after six decades in America, they still had Polish and Russian accents.

America, however, shaped the second generation from the outset. For the Nisei, assimilation was never an issue. "We are Americans, not by virtue of our birth in America, but by virtue of the social and cultural forces in America," witness Michio Kunitani told a congressional committee just weeks after Pearl Harbor. "We are Americans, not by mere technicality of birth, but by all the other forces of sports, amusements, schools, churches, which . . . affect our lives directly. Some of us are Yankee fans; some of us are Dodger fans. . . . We listen to Beethoven, and some of us even go through the *Congressional Record*." Nisei spoke Japanese at home, though seldom fluently, and English with American accents everywhere else. Often they called themselves by translations of their Japanese first names. In this way, Makoto became Mac, and Katsu (Victory) became Victor.[41]

Differences in outlook developed between parents and children. Yoshiko Uchida, born in 1921, gave a telling illustration. As a child in Berkeley, California, she was embarrassed if her mother acted "in what seemed to me a non-American way," the author recalled. "I would cringe when I was with her as she met a Japanese friend on the street and began a series of bows, speaking all the while in Japanese. 'Come on, Mama,' I would interrupt, tugging at her sleeve. 'Let's go,' I would urge, trying to terminate the long exchange of amenities. I felt disgraced in public." Mothers, however, objected when their daughters walked in the American manner, bounding along like frisky colts. "Why do you take such big steps," they'd scold. "You walk like a boy! Can't you be more feminine?"[42]

Nisei faced the questions we all must answer in growing up: What path should I take in life? How shall I earn a living? One thing, however, was never in doubt. Issei parents wanted their children to get an education—no matter what. Education, to them, was a magical key that would open America's doors of opportunity. Of all immigrant groups, only the Japanese did not send their children out to work. Recent Italian and East European Jewish immigrants, for example, often sent their children, usually daughters, into New York's garment factories. Irish children sold newspapers on street corners. Irish and Italian boys helped dig the city's sewers and subway tunnels. Their earnings helped put food on the table, but also bought steamship tickets for other family members to come to America. The Issei, on the other hand, scrimped and saved, even on necessities, for their children's education. "You have an opportunity your parents never had," they'd say. "Go to school and study. Don't miss that opportunity when it comes."[43]

Young Nisei might attend two schools: public schools on weekdays and Japanese schools on weekends. The Japanese schools aimed at passing the language, history, arts, and manners of the old country to the next generation. By the 1930s, some teachers at these schools were emphasizing pupils' loyalty to Japan and its world "mission." Daniel Inouye recalled his Japanese teacher lecturing on the Japanese "homeland," to which students owed total loyalty. "When Japan calls," the teacher told his students, "you must know that it is Japanese blood that flows in your veins." Such messages left little, if any, impression. After Pearl Harbor,

Inouye and his friends volunteered for the U.S. Army. He became a war hero and later a U.S. senator from Hawaii.[44]

Public school teachers found their Nisei pupils to be serious, diligent, and patriotic. School photographs show Nisei holding the Stars and Stripes at assemblies and pledging allegiance. It was almost unthinkable, a dreadful "loss of face," for a parent to be called to school about a child's grades or behavior. Parents took pride in their children's grades. "It was important to succeed in school," a Nisei recalled. "I enjoyed seeing those A's on my report card, but a big part of the pleasure came in seeing how pleased my parents were. I guess you might say I worked for good grades, because it made my parents happy."[45]

After graduating from high school, many Nisei went on to earn degrees from colleges and universities. Yet they found that good grades were not enough to break into the mainstream economy. Prejudices do not simply vanish by themselves, especially when stirred by large special-interest groups and the likes of William Randolph Hearst. Seldom could highly qualified Nisei professionals—doctors, dentists, and lawyers—follow careers outside their own community. Most graduates had to take jobs well beneath their qualifications, in Japanese shops, laundries, fruit stands, and the like. A common joke, told through clenched teeth, went like this: "Whenever you saw beautifully stacked apples in the grocery store, you knew they had been arranged by a college-trained engineer." One disappointed graduate described himself as "a professional carrot washer."[46]

CLOSING DOORS

Resistance to the "Japanese Invasion" continued. During the 1912 presidential election campaign, Woodrow Wilson, the Democratic candidate and an ardent white supremacist (born in Virginia, he was a son of the South), appealed to California voters by denying that the Japanese could "blend with the Caucasian race." The following year, President Wilson made segregation U.S. government policy. With the stroke of a pen, he forced black and white federal employees to use separate cafeterias and toilets. Wilson's actions further encouraged racists in California. The state legislature easily passed the California Alien Land Law of 1913, which banned non-citizens from owning farmland or leasing farmland for more than three years.

Because the word *non-citizens* could also mean whites, follow-up legislation, the California Alien Land Law of 1920, banned immigrants "ineligible for citizenship" from leasing farmland. The Issei responded in a most American fashion: they hired lawyers to find ways around these laws. The best way turned out to be the simplest: parents leased or bought land in the names of their American-born children.[47]

During the early 1920s, the anti-Japanese crusade grew nastier. In Washington State, for example, the *Seattle Star* ran sensational articles with inflammatory headlines: "Charge: Jap Choked White Woman," "Charge: Jap Stole White Wife's Love," and "One-Third of Our Hotels Jap Owned." The

Woodrow Wilson, as governor of New Jersey, shortly before running for president. (c. 1911)

American Legion and other patriotic organizations denounced Japanese "abuses." California, as usual, led the way. A slogan making the rounds said it all: "Keep California White." The Japanese were "breeding like rabbits," railed a state legislator; before long, "they will outnumber the white people." A circular warning Japanese to stay away from Hollywood read: "We don't want you with us so, get busy, Japs, and move out of Hollywood!" Roadside billboards bore messages in bold letters: JAPS: DON'T LET THE SUN SET ON YOU HERE. KEEP MOVING! A sign posted in San Francisco's Golden Gate Park stated JAPANESE ARE NOT ADMITTED.[48]

The agitation on the West Coast sparked a nationwide movement. Southerners, with their strong beliefs in white supremacy, joined the assault. Congress began debate on a proposal to bar Asian immigrants entirely. South Carolina senator Ellison DuRant Smith, a fiery speaker, set the tone: "We now have sufficient population in our country for us to shut the door and to breed up a pure, unadulterated American citizenship." He meant citizens who were undiluted, untainted members of the white race. Debate ended with passage of the Immigration Act of 1924. By wide majorities, Congress closed America's doors to all persons ineligible for citizenship. Translation: to all nonwhites, but chiefly to Japanese.[49]

Nobody in the Senate or the House of Representatives seemed to care that, without consulting Japan, the new law canceled the Gentlemen's Agreement negotiated by President Theodore Roosevelt. But the outburst that followed in Japan made the reaction to the 1906 San Francisco school segregation dispute seem tame.

Tokyo's ambassador to Washington resigned in protest, as did Washington's ambassador to Tokyo. Japanese newspapers branded the law "most humiliating to the Japanese race," an "unfriendly act," and "a wound that will hurt and rankle for generations and generations." The government declared an official "National Humiliation Day," and "Hate America" rallies rocked major cities. Over 10,000 people gathered in a Tokyo stadium to shout: "Start a war with America!" A mob broke through the gates of the U.S. embassy, hauled down the Stars and Stripes, cut it into shreds, and stomped on the pieces. As the mob's fury mounted, a student fell to his knees and slowly, deliberately, sliced his belly open. Worse yet, the Immigration Act of 1924 was a gift to extremists. It is hard to imagine an American action better suited to strengthen the military's grip on Japanese society.[50]

KIBEI

Meanwhile, the Issei feared that even their American-born children would never gain acceptance. Already, in the early 1920s, parents were sending hundreds of Nisei each year to live with relatives in Japan and complete their education there. Those who decided to stay in Japan after graduation, parents hoped, would qualify for better jobs than they were likely to get in the States. Hopefully, the others, called *Kibei* (pronounced *KEE-bay* and meaning "returned to America"), would be able to find jobs more easily with American branches of Japanese companies.

It was not to be. Nisei visitors felt out of place in Japan. Though they looked Japanese, they thought and acted like Americans. Japanese people, even their relatives, regarded them as loud, gum-chewing "foreigners." Visitors no doubt would have nodded in agreement had they read the letters of

Mary Kimoto Tomita. Born in 1918 in Ceres, a small farming town in California, at twenty-one Mary went to Japan to study. While there, she wrote dozens of letters to Miye Yamasaki, her best friend in California, and to Kay Oka, a fellow Nisei student in Tokyo. Mary's letters say nothing about politics. Instead, they portray Japan through the eyes of an intelligent woman at a critical time in its history.

Japan's overcrowding made Mary feel "like you can't even breathe." Outside the main cities, towns were depressing places. "Miye—you have no idea of what Japanese towns are until you see one. They are all the same. Narrow streets. No sidewalks. Small unpainted one-room shacks on either side of the street. . . . Dirty children with sores on their heads. Working men scantily dressed and browned and weather-beaten. Country girls with straight hair in a short pigtail with fat legs and thick ankles."[51]

Mary found Japanese women at once astonishing and infuriating. "Old ladies ride bikes," she wrote. "You see women nursing children everywhere. Lots of women go bare to the waist when cleaning house." In public, however, married women were expected to act humbly, meekly, walking a few steps behind their husbands. "I feel like punching those men, or sticking a pin in them to watch all their inflated hot gas ooze out. They give me a pain in the neck."[52]

The war in China, still raging, hung over Japan like a black cloud. Everyday items were expensive and hard to find: eggs, cooking oil, charcoal, pots, pans, soap, fruit. "Oh for some grapes and peaches—and green apples, I surely miss them," Mary wrote Miye. "Rice, rice and more RICE. Three times a day. Every day of the week. I don't see how they live on it." There is "always talk about save this or save that." But when it came to saving lives, the men in power were silent. By early 1941, nearly 400,000 Japanese men had died in China.[53]

Wherever Mary turned, she saw the war's human cost. She met young women doomed to spinsterhood because "most of the eligible men go off to China for cannon fodder." Her cousin's husband, on leave after three years at the front, seemed detached and numb. "He said that when you chop off a Chinaman's head, the blood spurts in two spots for a yard in the air." He usually moped around the house, mumbling the word *baka* (stupid) to himself. Mary heard about a woman who "saw her son in a dream bowing to her the very night that he was killed." Weekday mornings, on the way to class, Mary passed streetcars filled with men in snow-white kimonos, an outfit reserved for crippled soldiers. Time and again, the trains she boarded in Tokyo had "a lot of boxes . . . [and] each contained the ashes of a soldier." Only broken men and ashes came out of China. Like so many other Nisei, she could not stand Japan anymore.[54]

So Mary joined 200 "Nisei girls like me" aboard the *Tatsuta Maru* at Yokohama. Six days later, as it steamed across the Pacific, bound for San Francisco, an urgent radio message arrived: Turn around! Come back to port at once! It was December 7, 1941.[55]

THE PATH TO THE DARK SIDE

Fear is the path to the dark side. Fear leads to anger.
Anger leads to hate. Hate leads to suffering.
— JEDI MASTER YODA, *Star Wars: The Phantom Menace* (1999)

"REMEMBER PEARL HARBOR!"

It is difficult, after three-quarters of a century, to re-create the mood on December 7, 1941. In Japan, Emperor Hirohito hailed the Pearl Harbor attack with a declaration of war waged in Japan's "self-defense" to punish America for "disturbing the peace of East Asia." At the Navy Ministry in Tokyo, gleeful officers ran through the corridors, shouting, "We did it! We did it! The war's really begun!" As Radio Tokyo blared "The Battleship March" and other martial tunes, civilians reacted with "deep emotion" and "tears of thanks." Patriotic poets hailed the attack as the start of a "Holy War" fought by "divine heroes" against the "animal-like" Americans. A poet wrote:

The time has come
To slaughter America and England;
Ah, how refreshing:
The clouds in the four heavens
Have simultaneously cleared.[1]

Others disagreed but, mindful of the Tokko (Thought Police), spoke only to their diaries and to those they absolutely trusted. Author Nagi Kafu noted in his diary that Japan's leaders were "stupid and vulgar" men who despised the common people. A professor at Tokyo Imperial University whispered to a friend that, yes, the American fleet had been sunk, but "this means Japan is sunk, too." A Zero pilot thought the attack was justified yet was carried out dishonorably: "In the old wars, when the samurai drew his sword to attack the enemy, he shouted at him or otherwise drew his attention so that he could be ready to face him for the attack."[2]

Across the Pacific, December 7 began as a normal Sunday for millions of Americans. But as news of Pearl Harbor flashed from coast to coast, the world changed in ways they would remember for the rest of their lives. In the White House, Franklin D. Roosevelt, a distant cousin of former president TR, was furious. Moments after learning of the attack, the wheelchair-bound president, a victim of polio, was pushed down the hallway toward the Oval Office. Secret Service agent Mike Reilly, chief of the presidential security detail, saw him and later wrote, "His chin stuck out about two feet in front of his knees and he was the maddest Dutchman I or anybody ever saw."[3]

Next day, FDR, as he was called by everyone, gave his "date that will live in infamy" speech. I was nearly six years old when he addressed Congress and the nation. Besides the rich tone of his voice as it came over the radio, I remember the sound of breaking glass. Because my parents and our neighbors could not afford fine glassware, they bought the much cheaper Japanese product. Moments after FDR finished, it seemed that every family on our block was throwing their drinking glasses, teacups, plates, and saucers into the street. "Remember Pearl Harbor!" was on everyone's lips. Japan became the most hated enemy in American history. The nation closed ranks, vowing to grind Japan to dust.

Japanese Americans reacted with shock, anger, and anxiety. Mary Tsukamoto got the news in her small California farming community. "We just couldn't believe it. . . . I remember how stunned we were. And suddenly the whole world turned dark." As if in a daze, high school student Masao Hamamura murmured, "*They* are attacking *us.*"[4]

Rafu Shimpo, a leading Japanese-language newspaper, left no doubt where its readers' loyalties lay. Under the headline "All-Out Victory," it said:

> The bombing of innocent women and children in a surprise attack . . . can never be forgotten. The defeat of Japan is a certainty. By her cowardly and dishonorable stab in the back . . . she has sealed her doom. . . . Suspicion is frequently aroused because of our similarity in facial characteristics to the enemies. But blood ties mean nothing now. We do not hesitate to repudiate and condemn our ancestral country. . . . Fellow Americans, give us a chance to do our share to make this world a better place to live in![5]

Pledges of support from Japanese American groups poured into the White House, studded with declara-

The front page of the Monday-morning Extra edition of the *Los Angeles Times,* announcing the Japanese air attack on Pearl Harbor, Hawaii. The United States and Britain officially declared war on Japan later that day. (December 8, 1941)

tions of loyalty to "our land" and "our country." In Los Angeles, three Issei men committed suicide, unable to bear the shame of Pearl Harbor. One left a note saying: "I don't want to live any more since Japan has attacked this country. . . . I am a registered Japanese alien and I am ashamed."[6]

In Hawaii, Japanese Americans watched the first attack planes arrive

A propaganda poster created by the U.S. government calling for revenge for the Pearl Harbor attack. (c. 1942)

and the first bombs fall on Pearl Harbor. Masao Harold Onishi stood dumbfounded as the battleship *Arizona* exploded, sending chunks of hot steel into his yard. Onishi rushed his family into his car and stepped on the gas. "I looked out the car window and saw the flag of the Rising Sun on the planes. Then I realized it was Japan attacking us." Another man recalled his family running outside and pointing skyward; his mother told him "the 'Japs'

had come." Seventeen-year-old Daniel Inouye ran to help at his high school's first-aid station. Inouye, "choking with emotion," looked up at the sky and shouted, "You dirty Japs!" Inouye and other Nisei used this insulting term because they felt it did not apply to them. After all, they were Americans of Japanese ancestry, not *Japanese* Japanese.[7]

Their country, nevertheless, was at war with their parents' homeland, whose citizens their parents still were. That worried some Nisei. On December 7, the artist Miné Okubo was living in Berkeley, California, having returned from a year's study in Europe. While making breakfast, the twenty-nine-year-old switched on the radio and heard the bulletin: "Pearl Harbor bombed by the Japanese!" Turning to her brother Toku, Miné said, "Oh-oh! We're in trouble!" She was right, but the trouble did not start immediately.[8]

Now and then, there were scowls from passersby, but little open hostility toward Japanese Americans. In Stockton, California, Filipinos and Nisei had a fistfight. In Gilroy, California, shots were fired into a Japanese home, harming nobody. Quick thinking by folksinger Woody Guthrie may have avoided a riot. While performing in

San Francisco's Ace High Bar, he heard a plate-glass window shatter in the Imperial Bar next door, owned by an Issei couple. Guthrie ran outside, into the pouring rain, followed by several tipsy sailors. "Japs is Japs! Get 'em! Jail 'em! Kill 'em!" shouted the mob forming in front of the Imperial Bar. The sailors linked arms while Guthrie calmly strummed his guitar and gave out with an old union song:

> *We will fight together;*
> *We shall not be moved*
> *We will fight together;*
> *We shall not be moved*
> *Just like a tree*
> *That's planted by the water,*
> *We*
> *Shall not*
> *Be moved.*

When the police finally arrived, all they saw was rain-soaked men singing in front of a broken window.[9]

The press behaved responsibly. Most West Coast newspapers called for tolerance. Even the anti-Japanese *San Francisco Chronicle* remained calm. Its December 9 editorial urged readers to respect the feelings of the Issei and Nisei. "There is no excuse to wound the sensibilities of any persons in America by showing suspicion or prejudice.... [Our enemies] would like nothing better than to set the dogs of prejudice on a first-class American Japanese." Within days, however, opinion shifted dramatically. The *Chronicle* thundered: "We have to be tough, even if civil rights ... take a beating for a time." Why the change?[10]

ENEMY ALIENS

Foreigners have always come to America to work, to study, to join their families. For one reason or another, many do not apply for citizenship. In peacetime, the law defines them as "resident aliens"—people living in the United States but owing allegiance to another country. Though they cannot vote or hold government jobs, they pay taxes and enjoy the same protections as American citizens: trial by jury and the freedom to travel, to own property, and to live wherever they choose. However, if their country and the United States go to war, resident aliens become "enemy aliens," subject to internment, or confinement, until the conflict ends.

The use of internment is recognized by U.S. and international law. It can be applied not only to enemy aliens but also to seamen from an enemy country and to their ships in port on the day war is declared. When, for example, America entered the First World War in 1917, the Department of Justice carried out mass arrests of German aliens. After hearings by special panels, only 6,500 wound up in prison barracks located in army camps. A reporter described an upstate New York facility: "The prison contains three rows of barbed wire that enclosed the barracks. Placed at intervals along the barbed wire are twelve elevated sentry boxes with each box armed with a repeating shot gun, a rifle, and a machine gun." Though held in custody, internees had decent living quarters and three meals a day. To fight boredom, wardens encouraged boxing, wrestling, basketball, and the like. Camp libraries offered books; internees in several camps published their own newspapers. Their families in Germany were officially notified of their whereabouts.[11]

In June 1940, as war swept Europe and Asia, Americans feared that it was only a matter of time before the conflict reached their shores. At President Roosevelt's urging, Congress passed the Alien Registration Act. It ordered all resident aliens over the age of fourteen to register at post offices, have their fingerprints and photographs taken, and report any change of address or employment. Within four months, 4.7 million aliens had filed registration forms and received identification cards.

A Justice Department unit, meanwhile, compiled lists of certain groups' potential threats to national security, often based on incomplete or hearsay evidence. During the night of December 7, 1941, the White House set the machinery in motion. From coast to coast, Teletype machines clattered in Federal Bureau of Investigation offices. By midnight, December 9, FBI agents had arrested 865 German, 147 Italian, and 1,291 Japanese aliens. This was just the first batch; more arrests followed in the coming weeks and months.[12]

Though there were far fewer Issei than German and Italian aliens in the United States, Washington distrusted the Issei most. Their language, customs, and appearance had always set them apart. The Issei, moreover, had mixed feelings about Japan's actions in Asia. Though they had lived in the United States for decades, their race barred them from citizenship. Rejection hurt—and increased their pride in Japan. It was different with their children. Nisei were Americans; they did not identify with, much less have strong ties to, their ancestral land. Quite the opposite: some protested Japanese aggression in China, sparking family quarrels.[13]

As the war in China ground on, some Issei groups sent "comfort kits"—packages of dried fruit, candy, soap, and tobacco—to Japanese soldiers fighting there. In an extreme case, the Japanese Association of Pasadena, California, raised money to buy two scout planes for Japan. Such support owed more to lack of knowledge than to anything else. After the Rape of Nanking in 1937, Tokyo imposed a blackout on anything having to do with the atrocities. Propaganda bulletins from Japanese news agencies were reprinted word for word in the immigrant press, becoming the only source of war information for non-English readers. Even so, worsening Japan-U.S. relations did not translate into Issei hatred of their adopted country or a desire to harm it. Yet none of this mattered after Pearl Harbor.[14]

Working hastily from lists of prominent Issei men, FBI agents arrested officials of community organizations, lawyers, journalists, teachers, and clergymen, both Buddhist and Christian. Agents arrested others because they had money in U.S. branches of Japanese banks or worked for Japanese-owned import-export firms. Such arrests had a double aim: to eliminate security risks and to remove the Issei community's natural leaders. A Christian minister, Daisuke Kitagawa, described the effects: "In no time, the whole community was thoroughly panic-stricken; every male lived in anticipation of arrest by the FBI, and every household endured each day in fear and trembling."[15]

The dragnet might sweep you up anywhere. FBI teams nabbed men riding bicycles, walking to work, or stepping off a train. On the night of December 7, agents seized a dozen tuxedo-clad guests at a wedding reception. Mostly, though, they went directly to a man's home. (I cannot find instances of women being arrested.) Arrest teams usually struck at night or early in the morning, when men were sure to be home. A woman named Amy Hiratzka remembered that they first cut the telephone wires to isolate her house. Then came violent knocking at the door. "FBI! Open up!" Sometimes agents just broke down the door and stormed in with pistols drawn.[16]

Family members, bleary-eyed and frightened, were forced to sit at a table while intruders searched their homes.

Weapons and items useful for spying—knives, cameras, flashlights, and short-wave radios—went into evidence bags. So did anything written in Japanese: books, magazines, knitting instructions, personal letters. During one raid, agents took away sacks of sheet music for the *shakuhachi,* the Japanese bamboo flute. Others seized toy swords and plans for model airplanes![17]

Yuriko Hohri, a businessman's daughter, was twelve when the FBI came to her Long Beach, California, home. The experience of armed strangers violating her family's privacy seared itself into Yuriko's memory:

One man went into the kitchen. As I watched, he looked under the sink and he looked into the oven. Then he went into the parlor and opened the glass cases where our most treasured things were. . . . I followed the man into my mother and father's bedroom. Strangers do not usually go into our bedrooms when they first come. As I watched, he went into the closet and brought out my father's golf clubs. He turned the bag upside down. I was only concerned about the golf balls, because I played jacks with them. Then he opened the *tansu,* a chest of drawers. My mother and [three] sisters were weeping.[18]

The FBI left with the man of the house in handcuffs. Days, sometimes weeks, passed before officials revealed his whereabouts and allowed his family to visit. Peter Ota, fifteen at the time, saw his father, a leader in the Japanese Chamber of Commerce of Los Angeles, in the county jail. "When my father walked through the door, my mother was so humiliated. She didn't say anything. She cried. He was in prisoner's clothing, with a denim jacket and a number on the back. The shame and humiliation just broke her down. . . .

A Japanese American family on Terminal Island, California, looks on helplessly as an FBI agent searches through their belongings. (c. 1942)

Right after that day she got very ill and contracted tuberculosis. She had to be sent to a sanitarium. . . . She was there till she passed away."[19]

Eventually, enemy alien prisoners wound up in internment camps in out-of-the-way places like Fort Still, Oklahoma, and Missoula, Montana. Enemy alien hearing boards, made up of civilians chosen by the Department of Justice, took up each case. Families often had no idea where their loved ones were or if they were still alive. Hearings might last weeks before the board reached its decision. The accused had no right to a lawyer, to challenge the evidence against him, or to question the legality of the hearing. At last, the board released, paroled, or ordered him interned until the end of the war. Yet, for the Issei, things were about to get worse—a lot worse.[20]

THE POWER OF FEAR

"Heaven is with us," Radio Tokyo crowed. In the days and weeks after Pearl Harbor, Japanese forces struck targets thousands of miles apart. Each blow was a rude shock for the defenders, as is always the case when reality confronts arrogance. While awaiting at-

FBI agents arrest Japanese American civilians, including many community and religious leaders, on Terminal Island, California. (c. 1942)

tack in British-controlled Hong Kong, for instance, the British felt invincible. Irene Drewery, then a child of eight, recalled that "everyone was going round saying the Japanese wouldn't dare fight us, because they were only little . . . and they didn't know how to fight."[21]

On December 10, the British had their own Pearl Harbor experience when Japanese planes easily sank the battleship *Prince of Wales* and the battle cruiser *Repulse* in the South China Sea. As the planes approached, an officer aboard *Repulse* scoffed, "Oh, but they're Japanese. There's nothing to worry about." Hong Kong fell on Christmas Day. On December 26, American and Filipino troops abandoned Manila, capital of the Philippines, retreating to the

Bataan Peninsula for a last-ditch stand. The 100,000 soldiers in Singapore, Britain's stronghold in Malaya, surrendered on February 15, 1942, to a force less than half their number. In March, the Dutch East Indies fell. By the second week in April, after ferocious fighting, Bataan's defenders surrendered, an event that would have grave results. Admiral Yamamoto had kept his word. Within four months, Japan conquered an empire of ninety million people and vital natural resources.[22]

The war reached America's very doorsteps. German submarines roamed the Atlantic coast. At night, coastal communities saw the horizon lit by

Secretary of the Navy Frank Knox at his desk in Washington, D.C. (c. 1943)

blazing merchant ships and oil tankers. The undersea raiders came so close to shore, reporter Eric Sevareid wrote, "that a chorus girl in a Miami penthouse could see men die in flaming oil." On the western side of the country, long-range Japanese submarines lurked off the California coast, sinking few ships but spreading panic ashore. These attacks caught the U.S. Navy unprepared—"with its pants down," some said. It had only two destroyers and forty-five modern fighter planes to guard the entire Pacific coastline, from northern Washington to southern California. Civil defense was a mess, too, as many cities lacked basic equipment, including air-raid sirens.[23]

A high government official added to the public's anxiety. On December 9, Secretary of the Navy Frank Knox flew to Pearl Harbor to inspect the damage. Knox, formerly general manager of the Hearst newspaper chain, deeply resented Japanese people. After thirty-six hours in Hawaii, he dropped his own bombshell. During a press conference, Knox declared that the attackers had received help from a "fifth column"— that is, from undercover groups weakening America from within. These groups, Knox declared, consisted of people of Japanese descent who had lived in Hawaii for generations. The secretary offered no proof of this damning charge, other than to repeat rumors he'd heard in Honolulu: traitors had cut arrows in sugarcane fields to direct the raiders to their targets, had blocked roads around Pearl Harbor, and had rammed trucks into planes parked on runways. As if that were not bad enough, local Japanese had supposedly driven milk trucks onto military bases, let down the trucks' sides to expose machine guns, and then mowed down hundreds of unarmed soldiers.[24]

Knox's charges struck raw nerves. Mainland newspapers began to print alarmist headlines: "Secretary of the Navy Blames Fifth Columnists for the Raid," "Fifth Column Prepared Attack," "Fifth Column Treachery Told." The New York Times repeated the wildest rumors as fact and even added rumors to the list: Advertisements in Japanese-language newspapers contained coded orders to fifth columnists! Ham radio operators sent information to the Japanese strike force! "Some of the Japanese aviators shot down were wearing the rings of Honolulu high schools and of Oregon State University." None of this was true, but the climate of fear and anger it promoted was all too real. Sadly, these myths were to have long lives. When I was in high school in the early 1950s, my American history teacher, a well-educated man, taught them to us as proven facts. To this day, these "facts" come up in conversations among people of the Pearl Harbor generation.[25]

No instance of sabotage or spying by Japanese Americans has ever been found. Nevertheless, there were Nisei spies in Hawaii—American spies. Orange Group was the code name given to 100 volunteers who reported suspicious persons to the FBI and to the army's intelligence-gathering unit (known as G2) in Honolulu before the Japanese attack.[26]

Tokyo's only military spy assigned to Pearl Harbor was a naval officer named Takeo Yoshikawa. An undercover operator with the Japanese embassy, Yoshikawa was ultra-cautious, avoiding Japanese Americans like poison. "You see," he explained after the war, "I couldn't trust them in Hawaii to help us. They were loyal to the United States." Instead, he got his information from sources available to anyone. The spy read everything he could find about the naval base in military journals and newspapers. He bought tourist guides, detailed maps, and postcards of Honolulu and its surrounding area. On weekends, he hired private planes and flew over the base, snapping photos of its defenses and the location of each warship in its berth. Equally important, Yoshikawa logged ships' comings and goings from the second floor of a restaurant on a hilltop overlooking the harbor. As a courtesy, the restaurant provided telescopes so tourists could get a better view. The information he sent enabled Japanese experts to build a scale model of the base, exact in every detail, to use for planning and training the attack pilots.[27]

Meanwhile, charges of disloyalty in Hawaii turned public opinion against the West Coast Japanese. By mid-January 1942, a barrage of rumors was stoking invasion fears. Fantastic stories seemed to come out of thin air, growing scarier with each telling: Issei farmers had planted rows of tomatoes as "arrows" pointing at airfields! Other Issei ignited "fire-arrows" aimed at Seattle and set fire to trees—"signal fires"— atop cliffs overlooking the Pacific! Traitors tore down exposed telephone lines! Army listening posts in California heard mysterious radio signals beamed out to sea! All this made "sense," because air patrols had spotted a Japanese "battle fleet" exactly 164 miles west of San Francisco! Nor was there a shortage of people to confirm these "facts," because they had heard them from a friend of a friend of an "eyewitness."[28]

GREED, HATRED, RACISM

Since the 1890s, various groups had hyped Imperial Japan's threat to the West Coast. For them, the attack on Pearl Harbor was a godsend. To exploit the disaster for their own ends, they played on fears of a fifth column to demand the expulsion of Japanese Americans.

Farmers, especially, had always resented the economic success of the Issei. Now, by using the war as an excuse, they set out to smash their competitors and take over their land. The Grower-Shipper Vegetable Association of Salinas, California, was brutally frank about its goal. "We're charged with wanting to get rid of the Japs for selfish reasons," it said in a press release. "We might as well be honest. We do. If all the Japs were removed tomorrow, we'd never miss them in two weeks, because the white farmer can take over and produce everything the Jap grows. And we don't want them back when the war ends either."[29]

Racists, true to form, hopped onto the kick-out-the-Japanese bandwagon. For sheer nastiness, however, few equaled Henry McLemore, a columnist for the Hearst newspaper chain. On January 29, 1942, McLemore wrote in the *San Francisco Examiner:*

> I know this is the melting pot of the world and all men are created equal and there must be no such thing as race or creed hatred, but do those things go when a country is fighting for its life? Not in my book. . . . I am for the immediate removal of every Japanese on the West Coast to a point deep in the interior. I don't mean a nice part of the interior either. Herd 'em up, pack 'em off and give 'em the inside room in the badlands. Let 'em be pinched, hurt, hungry and dead up against it. . . . Personally, I hate the Japanese. And that goes for all of them.[30]

Cartoonists inflamed the public's fears, too. During the 1940s, most newspapers ran cartoons illustrating current issues in humorous ways. After Pearl Harbor, one cartoonist earned a unique anti-Japanese reputation, all but forgotten today. Theodor Seuss Geisel, best known as Dr. Seuss, later became famous for his whimsical children's books like *Yertle the Turtle* and *The Cat in the Hat.* Geisel also worked for *PM,* a popular New York newspaper. His most biting cartoon, "Waiting for the Signal from Home," depicts an endless line of identical, grinning West Coast Japanese men approaching a booth bearing the sign HONORABLE 5TH COLUMN. A slant-eyed traitor hands each man a package of TNT (a powerful explosive) as he passes. The army

An anti-Japanese cartoon created by Theodor Seuss Geisel, best known as Dr. Seuss. (February 13, 1942)

later sent Geisel to Hollywood to work on anti-Japanese propaganda films.[31]

Hollywood went all out to whip up hysteria. By the summer of 1942, movie studios had released at least a dozen films with titles like *Betrayal from the East, Across the Pacific, Black Dragon,* and *Behind the Rising Sun. Air Force,* from Warner Bros., depicted "traitorous fifth columnists" doing dirty deeds at Pearl Harbor. *Little Tokyo, U.S.A.,* a Twentieth Century-Fox release, assumed that anyone of Japanese descent, Issei or Nisei, was loyal to Emperor Hirohito and posed a threat to America. The movie hammered away at the theme of a "vast army of volunteer spies" engaged in "mass espionage" in the United States for "more than a decade." Children heard on the radio a new version of the dwarfs' work song from Walt Disney's 1937 movie *Snow White and the Seven Dwarfs:*

> *Whistle while you work*
> *Hitler is a jerk*
> *Mussolini is a meanie*
> *And the Japs are worse.*[32]

Earl Warren, as governor of California. A vocal advocate of the uprooting of Japanese Americans, Warren later went on to become chief justice of the United States. (c. 1943–1953)

THE POLITICIANS

Politicians backed demands to uproot the West Coast Japanese. On the state level, we need only focus on Earl Warren, because few had his influence and intellect. A gifted lawyer, Warren was also a shrewd politician and California's attorney general. In later years, he became California's governor and chief justice of the United States.

Warren disliked Japanese people. As a young man, he joined the Native Sons of the Golden West and other anti-Asian groups. Like them, he believed the Japanese could never be loyal Americans. They had, he claimed, "racial characteristics" that set them apart,

binding them forever to Japan. After Pearl Harbor, according to Warren, "an entire race of people, men, women, and children alike—especially United States citizens of Japanese ancestry—[are] poised to take disloyal action against the United States at any moment." Yet nothing happened. Why? Obviously, Warren concluded, the fifth column was biding its time. By his twisted logic, no attack *now* proved that an attack was sure to come *later*. All the traitors needed was "some mysterious signal to be issued by the Japanese enemy." For Warren, then, the choice was between security and what he vaguely called "some principle of law." He chose security by uprooting the West Coast Japanese.[33]

In the meantime, members of the House of Representatives and senators from California, Oregon, and Washington joined forces with their southern colleagues. Their most vocal ally, Representative John Rankin of Mississippi, was a racist to his fingertips, and proud of it. Dubbed the "shoutin'est member of the House of Representatives," Rankin despised anyone who was not a white Protestant. His hate list included Roman Catholics, Jews, and blacks. He called slavery "the greatest blessing the Negro had ever known." And he declared, "Once a Jap, always a Jap. Damn them! Let us get rid of them now!" To reduce their birthrate, Rankin called for Japanese men and women to be locked away in separate prison camps.[34]

VOICES OF REASON

In the weeks before and immediately after Pearl Harbor, some Americans refused to give way to fear, rumors, and racism.

Curtis B. Munson was a special State Department representative acting under White House orders. In October and November 1941, Munson set out to gather information about the loyalty of Japanese Americans. A careful investigator, he had the cooperation of several reliable sources: the FBI, Army and Navy Intelligence, educators, religious leaders, and informants within the Japanese community.

Titled "Japanese on the West Coast," Munson's twenty-five-page report was an accurate description of the West Coast Japanese on the eve of war. "Their family life is disciplined and honorable," the author noted. "The children are obedient and the girls virtuous." The Issei had made America their home and, if allowed, would rush to become citizens; should war come, they "hope that by remaining quiet they can avoid concentration camps or irresponsible mobs." As for the Nisei, they "show a pathetic eagerness to be Americans." Without knowing about the spy Takeo Yoshikawa, Munson drew the same conclusion as he had: that the Japanese "are afraid of and do not trust the Nisei." Though "horrified" by the lax state of civil defense, Munson had confidence in the Japanese community. "There is," he concluded, "no Japanese 'problem' on the Coast. There will be no armed uprising of Japanese."[35]

U.S. Navy lieutenant commander Kenneth D. Ringle, who advised against placing Nisei in camps. (Date unknown)

Kenneth D. Ringle agreed. The Office of Naval Intelligence had assigned Ringle, a U.S. Navy lieutenant commander, to double-check Munson's findings. Ringle's report, turned in three weeks after the Pearl Harbor disaster, was based on contacts he had developed over the years. Ringle, a fluent Japanese speaker, noted that the Japanese "do not themselves trust the Nisei." Though racism clouded people's thinking, there was no more reason to doubt the loyalty of the vast majority of Japanese than of German and Italian Americans. Ringle ended by saying that uprooting them and placing them in camps was "not only unwarranted but very unwise," bound to create problems where none existed before.[36]

The Munson and Ringle reports were not made public. Nor were the findings of J. Edgar Hoover's FBI. A tough-minded lawman, for years Director Hoover had waged war on crime. During the 1930s, desperadoes like bank robber John Dillinger died in hails of bullets fired by his agents. Hoover's "G-men" (government men) also gathered information on individuals and groups likely to threaten national security.

In the weeks after Pearl Harbor, Hoover carried out his own investigation of the West Coast Japanese. Instead of disloyalty, his agents found explanations for nearly every rumor. "Signal fires," for example, were merely piles of brush burned by farmers. Not saboteurs but "cattle scratching their backs on the wires" brought down telephone lines, as they had always done. Radio messages detected by listening posts had nothing to do with Japan. Communications experts found the posts staffed by "unskilled and untrained" operators ignorant about tracing the source of radio signals. In this comedy of errors, the army and navy were reporting each other's signals as those of the Japanese.[37]

All those FBI raids on private homes had produced no incriminating evidence—none. According to the Justice Department, "We have not found a single machine gun, nor have we found any gun in any circumstances indicating that it was to be used in a manner helpful to our enemies. We have not found a single camera which we have reason to believe was for use in espionage."[38]

Hoover's conclusion: Calls to uproot the West Coast Japanese were "based

Director of the FBI J. Edgar Hoover, whose investigation of the West Coast Japanese Americans found no factual data to support the need to uproot them. (April 5, 1940)

primarily upon public and political pressure rather than on factual data." Their fate, however, did not lie with the FBI director or the other investigators. It lay with the man in the White House.[39]

MR. PRESIDENT

The website of the Franklin D. Roosevelt Presidential Library and Museum in Hyde Park, New York, claims that the president bowed to irresistible pressure to uproot the Japanese. The pressure was real. But did he simply give in to it? The facts paint a complex and disturbing picture.[40]

FDR had always liked China and distrusted Japan. He inherited his

affection from his mother, Sara. Her father, Warren Delano, was a partner in Russell & Company of Boston, the nation's leader in the "China trade," a polite term for the opium business. (The *D* in FDR stands for Delano.) As a child in the 1860s, while her father made the family's fortune, Sara lived in his Hong Kong mansion. At the age of twenty-six, she married James Roosevelt, a wealthy widower of Dutch descent, and moved to Hyde Park, his New York estate, where she gave birth to Franklin in 1882. There he grew up

among cherished mementos of China. A bronze bell announced each meal. Antique Chinese furniture filled the rooms. The boy's mother and grandfather filled his head with tales of their happy years in China and their fondness for the Chinese.[41]

Roosevelt held strong opinions about race. Such opinions were not unusual for his time and social position. In the late 1800s, America's upper classes fancied themselves the "best people," divinely chosen to rule and prosper. So did the future president. Roosevelt's people—rich, white, and Protestant—had what he called "blood of the right sort." The Japanese did not.[42]

Roosevelt put his opinions about Japan into print. An article by him titled "Shall We Trust Japan?" was published in the July 1923 issue of *Asia,* a respected current affairs magazine. (FDR's preferred title, "The Japs—a Habit of Mind," had been rejected by the editors.) Then, a year after the Immigration Act of 1924 had banned Japanese immigrants, he wrote nine editorials, all titled "Roosevelt Says," for the *Macon Telegraph.* At the time, FDR, a former assistant secretary of the navy, was in Warm Springs, Georgia, where he owned a rehabilitation facility, trying to recover the use of his legs after a polio attack.

In one of these articles, Roosevelt showed that he viewed people of Japanese origin racially—as a group—not as individuals. Japanese were Japanese in his eyes; they could no more change their nature than a zebra could change its stripes to polka dots. "Japanese immigrants are not capable of assimilation into the American population," FDR declared. "Anyone who has traveled in the Far East knows that the mingling of Asiatic blood with European

and American blood produces, in nine cases out of ten, the most unfortunate results." Admitting more Japanese to the United States, therefore, would "threaten blood purity." The author took such pride in these articles that he had copies bound in pigskin embossed with gold lettering.[43]

Roosevelt was elected president in 1932 and again in 1936. Japan's invasion of China in 1937 intensified his hostility. Even before FDR imposed economic sanctions, he insisted that the Japanese were a "treacherous people" and that aggression "was in the blood" of their leaders. He repeated, with a chuckle, a Chinese folktale about the origins of the Japanese: "A wayward daughter of an ancient Chinese emperor left her native land . . . and finally reached Japan, then inhabited by baboons. The inevitable happened and in due course the Japanese made their appearance." Common racist terms for Japanese people, as for blacks, were "apes," "monkeys," and "baboons."[44]

Roosevelt had conversations secretly recorded in the Oval Office. On several occasions, he spoke scornfully of "the Japs" and "any damn Jap." In public statements, he denounced the brutality of "the Nazis and the Japs." The man in the White House went further, asking a scientist at the Smithsonian Institution, Ales Hrdlicka, to explain why the Japanese were so bad. The reason that Hrdlicka gave, and FDR accepted, was quite simple. Their skulls, Hrdlicka said, "were some 2,000 years less developed than ours." This meant that small-brained Japanese, being less logical, were more prone to emotional outbursts and violence than whites—an absurd notion disproved by history and science.[45]

Recent research has shown that Roosevelt held yet more extreme racial views. The best way to deal with Puerto Rico's high birthrate, he said in a tasteless joke, was to sterilize those of childbearing age by using "the methods which Hitler used so effectively" on German people he deemed "defective." To prevent Germany from starting another war, he told Secretary of the Treasury Henry Morgenthau, in all seriousness, "you either have to castrate the German people or you have to treat them in such a manner so they can't go on reproducing people who want to continue the way they have in the past."[46]

THE DECISION

The president never shared his racial views with American voters. Nor did he voice his true opinions on civil liberties in wartime. Publicly, he said all the right things. On December 15, 1941, FDR announced that, whatever the threat, Americans would never abandon the liberties "our forefathers framed for us in the Bill of Rights." During his State of the Union address in January 1942, he urged the nation to be "particularly vigilant against racial discrimination in any of its ugly forms." In reality, Roosevelt worried that too much concern for civil liberties would undermine the war effort. He believed these were luxuries the nation could ill afford in its struggle for survival. The president would do anything to protect national security, as he understood it, and win the war.[47]

Attorney General Francis Biddle, the nation's chief legal officer, had known his boss since they were schoolboys. Biddle wrote that FDR had an iron rule: "What must be done to defend the country must be done." The president "thought that rights should yield to the necessities of war. Rights came after victory, not before." For without victory, Americans would have

A letter from Attorney General Francis Biddle to Secretary of War Henry L. Stimson, stating that "the Department of Justice has no power or authority to evacuate" American citizens, and legal problems could arise if they moved forward with this action. (February 12, 1942)

no rights. If dealing with the wartime emergency meant suspending parts of the Constitution, then so be it! Abraham Lincoln had done the same, closing opposition newspapers during the Civil War.[48]

In 1936, a year before the Rape of Nanking, Roosevelt had thought about launching a massive crackdown in Hawaii. Japanese merchant and passenger ships routinely stopped at Honolulu, the home of the Pearl Harbor naval base. FDR ordered the U.S. Navy to keep a list of every Japanese, "citizen or non-citizen," who met the ships. If war came, he said, they "would be the first to be placed in a concentration camp"—a place where prisoners are confined without trial and kept under harsh conditions.[49]

On the day Japan attacked, Hawaii's governor placed the islands under martial law. The military took charge during the emergency, having the authority to make and enforce civil and criminal laws. The writ of habeas corpus, which safeguards people from being imprisoned unlawfully, was suspended. The military closed civilian courts and could arrest, try, and convict anyone in its own courts.

The president wanted to ship all Hawaiian Issei and Nisei to the mainland, but the arithmetic was wrong. The islands had a population of 500,000, of whom 160,000 (32 percent) were of Japanese heritage. Unlike on the mainland, they were woven into the fabric of life in the islands. Japanese, native Hawaiians, and whites got along pretty well. Japanese was the unofficial second language. There were Japanese newspapers, movie houses, and theaters; most radio stations had a "Japanese hour." If it had been possible to ship everyone across 2,000 miles of ocean in wartime—which it was not—the Hawaiian economy would have collapsed. Issei and Nisei made up over 90 percent of the islands' carpenters, nearly all their transportation workers, and the bulk of their farm laborers. What's more, a U.S. Army general noted, mechanics of Japanese descent were "absolutely essential" to repairing the naval base and keeping it running smoothly.[50]

FDR stubbornly insisted that the safety of the Hawaiian Islands came first and that the labor situation "should not be given any consideration whatsoever." But the president soon realized, angrily, that his priorities were unrealistic; safeguarding the islands would be impossible without Japanese labor. So he settled for arresting 1,037 enemy aliens—that is, Issei

men. First imprisoned on Sand Island in Honolulu Harbor, inmates had a rough time. "They stripped us down," one recalled. "We were completely naked. Not even under shorts. They even checked our assholes." Another described how trigger-happy guards lined them up against a wall, threatening to shoot if they dared question, let alone disobey, orders. Eventually, they were sent to the mainland, where enemy alien hearing boards ordered them placed in camps run by the army.[51]

This left some 110,000 West Coast Japanese, of whom over 72,000 were U.S. citizens. What to do about them? Various special-interest groups and politicians called for their uprooting, but it was the army that spoke with the greatest authority.

Army officers had been caught up in the hysteria following Japan's victories, and none more than General John L. DeWitt. Short, balding, and nearsighted, the sixty-two-year-old headed the Western Defense Command. A specialist in logistics, or getting the right supplies to the right places on time, the general had earned a reputation for thoroughness and efficiency during the First World War. General John J. Pershing, supreme commander of U.S. forces in France, praised him for having "displayed rare ability in meeting the tremendous demands and overcoming the difficulties of transportation" of vital supplies to the front-line troops. However, having spent his career behind desks, DeWitt was high-strung and fussy, easily panicked, and given to temper tantrums. On the night after Pearl Harbor, he alarmed the entire city of San Francisco. Until daybreak, giant searchlights scanned the sky for a rumored flight of thirty Japanese bombers. When none appeared, he yelled about the "fools," military and civilian, who refused to take the war as seriously as he.[52, 53]

DeWitt checked with California attorney general Earl Warren, a close friend. He shared Warren's topsy-turvy logic. Obviously, no violence by Japanese Americans proved they were poised to unleash what DeWitt called "a second Pearl Harbor," this time on the mainland. Like Warren, he, too, saw the Japanese not as individuals with their own minds, but collectively, as a race with inborn traits impossible to change. "A Jap's a Jap," DeWitt famously said. "The Japanese race is an enemy race and while many second- and third-generation Japanese born on

General John L. DeWitt was an early and vocal supporter of Japanese internment and was instrumental in carrying out Executive Order 9066. (Date unknown)

United States soil, possessed of United States citizenship, have become 'Americanized,' the racial strains are undiluted." Thus, the only thing to do, he said, was to uproot them from the West Coast. Get rid of the lot—every man, woman, and child, enemy alien and citizen![54]

The general made this recommendation to Henry L. Stimson, his civilian chief. Stimson was among the most respected public servants of his day. Now secretary of war, he had been a top Wall Street lawyer and also secretary of state. Like many of America's elite, Stimson was biased against nonwhite, non-Protestant minorities. The secretary feared "race equality" (his term) with blacks, and he resented "Jewish influence" in business and politics. As for the Japanese, he thought them treacherous by nature. "Their racial characteristics," he claimed, made it impossible to "understand or trust even the citizen Japanese." They were born outsiders, and would remain so forever, he believed.[55]

On February 11, Stimson telephoned the White House. Roosevelt, he noted in his diary, was "very vigorous" and told him to do whatever he thought best with regard to the West Coast Japa-

nese. FDR promised to support his actions, because the charges of disloyalty squared with his own ingrained beliefs. So on February 19, 1942, another date that will live in infamy, the president signed Executive Order 9066.[56]

The order was written in bland language to allow for the most flexible interpretation—"wiggle room," as we would say today. Fighting the war, it said, required vigorous safeguards against spying and sabotage. Therefore, the secretary of war, or the commander he chose, was authorized to define military areas "from which any or all persons may be excluded." The military would see that those excluded had proper transportation, shelter, and food, "until other arrangements are made to accomplish the purpose of this order." The phrase "other arrangements" was filled with menace, for it implied that military commanders could do *whatever* they thought necessary.[57]

The order said nothing about Japanese Americans—about uprooting them from the West Coast, or imprisoning them. Yet everyone assumed they were its targets. Attorney General Francis Biddle, who reluctantly supported Roosevelt's action, admitted as

Secretary of War
Henry L. Stimson. (c. 1940)

much. "American citizens of Japanese origins," he wrote years later, were handled "as untouchables, a group who could not be trusted and had to be shut up only *because* they were of Japanese descent."[58]

Executive orders have the force of law, though not the power to impose penalties for their violation; only Congress has that power. On March 21, Congress put teeth into Roosevelt's order. Without a single "nay" vote, or a minute's debate, the House of Representatives and Senate passed, and FDR signed, Public Law 503. This made any violation of Executive Order 9066 a federal offense, punishable by a $5,000 fine ($79,837 in 2016 dollars) and a jail term.

The presidential order and the law that confirmed it were unjust. The American ideal of justice is based on *individual* rights and equality before the law. It rejects any notion of group guilt. We are responsible for what we do personally, not for who we are or how we look. Innocence or guilt cannot depend on race, ancestry, religion, language, family, social class, sex, wealth, politics, feelings, or ideas. In violating this core principle, decision makers failed to discharge their first duty: to protect all the people equally. Rather than confront fear and rumor with facts and reason, they let them run wild, even fed them in the name of "national security." Leaders' failures set the stage for untold personal tragedies, casting doubt on the very essence of America.

CHAPTER 4

SORROWFUL DAYS

*Moving day was the most lamentable and sorrowful day in all our life on the
Pacific Coast—our foundation, built by fifty years of hard toil and planning,
was swept away by Army's Order. It was Awful Nightmare!*
—JOURNAL OF "MR. H." (1942)

"KICK THEM OUT!"

Secretary of War Stimson moved quickly. On February 20, 1942, the day after FDR
signed Executive Order 9066, he put General DeWitt in charge of carrying it out.
DeWitt's headquarters were at the Presidio, the largest military post in the West,
overlooking the Golden Gate Bridge and San Francisco Bay. From Building 35, he
directed the entire operation.

It was still a time of high anxiety. There were more "sightings" of the Japanese
fleet, obviously the prelude to a full-scale invasion! At any moment, rumor had it,
Japanese paratroops would drop into San Francisco! And in fact, on February 23,

a submarine surfaced off Goleta, California, during a nationwide broadcast by the president. For a quarter of an hour, it lobbed shells at an oil refinery but did no damage. It did, however, frighten William Randolph Hearst, who fled from his castle at nearby San Simeon. Hearst swore that the Japanese had targeted him personally for the hatred his newspapers had spewed against the Issei and Nisei.[1]

On the night of February 24–25, DeWitt's troops fought the so-called Battle of Los Angeles. Sleepers were jarred awake by booming antiaircraft guns aimed at "swarms" of Japanese "bombers." Shells exploded in fiery balls, their falling fragments damaging property. Five people died of heart attacks and in auto accidents in the blacked-out streets. By dawn, the sky was clear, because it was all a false alarm; the bombers did not exist. Local newspapers, however, took the "air raid" seriously, without any evidence that it had transpired. The *Los Angeles Examiner* led with a banner headline: "Air Battle Rages over Los Angeles," adding that gunfire had downed an enemy plane on a city street. Not to be outdone, the *Los Angeles Times* printed an extra with the headline "LA Area

Raided." It went on to say that "Jap Planes Peril Santa Monica" and other coastal cities. Army investigators soon decided the gun crews had mistaken weather balloons for bombers. Yet no officials explained the error to the public, probably because they would have revealed the weakness of West Coast air defenses. Letting the story stand, however, proclaimed that Japan had

The *Los Angeles Times* coverage of the "Battle of Los Angeles" and its aftermath. (February 26, 1942)

attacked the mainland, spawning more scare headlines and fifth-column fears.[2]

DeWitt, meanwhile, feverishly marked out sensitive military areas, or "exclusion zones," on his maps. Area No. 1 was a 100-mile-wide strip of the Washington, Oregon, and California coastline, plus southern Arizona bordering Mexico. This area, in turn, was divided into ninety-nine smaller, easier-to-manage sections. Later, the general carved out Area No. 2, which included all of California.

It became clear whom Executive Order 9066 meant by the phrase "any or all persons." *Not* Germans or Italians. Some 22,000 German and 58,000 Italian aliens lived on the West Coast, out of the approximately one million in the entire country. Uprooting them all, rather than just those on the lists of security risks, would have sparked resentment among their millions of naturalized and American-born relatives, who voted. Besides, their removal, like that of the Japanese in Hawaii, would have disrupted the war effort.

As regards Italian aliens, the president did not think them dangerous. "I don't care much about the Italians," he told Francis Biddle. "They are a lot of opera singers." Baseball players, too.

The parents of New York Yankees star Joe DiMaggio, the "Yankee Clipper," were aliens, having spent forty years in America without applying for citizenship. Locking them up would have caused an uproar. So on October 12, 1942, Columbus Day, a day of pride for Italian Americans, the attorney general announced that no Italian aliens would be considered enemies. President Roosevelt, ever the politician, immediately gave Biddle's action his blessing, calling it "a masterly stroke of international statesmanship and good politics."[3]

There was another, hush-hush reason for not offending Italians. In the three months after Pearl Harbor, German submarines sank scores of ships off the Atlantic coast. They struck boldly, as if they were receiving information from spies in the Port of New York, the hub for Europe-bound war supplies. The Office of Naval Intelligence, desperate to root them out, replied by launching Operation Underworld. Early in 1942, it made a deal with the Mafia, the Italians-only criminal organization that, in addition to activities like selling narcotics, ran the waterfront. It so happened that Mafia chieftain Charles "Lucky" Luciano was serving a long sentence in an upstate New York prison. The gangster agreed to help Naval Intelligence, in return for its promise to help reduce his sentence. On Luciano's orders, his lieutenants, thugs like Albert Anastasia of Murder Inc., notorious killers for hire, set their gangs to work. Using their own methods—snitches, kidnapping, beating, torture—they uncovered spies. Bullet-riddled bodies soon began turning up in waterfront alleys, and the number of ships sunk plummeted.[4]

Japanese Americans had no politician, general, or gangster to speak up for them. So DeWitt asked them to leave the exclusion zones voluntarily. But this was easier said than done. Leavers needed a place to go, and a way to earn a living once they got there. To make matters worse, they ran into a wall of hatred.

As they went inland, usually in their own automobiles, newspapers let them know they were unwelcome. In the *Kansas City Star,* for example, a cartoon titled "Plague of Japanese Beetles" showed Uncle Sam chasing bucktoothed insects out of California, while Kansans held up signs reading WE DON'T WANT 'EM and KEEP 'EM FLYING—IN ANOTHER DIRECTION. Protesters in Idaho cried, "We're all white

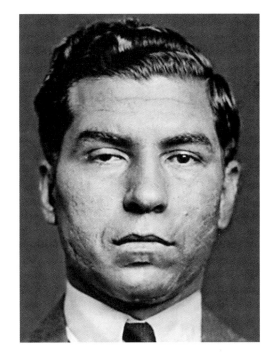

Mobster Charles "Lucky" Luciano's New York Police Department mug shot. (c. 1936)

folks." Roadside diners in Arizona posted a sign: THIS RESTAURANT POISONS BOTH RATS AND JAPS.[5]

Governors of some western states— Arizona, Idaho, Nebraska—urged the army to drag "the lousy Japs" off to concentration camps. Even New York City's 2,000 Japanese became targets. They lost jobs, and boycotts forced their businesses to close. Rumors spread that Japanese restaurants served chopped-up rats and stale filth in spicy sauce. The city's popular mayor, Fiorello La Guardia, warned the Japanese to stay off the streets and buses and to avoid the subways for their own good. Only Colorado governor William Carr welcomed the refugees. By turning them away, he warned, "we are tearing down the whole American system."[6]

DeWitt realized that few could leave the exclusion zones on their own, let alone leave fast enough to suit his superiors in Washington. So on March 24, five weeks after FDR signed Executive Order 9066, the general announced a curfew from 8:00 p.m. to 6:00 a.m. for all Issei and Nisei. Three days later, he went further, ordering them to stay in their exclusion zones until further notice. This effectively made them prisoners in their own homes and neighborhoods. However, it was just the beginning.

In the 1830s, during the presidency of Andrew Jackson, the army began to drive Native Americans off their tribal lands in the South and on the Great Plains. Inevitably, their "Trail of Tears" led to reservations, open-air prisons set on the poorest-quality lands. The completion of Indian removal took decades, and the numbers were small, no more than a few hundred at a time. Now, in the spring and summer of 1942, the army carried out the largest forced migration in American history.

WHO MUST GO?

The uprooting was to be a two-stage process. In Stage 1, General DeWitt planned to have the army expel Japanese Americans and confine them in temporary facilities. Stage 2 would depend on a civilian agency. The War Relocation Authority, created by Executive Order 9102, was to handle the uprooted long term. The WRA would house its charges in new and better facilities and provide basic services: food, health care, education, recreation, and the like.

Stage 1 began with printed notices. You knew your life was about to change when you saw soldiers riding around your neighborhood in jeeps. At each

Civilian Exclusion Order No. 5, posted at First and Front streets in San Francisco, directing removal by April 7, 1942, of persons of Japanese ancestry. (April 1, 1942)

stop, they tacked a "civilian exclusion order" onto a telephone pole, lamppost, or billboard. These orders required an adult member of every Japanese family to report by a given date to the local "civil control station": a school, community center, Christian church, or Buddhist temple.

People tried to grasp the orders' meaning. They knew they had done nothing wrong, but the orders implied the government had something bad in store for them. "Although I was just a child," a Nisei recalled, "I knew and could sense the terror . . . in my mother and father's eyes." Yet there was no escaping the long arm of the army. Federal agencies, notably the Census Bureau, helped it carry out Stage 1 in key ways. During the 1940 census, the bureau compiled detailed information on each Japanese family: address, size, and members' names, ages, and occupations. It also had detailed maps pinpointing each family's location. Though supposedly confidential, this information was shared with the army.[7]

Civil control stations were not friendly places. To enter, you had to pass between stern-faced soldiers armed with rifles. Once inside, you found rows of tables and chairs. Often social workers—professionals trained to help people with personal, family, and financial problems—sat at the tables within reach of piles of printed forms. Yoosun Park, a scholar who studied their role in the uprooting, found that most social workers believed official claims of military necessity. This belief, Park insists, made them "accomplices of the government" and thus "legitimized the bigoted policies of racial profiling."[8]

During registration, the "client" (the official term) received an identification tag for each family member, with the family's special number, and for each piece of baggage the family needed. A document listed what should and should not be taken. Take only what you can carry: bedding, towels, extra clothing, toiletries, kitchen utensils, and personal articles. "No pets of any kind will be permitted."[9]

There were no exceptions. Doctors and lawyers, businesspeople and fishermen, farmers and day laborers, young and old: all had to leave. This meant that Harry Sumida, a bedridden veteran of the Spanish-American War of 1898 and one of the first Nisei born in the United States, was carried out of a Veterans Administration hospital and sent away. Race alone determined a

Japanese Americans file forms containing personal data, two days before expulsion, at a civil control station. (April 4, 1942)

person's fate. "We Caucasians are patriots by virtue of our skin," declared Colonel Karl R. Bendetsen, a top aide to General DeWitt. People of Japanese heritage, however, were inclined to treason because of their race, he told a Catholic priest. "If they have one drop of Japanese blood in them, they must go."[10]

The result was a tangle of rules based on the amount of "Japanese blood" flowing in one's veins. What makes this policy all the more chilling is that in 1942, Adolf Hitler's henchmen were selecting Jews on the same basis. Those with the slightest "taint," with a Jewish look—including children of "race-mixed" Jewish-gentile marriages—were being identified, uprooted, and herded together to be murdered.[11]

There was no question that "pure-blood" Japanese families—husbands, wives, and their children—had to go. So did childless couples and children in orphanages, notably the Los Angeles Japanese Children's Home, and in foster care with Caucasian families. Japanese families of "mixed blood," however, raised a special issue. Where, exactly, to draw the line? DeWitt's staff decided that anyone who was one-sixteenth Japanese—that is, who had at least one Japanese great-grandparent—had to leave. The results might seem laughable, if they were not so tragic. An Irish laborer named Hayward, for example, had twenty family members, each white-skinned, blue-eyed, and red-haired. But since Haywood had a Japanese grandparent, his whole family had to go.[12]

There were around 1,400 interracial families living on the West Coast as well. Social workers gave those with children of white fathers and Japanese mothers a choice. Either parents and children could be confined as a family, or parents could separate for the duration of the war. If parents chose to separate, the Japanese mother could take the children with her to a confinement facility, or her white husband could stay at home with their children while she went away. More often than not, white fathers stayed home with their children. This involved a cruel choice between love and necessity. The wife's going away was the price paid to keep their children's lives as normal as possible. While she stayed in a facility, her husband tended to the family's house and worked at his regular job.[13]

Families with Japanese fathers and white mothers were in a different category. If the children had been living almost entirely among whites, the army did not wish them, it said, "to be tainted by contact with Japanese people" or "exposed to *infectious Japanese thought*." These families needn't stay in a confinement facility, but they could not stay home, either. They had to leave the West Coast. If they could not, they had to enter a facility after all.[14]

LEAVING HOME

At the end of each area's registration period, soldiers posted another order. Addressed in bold letters to "All Persons of Japanese Ancestry, Both Alien and Non-Alien," it revealed a great deal without saying much directly. It made clear that the Issei should not expect to be treated as legal enemy aliens.

Unlike those arrested after Pearl Harbor, they would not have their cases heard individually, with evidence presented to special boards. The authorities had simply lumped them together because of their Japanese "blood." Nor did American citizenship count for their Nisei children. The constitutional right to "equal protection of the laws" no longer applied to them. Like their parents, they had been judged not by their individual actions but as a mass with only race in common.

The order told families to prepare to leave within six days to two weeks. While no family experienced exactly what is described below, this account shares elements of every family's experience.

Waiting to leave home was hectic and nerve-racking. There was so much to do, and so little time to do it. Families had to dispose of everything they could not carry in a couple of suitcases and duffel bags. President Roosevelt, an aide noted, was blasé, indifferent

Japanese Americans wait for a bus at a civil control station as part of the first group to be evacuated from San Francisco. (April 6, 1942)

to "what happened to their property" after they moved. As a result, the uprooted had to use their wits to try to preserve whatever they could.[15]

Some left their property with white neighbors for safekeeping. "I gave my pictures to the camera club friends," one said, "the piano I put in the church parlor, the washing machine and dishes went into the basement of one friend, the books into the basement of another friend. Here and there our boxes were scattered all over the town." Others stored their property in unsecured federal warehouses, hoping to find it there when they returned. Most decided to sell everything for ready cash.[16]

Sales attracted "vultures in the form of human beings." These scavengers preyed upon uprooted people's anxiety and confusion. Con artists posing as FBI agents and "immigration counselors" urged people to sell at fire-sale prices and threatened to "arrange" for the FBI to seize everything of those that wouldn't. Most buyers, however, were ordinary folks looking for bargains. Nevertheless, they had the upper hand. Time is running out! Sell while you can! If you don't sell to me, this minute, you will have nothing! Owners settled for a fraction of their possessions' value.

Some sample prices: $150 for a brand-new automobile, $50 for a piano, $20 for a tea set, $50 for a living room furniture, $10 for a washing machine, $5 for a refrigerator. One woman sold her twenty-six-room hotel for $500 ($7,984 in 2016 dollars)![17]

These were not merely objects, things, but embodied lifetimes of work, sacrifice, and memories. Thus, trifling offers felt like insults, verbal slaps in the face. Jeanne Wakatsuki Houston remembered her mother's reaction to an offer of $15 for a set of elegant china. She began to break it, piece by piece. "Mama took out another dinner plate and hurled it at the floor, then another

The Japanese American owner of an Oakland, California, store placed this sign in the window the day after Pearl Harbor. The store was closed and later sold when the owner, a University of California graduate, was forced to leave. (c. March 1942)

and another, never moving, never opening her mouth, just quivering and glaring at the retreating dealer, with tears streaming down her cheeks.... When he was gone she stood there smashing cups and bowls and platters until the whole set lay in scattered blue and white fragments across the wooden floor." A man wanted to set fire to his house, but he didn't because his wife reminded him, "We are civilized people, not savages." Many just boarded up their homes and hoped for the best.[18]

Land was the only property that could not be sold, destroyed, or abandoned. A federal agency, the Farm Security Administration, took a hard line. Until it rented some 6,000 farms to whites, it ordered their owners to keep working until E-Day—Evacuation Day. A spokesman for General DeWitt reminded owners of their patriotic duty

Children at the Raphael Weill Public School in San Francisco pledge allegiance to America shortly before being relocated with their families. (April 20, 1942)

to grow food for the war effort. Refusing to do so was an act of sabotage, punishable by a fine and a jail term.[19]

The uprooted left home with mixed feelings. With dignity, "everyone was dressed in their Sunday best, men in suits and women in dresses and hats," one recalled. With pride, children waved tiny American flags. A little boy wore a cap stitched with the motto "Remember Pearl Harbor." Old people said things like *"Shikata ga nai"* ("It can't be helped") and exhibited *gaman,* an attitude of endurance, of taking what comes without flinching. Being "tagged like a dog," however, sparked anger. Shuji Kimura remembered feeling utterly humiliated. "Mother began to cry," he wrote. "I couldn't see through my tears either." Despite their fears, one thing seemed not to cause worry. "You had an uncertainty about where you were going and what was going to happen, but you knew you weren't going to be killed."[20]

Soldiers in battle dress met them at the local civil control station. Upon arrival, soldiers and local police searched their baggage, spilling items onto the floor or sidewalk. From there, buses took them to a train station. Crowds might line the route, some members

shouting, "Out, Japs!" and "Good riddance, I'm glad you're leaving!" Yet others were appalled at the scene. "This is wrong," they said out loud. White friends gave small goodbye presents. It meant so much, Betty Morita said years later, that her third-grade teacher "had all the kids in my class go out and pick wildflowers and gave me a bouquet. I'll never forget that."[21]

The uprooted became part of an event that would stay with them for the rest of their lives. Conditions at the train station were frantic, the air crackling with tension and worry. Hospital patients on stretchers were being loaded onto trains through open windows. Meanwhile, rows of soldiers stood

Members of the Mochida family, tagged for expulsion and awaiting the bus. Before his relocation, Mochida operated a nursery and five greenhouses. (May 8, 1942)

shoulder to shoulder, rifles at the ready, eyeing their charges as they lined up to board, each tagged as required, many holding infants in their arms. Her family's leaving Los Angeles branded itself into Grace Nakamura's memory. Forty years later, she recalled the scene:

> On May 16, 1942 at 9:30 a.m. we departed for . . . an unknown destination. To this day I can remember vividly the plight of the elderly, some on stretchers, orphans herded on the train by caretakers, and especially a young couple with four preschool children. The mother had two frightened toddlers hanging on to her coat. In her arms, she carried two crying babies. The father had diapers and other baby paraphernalia strapped to his back. In his hands he struggled with a duffel bag and suitcase. The shades were drawn on the train for our entire trip. Military police patrolled the aisles.[22]

A child waits with the family's belongings as they prepare to relocate. (c. April 1942)

The uprooting lasted from March 31 to August 7, 1942. During that time, the army moved 110,000 people. Everything went smoothly, with military precision. There were no protests or demonstrations. Nobody died, except for two Issei who committed suicide out of despair. Hideo Murata put a bullet into his head. In his hand, the Californian held a "Certificate of Honorary Citizenship" given by Monterey County "for your loyal and splendid service to the country in the Great World War. Our flag was assaulted, and you gallantly took up its defense."[23]

Whole neighborhoods now stood empty. It was eerie. You could walk along darkened streets and hear only echoes of your own footsteps. Just six Japanese remained in San Francisco, all seriously ill in a hospital. If they re- covered, they, too, would be sent away. On May 21, the *San Francisco Chroni- cle* reported: "For the first time in 81 years, not a single Japanese is walking the streets of San Francisco.... Last night, Japanese Town was empty. Its stores were vacant, its windows plas- tered with 'To Lease' signs.... A col- orful chapter in San Francisco history was closed forever." A *Chronicle* reader saw this as the result of "racial preju- dice and filthy politics."[24]

ASSEMBLY CENTERS

The uprooted felt as if they had stepped out of one world and into another.

A map of the war relocation centers and other notable sites for the internment of Japanese Americans.

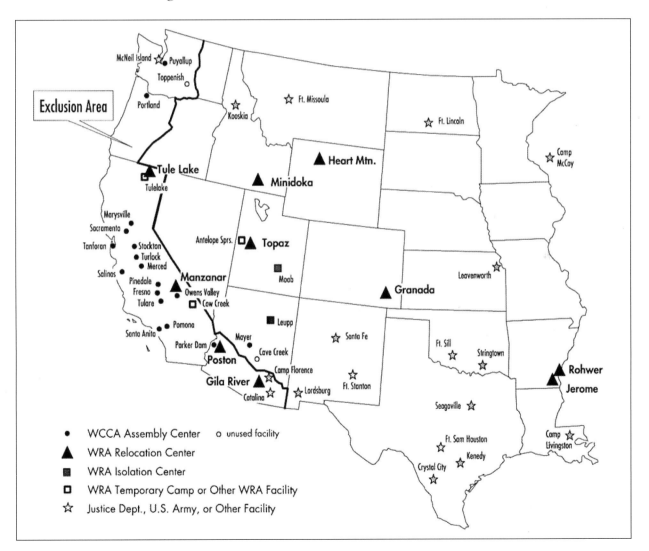

Exclusion Area

McNeil Island ☆ ● Puyallup
Toppenish ○
Portland ●
☆ Ft. Missoula
Kooskia ☆
☆ Ft. Lincoln
☆ Camp McCoy
▲ Heart Mtn.
▲ Tule Lake
□ Tulelake
▲ Minidoka
Marysville ●
Sacramento ●
Tanforan ●
Stockton ●
Turlock ●
Merced ●
Salinas ●
Pinedale ●
Fresno ●
Tulare ●
Antelope Sprs. □ ▲ Topaz
■ Moab
Leavenworth ☆
▲ Manzanar
Owens Valley
□ Cow Creek
■ Leupp
▲ Granada
Santa Anita
Pomona ●
Parker Dam ● ▲ Poston
Mayer ●
Cave Creek ●
○ Camp Florence
Gila River ▲ ● ☆
Catalina ☆
☆ Santa Fe
Ft. Stanton ☆
☆ Lordsburg
Ft. Sill ☆
Stringtown ☆
▲ Rohwer
Jerome
Seagoville ☆
Camp ☆ Livingston
Ft. Sam Houston ☆
Kenedy ☆
Crystal City ☆

● WCCA Assembly Center   ○ unused facility
▲ WRA Relocation Center
■ WRA Isolation Center
□ WRA Temporary Camp or Other WRA Facility
☆ Justice Dept., U.S. Army, or Other Facility

During Stage 1, the army expelled so many people that it had to send them to fifteen temporary "assembly centers," which were to be used until larger, more permanent ones could be built.

Expulsions took place so rapidly that it was necessary to use existing facilities designed to hold large crowds. Racetracks and fairgrounds seemed ideal, since they already had electricity and water. Parking lots gave extra space for quickly built shacks, derisively called "chicken coops." California, the state with the most Japanese Americans, had twelve assembly centers: Marysville, Sacramento, Stockton, Tanforan, Turlock, Merced, Salinas, Pinedale, Fresno, Tulare, Santa Anita, and Pomona. The other three were located in Puyallup, Washington; Portland, Oregon; and Mayer, Arizona. While these filled, Stage 2 got under way as work began on centers meant to last for the duration of the war.

Assembly centers looked and felt like prisons. Passing through gates in chain-link fences topped with barbed wire, new arrivals walked between ranks of soldiers, young draftees often away from home for the first time. At Santa Anita, a racetrack in Arcadia, Private Leonard Adams was deeply

touched by the sight of the "many weeping or simply dazed, or bewildered by our formidable ranks." A child cried, "Mother, I don't like Japan. Let's go back to America." Another noticed a stray dog following her. "Don't come here, little dog," she said. "You won't be able to go back to America."[25]

The experiences of Miné Okubo were typical. Unlike most other inmates, however, she was a talented artist. Okubo and her brother Toku arrived by bus at Tanforan Racetrack in San Bruno, just south of San Francisco. Tanforan infuriated her but also sparked her creativity. The result was a book titled *Citizen 13660,* published in 1946, the first to describe the lives of the uprooted in words and drawings. An invaluable human document, *Citizen 13660* is more than just words and pictures. It is a warning about what can happen in times of fear and hysteria.

Arriving inmates were "processed": searched, fingerprinted, given a quick medical exam, vaccinated against smallpox, and assigned living quarters. A guide took Okubo and her brother to barrack 16, room 50—formerly stable 16, stall 50—fixed up to house people. Her drawings and captions let us see, even smell, this place in our imagination:

We walked in and dropped our things inside the entrance. The place was in semidarkness: light barely came through the dirty window on either side of the entrance. A swinging half-door divided the 20 by 9 ft. stall into two rooms.... The rear room had housed the horse and the front room the fodder. Both rooms showed signs of hurried whitewashing. Spider webs, horsehair, and hay had been whitewashed with the walls. Huge spikes and nails stuck out all over the walls. A two-inch layer of dust covered the floor, but on removing it we discovered that linoleum the color of redwood had been placed over the rough manure-covered boards.... We had to make friends with the wild creatures ... especially the spiders, mice, and rats, because we were outnumbered.[26]

Okubo drew grim-faced people lined up for everything. They ate in

Miné Okubo's drawing of her barracks at the Tanforan Assembly Center in San Bruno, California. (c. 1972)

The mess hall at the Fresno Assembly Center in Fresno, California. (c. 1942)

mess halls, dreary rooms swarming with horseflies—big, buzzing, biting brutes with blue tails—despite the coils of sticky flypaper dangling from ceilings. Three times a day, inmates shuffled along, holding up their trays for whatever the cooks scooped out of (clean) garbage cans. Generally, it was tinned hash, frankfurters and beans, a slice of bread, and, on a good day, canned fruit in sweet syrup. A Tanforan specialty was thick slabs of salted liver of a brownish-purplish color. "Table manners were forgotten. Guzzle, guzzle, guzzle; hurry, hurry, hurry," Okubo wrote.[27]

Keeping clean was a challenge. The army had rigged up showers in rooms intended for hosing down horses. Though men and women showered separately, they stood crowded among strangers. "The older women preferred the good old-fashioned bathtubs to showers. It was a common sight to see them bathing in pails, dishpans, or in tubs made from barrels," Okubo wrote. Latrines were awful. Women were shocked to see toilets without doors or partitions ranged side by side, running the length of a large room. Often they became constipated, unable to go because they were too embarrassed.

Some hid behind newspapers and pieces of cardboard; others waited until late at night, when, they hoped, the coast was clear. "Many of the women could not use the community toilets," Okubo noted. "They sought privacy by pinning up curtains and setting up boards." From time to time, the plumbing broke down, so the latrines smelled to high heaven.[28]

Few enjoyed a good night's sleep. The uprooted literally "hit the hay," lying on army cots, their springs covered by loosely sewn bags filled with straw. Okubo explained: "Because the partitions were low and there were many holes in the boards they were made of, the crackling of the straw and the noises from the other stalls were incessant. Loud snores, the grinding of teeth, the wail of babies, the murmur of conversations—these could be heard the full length of the stable."[29]

Nisei doctors saw to fellow inmates' health needs. They did their best, despite the lack of supplies. Sometimes the only "medicines" available were mineral oil, iodine, aspirin, alcohol, and a chalky substance called Kaopectate— for diarrhea, a common complaint. Conditions were especially hard on expectant mothers and newborns. At Tanforan, for instance, women could not get permission to go to a hospital in San Bruno. So they gave birth in a horse stall, on a table covered with a towel. For want of cribs, newborns slept in cardboard boxes. Childhood diseases raced through assembly centers. Doctors constantly battled outbreaks of chicken pox, measles, mumps, and whooping cough.[30]

Gradually, conditions improved, mainly because of the inmates' own efforts. People scrounged for scrap lumber, which they used to build chairs, stools, and tables. At Tanforan, Issei landscapers built a miniature park with a bridge and a public walkway. Elsewhere, former gardeners planted flowers with seeds they had brought.

Inmates found laughter a medicine that drove away the blues, at least temporarily. Okubo explained: "Humor is the only thing that mellows life, shows life as the circus it is. After being uprooted, everything seemed ridiculous, insane, and stupid." It felt good to call guards "blockheads" or stick out your tongue behind their backs. To protect her privacy while she worked, Okubo claimed to have hoof-and-mouth disease. She tacked a large sign on her stable door: QUARANTINED—DO NOT ENTER.[31]

RELOCATION CENTERS

On average, inmates stayed in assembly centers for about ninety days. Just as they were getting used to their surroundings, Stage 2 began. Without warning, bulletin boards ordered them to prepare for their second uprooting.

The army had nearly finished work on ten camps, officially known as "relocation centers" for "evacuees": Manzanar and Tule Lake (California), Poston and Gila River (Arizona), Topaz (Utah), Minidoka (Idaho), Granada (Colorado), Heart Mountain (Wyoming), and Jerome and Rohwer (Arkansas).

Center sites had not been selected for inmates' comfort. They were located where nobody wanted to live.

A dust storm among the barracks at the Manzanar War Relocation Center. (July 3, 1942)

However, they met the standards set by the army and the War Relocation Authority. Built on unused federal land, they were far from military bases, airfields, bridges, power stations, and dams. Though isolated, they had access to electricity and water. Each center could hold a minimum of 5,000 and a maximum of 10,000 people.[32]

From August to November 1942, an average of 3,700 people left for the relocation centers each day. Their journey lasted up to ten days, aboard slow, "ratty" old trains; the newer trains sped troops and supplies to the West Coast and the Pacific battles. With windows shut and covered by black shades, the trains rattled along, day and night. Military Police (MPs) patrolled the coaches. Food and drinking water often ran short or spoiled. Toilets overflowed. Now and then, the trains stopped for a half hour so inmates could stretch their legs in narrow fenced-in areas guarded by MPs. Most of the time, they sat upright, muscles stiff and bones aching, in mind-numbing boredom. "The trip was a nightmare," Miné Okubo recalled. "The train creaked with age. . . . The first night was a novelty . . . [but] I could not sleep and I spent the entire night taking the chair apart and readjusting it. Many became train sick and vomited. The children cried from restlessness."[33]

These were not the only children to cry. Canada had 22,274 people of Japanese descent, 80 percent of them citizens, living in British Columbia, a province on its west coast. White Canadians resented them for the same reasons that Californians did. Organizations like the White Canada Association flourished, and the slogan "No Japs from the Rockies to the Seas" became popular. On February 24, 1942, five days after FDR signed Executive Order 9066, Canada ordered "All Persons of Japanese Racial Origin" expelled from a 100-mile-wide coastal zone. Officials separated families, scattering them among ten lumbering camps, mining camps, and decrepit ghost towns. The government in Ottawa did nothing to protect their property. Instead, it auctioned off every car, fishing boat, house, farm, and stick of furniture. To add insult to injury, it used the money to pay for the inmates' upkeep.[34]

Meanwhile, in the United States, upon arrival at a train station, inmates were bused to a relocation center, a journey of several more hours. First impressions were not good. The climate was very different from that of the West Coast. Southern California is dry, sunny, and warm for much of the year. Northern California, Oregon, and Washington are cool, damp, and drizzly, even in summertime. Nothing had prepared the uprooted for relocation-center life. The Arkansas centers were in swampland, hot and humid in summer, cold, wet, and muddy in winter. At Rohwer, an inmate said, rainstorms imprisoned them in their living quarters. "The water stagnated at the front steps. . . . The mosquitoes that festered there were horrible. . . . Rohwer was a living nightmare."[35]

Other centers experienced Arctic-like weather—"Little Siberias." Tule Lake lay not by a lake but on a dry, sandy old lake bed 4,000 feet above sea level. In summer, the place was bearable, though hot. In winter, however, temperatures fell to twenty-nine degrees below zero. At Topaz, Miné Okubo noted, most families spent as much time as they could around potbellied stoves. Blizzards at Heart Mountain, "a godawful place," lasted for days. Inmate Miyuki Aoyama wrote:

Snow on the rooftop,
Snow upon the coal;

Winter in Wyoming—
Winter in my soul.[36]

By contrast, the desert centers sweltered. At Poston and Gila River, daytime summer temperatures soared to 120 degrees in the shade. The landscape shimmered in the heat, and searing winds made you feel as if you were standing at the mouth of a blast furnace. A guard at Poston died of heatstroke, while others keeled over at their posts. "Truthfully," an inmate wrote, "I must say this scorching Hell is a place beyond description and tears." Inmates carried umbrellas during the day; they swaddled infants in wet bedsheets to keep them cool. When babies wet their cloth diapers, they dried in no time. You also had to watch for venomous creatures: Gila monsters, rattlesnakes, scorpions, centipedes, tarantulas, and fire ants with stings like electric shocks.[37]

Located about 200 miles north of Los Angeles, in Owens Valley, Manzanar had the most scenic setting. It had once been fertile farmland; *huertos de manzanas* is Spanish for "apple orchard." Early in the century, however, the streams in the valley had been diverted to nourish Los Angeles, leaving the valley a semi-desert. The lowest spot in the

Western Hemisphere, Death Valley, lay just to the east. The snowcapped Sierra Nevada, crowned by Mount Whitney, dominated the western horizon.

Manzanar struck a child, Itsuko Taniguchi, as the most dismal spot on the planet:

My Mom, Pop, & me
Us living three
Dreaded the day
When we rode away,
Away to the land
With lots of sand
My Mom, Pop, & me.[38]

Sandstorms hid the sun at noontime and blasted the paint off metal signs. If you were unlucky enough to be caught outdoors, the tiny windblown grains felt like lit matches on bare skin, filled noses and ears, and crunched between teeth.

The relocation centers followed standard plans drawn up by army engineers. Each had several large units called "wards." Each ward had four housing "blocks" of sixteen to twenty-four barracks per block, built in rows along unpaved streets. Each block had its own facilities: kitchen, mess hall, laundry, showers, toilets, infirmary,

Jim Morikawa sprays water in an attempt to settle the dust after a dust storm at the Poston War Relocation Center in Poston, Arizona. (May 10, 1942)

meeting rooms, school, recreation areas, and houses of worship.

Barracks were built of wooden boards covered with tar paper—heavy paper soaked in tar for waterproofing. Each unit was 20 feet wide by 120 feet long, divided into five or six single-room "apartments," one per family. Since the apartments had no plumbing, inmates had to carry water in buckets from outside storage tanks. Furnishings were simple: cots, straw-stuffed bags, and thin woolen blankets. A bare lightbulb lit each apartment. Floors and walls made of raw, uncured lumber quickly warped, opening gaps that let in sand and vermin. The sameness of the rows of barracks confused inmates. A drawing by Miné Okubo shows a man gazing in despair, with the caption: "All residential blocks looked alike; people were lost all the time."[39]

The War Relocation Authority was in charge. Each center had a civilian director and around eighty white assistants to handle legal, health, housing, welfare, and educational matters. WRA police officers took care of internal security; MPs saw that nobody left or entered without permission. Inmates

The living quarters at the Poston War Relocation Center. (June 1, 1942)

elected a variety of boards, councils, and committees. These reported problems, filed complaints, and made suggestions, but they had no more power than student government in an elementary school. Their main job was to relay orders and information from the managers to the inmates.

The white staff members were the centers' aristocracy. Free to come and go, they lived in solidly built houses in a segregated area. They and their families ate hearty meals in a private mess hall and relaxed at a private recreation club. Washrooms in some centers had signs saying CAUCASIAN ADMINISTRA-TIVE STAFF ONLY. Staffers might hire female inmates, at cut-rate prices, to clean house and look after their children. During a visit to Tule Lake, a WRA inspector noted: "I discovered that a slave labor racket was being carried on and had been continuously carried on since the inception of that Center."[40]

As they had in the assembly centers, the uprooted got used to the daily routines in the relocation centers. Each morning, a "screaming" siren woke them. After roll call, inmates filed into the mess hall for breakfast. Food was not much better, and sometimes worse, than in the assembly centers. At Manzanar, for example, inmates ate "SOS," short for "same old slop." Almost everyone had visits from the "Manzanar Twins," Diar and Rhea—diarrhea. Yet this did not prevent congressmen who had never been inside a center from claiming inmates ate steak and drank wine. Newspapers printed this and other charges without bothering to check if they were true.[41]

Children attended school. Though the WRA meant well, center schools had many shortcomings. An official report from Rohwer pointed to defects common to other centers as well. Rohwer's schools lacked "supplies, equipment, high school textbooks and . . . enough teachers. The pupils sat on crude benches built to meet the emergency. Since there were no desks or tables, they often sat on the floor using the benches as desks." Mornings began with the Pledge of Allegiance to "one nation, indivisible, with liberty and justice for all."[42]

Classroom teachers were white, though Nisei women with early childhood training often ran nurseries and kindergartens. Older children took the standard subjects: math, science, English, social studies. In creative writing classes, they wrote essays and poems. These often drew inspiration from the physical environment. Observing the desert, for instance, could yield valuable life lessons. Kimii Nagata's poem "Be Like the Cactus" advises youngsters like herself to draw strength from the example of this hardy plant:

> *Let not harsh tongues,*
> *   that wag in vain,*
> *Discourage you.*
> *   In spite of pain,*
> *Be like the cactus,*
> *   which through rain,*
> *And storm, and thunder,*
> *   can remain.*

Tokiko Inouye's "The Desert Is My Home" expresses love for the harsh yet also beautiful land:

> *The desert is my home;*
> *I love its sun and sands,*
> *I love its vastness, century's sleep;*
> *It challenges, commands! . . .*
>
> *And this will be my home;*
> *The desert sands I'll plod,*
> *Far out beneath its skies and stars,*
> *To be alone with God.*[43]

No inmate was forced to work, but many took jobs to keep busy and earn money for the little extras—soap,

High school students and
their teacher at the Heart
Mountain War Relocation
Center in Wyoming.
(c. June 1943)

shampoo, and the like—sold in the camp store. Inmates earned $8 a month for unskilled jobs like delivering mail, washing dishes, and doing basic office work: filing, typing, and answering telephones. Skilled workers, such as electricians and mechanics, earned $12 a month. Professionals—doctors, dentists, and nurses—made $16 a month. Yet even the highest pay was pitifully low, compared to what whites earned for the same job. California's minimum wage was 45 cents an hour, or $72 a month for a forty-hour workweek. While on overseas duty, an army private first class and navy seaman second class earned $49.80 a month. My father brought home a princely $75 a week from a shipyard, where he did dangerous work that took lives.[44]

Despite harsh conditions, every relocation center had some land set aside for farming. Inmate-grown crops were important, because the WRA could spend only 45 cents per day (about $7.19 in 2016 dollars) to feed each person. Depending on local conditions, inmates grew cabbages, turnips, squash, watermelons, cucumbers, lettuce, and tomatoes. At Manzanar, inmates also harvested thousands of bushels of apples from trees abandoned years earlier by failed white farmers. Some centers raised pigs and cattle.[45]

Inmates also applied for "seasonal leave," permission to work outside their center for a given time. By the fall of 1942, a severe labor shortage had developed as white farm laborers went off to war. Accordingly, the WRA urged inmates to help with the harvest. No fewer than 10,000 volunteered. Their efforts saved the sugar beet crop in Utah, Idaho, Wyoming, and Montana, as well as Arizona's cotton crop. "We felt wonderful to have our freedom once more," a worker recalled. "It was such a good sensation to be moving along those dirt roads away from camp. I filled my eyes with the sight of green lawns, individual homes, [and] paved streets. . . . I never realized how much

A photograph of farming at the Manzanar War Relocation Center, taken by Ansel Adams. (c. 1943)

I missed those things that I had seen so often in San Francisco."[46]

Confined as they were, the uprooted tried to create a sense of structure and normality. This was important, because it helped them feel they were in control of their own lives, at least in certain respects. People changed their surroundings in small but significant ways. They did this by laying out rock gardens—native plants grown in pockets of soil among rocks, or just rocks set in geometric patterns, Japanese-style. Jeanne Wakatsuki Houston remembered how Issei gardeners diverted water from an aqueduct to build a "small park" at Manzanar "with mossy nooks, ponds, waterfalls and curved wooden bridges. Sometimes in the evenings we could walk down the raked gravel paths. You could face away from the barracks . . . and for a while not be a prisoner at all."[47]

Inmates filled their leisure time in other ways, too. Camps had baseball, basketball, and football teams. Manzanar had a children's zoo stocked with owls, magpies, chipmunks, and rabbits. Issei enjoyed watching *sumo,* a Japanese form of wrestling in which only one's feet could touch the ground. Patriotic holidays, especially the Fourth of July, were celebrated with parades and sports contests. Youngsters had their own organizations: Cub Scouts, Boy Scouts, Camp Fire Girls, and Girl Scouts. There were drama clubs, movies, and Saturday-night dances, where teenagers jitterbugged. Adults took classes in pottery, wood carving, calligraphy, weaving, and *ikebana,* traditional Japanese flower arranging. Experts taught *origami,* the art of folding paper into decorative figures such as birds and flowers. Miné Okubo taught drawing classes.[48]

Issei women enjoyed certain aspects of camp life. From the moment they'd arrived in America as picture brides, they had worked in their husbands' businesses or fields. Now they had leisure to develop interests and make new friends. One wrote:

Fortunate me; Indifferent
To the fierce fighting
All over the world,
Here I am, learning
Flower arrangement, writing, and
  embroidery.[49]

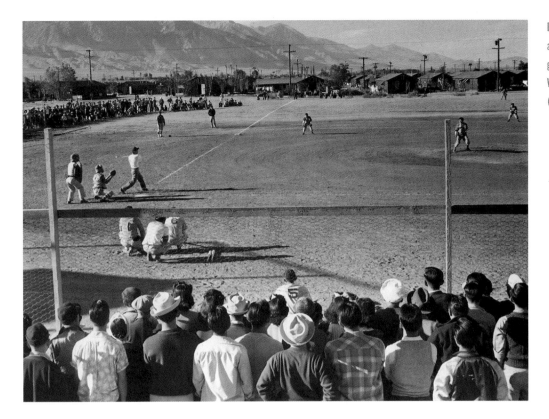

Detainees participate in—and observe—a baseball game at the Manzanar War Relocation Center. (c. 1943)

A PRISON IS A PRISON

Listing these activities may give a false impression. Relocation centers were hardly vacation resorts. Wherever the uprooted turned, they saw reminders that they were not free. Inmates had no privacy. WRA police were always on the lookout for rule breakers. "Day and night," Miné Okubo grumbled, "Caucasian camp police walked their beats within the center," peering through windows. Searches were as intrusive as any carried out by FBI agents after Pearl Harbor. During them, police offi-

cers seized anything that might serve as a weapon: scissors, pocketknives, nail files, and knitting needles.[50]

Like the assembly centers, the relocation centers resembled prisons—only more so. Guard towers, placed at intervals along tall barbed-wire fences, overlooked everything. Each tower had a powerful searchlight and a heavy machine gun pointing toward the barracks and open areas. Soldiers with rifles and fixed bayonets patrolled the outer perimeter. An inmate, Ted Nakashima, wrote:

The resettlement center is actually a penitentiary—armed guards in towers with spotlights and tommy guns, barbed-wire fences, everyone confined to quarters at nine, lights out at ten o'clock. The guards are ordered to shoot anyone who approaches within twenty feet of the fences.

Looking up at the men in the towers, a child asked: "Mommy, who are they afraid of?" Guards rarely fired, though when they did, their targets often died. At night, crisscrossing searchlight beams shone through barracks' windows, disturbing sleep.[51]

Everyone hated the barbed-wire fences. More than even the guard towers, these were reminders of captivity. "That Damned Fence," the work of an anonymous poet, expresses their feelings:

*We're trapped like rats in a wired
  cage,
To fret and fume with impotent rage;
Yonder whispers the lure of the night,
But that DAMNED FENCE assaults
  our sight.*

*We seek the softness of the midnight
  air,*

*But that DAMNED FENCE in the
  floodlight glare
Awakens unrest in our nocturnal
  quest,
And mockingly laughs with vicious
  jest. . . .*

*We all love life, and our country best,
Our misfortune is here in the west,
To keep us penned behind that
  DAMNED FENCE,
Is someone's notion of NATIONAL
  DEFENCE!*[52]

Confinement took an emotional toll. The continual stress broke people's spirits. "My dad lost everything," recalled Angie Nakashima. "He turned gray almost overnight." Inmates grew short-tempered and quarrelsome. Normally soft-spoken parents shouted at their children and at one another. Jim Matsuoka described how Manzanar changed his mother, until then a warm, outgoing person: "All of a sudden she burst into tears. That really stunned me. I couldn't figure out what was wrong. Little bits of things becoming frayed. The tension and stress poking through." Young married couples wondered if they should have children. "This is crazy," a pregnant wife told her husband. "You realize there's no future for us and what are we having kids for?" No wonder inmates ran twice the risk of stress-related illnesses—bleeding ulcers, high blood pressure, heart attack, and stroke—of the rest of the U.S. population.[53]

CIVILIAN PRISONERS OF THE RISING SUN

Radio Tokyo gave Japan's view of the relocation centers. Its broadcasts denounced America's "diabolic savagery" toward those who'd made "the fatal mistake of being born a member of the Japanese race." While this charge had the sting of truth, it also reeked of hypocrisy.[54]

Japan's advancing armies swept up over 130,000 Western—British, Dutch, Australian, and American—civilians. Before their capture, adults had been doctors, nurses, teachers, businesspeople, engineers, construction workers, journalists, and missionaries. Now they found themselves in prison camps, sometimes deep in the jungle, dotted across Asia and the Pacific islands.[55]

Some camps held only families; in others, men and women were separated, though young children stayed with their mothers. However, when boys turned ten, the "Little Adults,"

Young detainees at the barbed-wire fence in Manzanar. The photographer, Toyo Miyatake, was a prisoner there as well. (c. 1943)

as Japanese officials called them, went to the men's camps. Wherever they wound up, conditions in these camps were appalling. Civilians died in droves, victims of tropical diseases, lack of medical care, forced labor, and brutality. Food was so scarce, a former prisoner recalled, that "garbage ceased to exist." Weeds and worms, grubs and mice, snakes and monkeys, went into cooking pots.[56]

Children grew up fast in the Japanese camps. Ernest Hillen, a Dutch boy, could not recall a moment when he wasn't afraid. Every day, he saw guards slap and kick women and children, as their superiors had brutalized them. Ernest became so hardened that he "could walk down our barrack past women and children with broken teeth and bleeding gums . . . boils as big as ping pong balls and oozing tropical ulcers, and not let myself *see* them: pain was pain."[57]

President Roosevelt had already approved plans to help at least some American captives. Since the 1880s, German and Italian immigrants had flocked to Latin America in search of opportunity. After the Immigration Act of 1924 closed America's doors, thousands of Japanese settled there, too. Many did not become citizens.

In the summer of 1941, the U.S. State Department pressured several Latin American governments into drawing up *listas negras* (black lists) of aliens to be deported in case of war. Secret memos revealed the department's intention to use these people as a "reprisal reserve" for "bargaining purposes." In other words, America would kidnap them for use as hostages to trade for U.S. civilians in enemy hands. Our history textbooks do not discuss this effort.[58]

After Pearl Harbor, Latin American countries arrested 4,048 Germans, 2,264 Japanese (1,799 from Peru), and 288 Italians. As a policeman said while making an arrest, "I'm sorry we have to do this, but it's under the order of the United States." Soldiers herded entire families aboard rusty tubs guarded by the U.S. Marines. "All we had to eat was hot dogs and beans every day," Elsa Higashide, then seven, recalled years later.[59]

Upon arrival at New Orleans after several weeks at sea, a prisoner recalled, "all the women and some of the younger boy children were [put] in this huge warehouse-like place with open showers. We all had to be naked. Then they sprayed us with disinfectant from top to bottom." Immigration officers also took away their passports. So, technically, they entered the country illegally, providing an excuse for the U.S. government to detain them during the war and deport them afterward.[60]

From New Orleans, they went to Justice Department camps, where they lived in army-style barracks behind barbed-wire fences. Like the WRA's relocation centers, these camps were in remote places such as Missoula, Montana, and Santa Fe, New Mexico. The largest was located outside Crystal City,

Texas, a spot noted for its heat, black widow spiders, and scorpions. Eventually, Adolf Hitler traded 2,000 Latin American Germans for an equal number of American civilians. Japan agreed to exchange nearly 900 American captives but halted further exchanges, apparently to protest the relocation centers.[61]

PROTESTING—OR NOT

Secretary of War Stimson was worried. Though he'd called for the uprooting, as a lawyer he feared it would "make a tremendous hole in our constitutional system." John J. McCloy, Stimson's right-hand man at the War Department, was not as concerned as his boss. This bureaucrat, a former Wall Street lawyer, had little regard for the Constitution, the foundation of the American system of government. "If it is a question of the safety of the country, or the Constitution of the United States, why the Constitution is just a scrap of paper," he said. McCloy was not alone in his willingness to cast aside the Constitution when he thought it "necessary." Other highly placed officials, like General Allen Guillon, the army's provost marshal, or chief law officer, used

First Lady Eleanor Roosevelt, a civil rights activist both during her husband's time in office and afterward, visits the internment center at Gila River, Arizona, with Dillon S. Myer, director of the War Relocation Authority. (c. April 23, 1943)

almost the same words, declaring, "The Constitution is just a scrap of paper to me" in times of national emergency.[62]

Eleanor Roosevelt, however, shared Stimson's view. The First Lady had a reputation, well earned, as a champion of civil liberties. She questioned the wisdom of Executive Order 9066, calling the uprooting "absurd," "vicious," and "pathetic." The West Coast Japanese "are good Americans," she told her husband, "and have the right to live as anyone else." The president, though, did not take criticism lightly—from anyone. Now he gave his wife a frigid look, meaning she should not bring up the subject again. She didn't.[63]

FDR had incredible moral authority. Everyday folks loved him—

worshiped him, according to many observers. Roosevelt had used federal power to fight the Great Depression. Thanks to his efforts, Americans got Social Security, a federal program that helps retired workers and their families achieve a degree of economic security. Audiences of sixty million tuned in to his evening "fireside chats," radio talks in which he explained important issues in ways anyone could understand. Yet he said nothing to soften the blow of the uprooting. Instead, he defended it, deepening the public's fears.

In September 1943, with the relocation centers filled, Roosevelt told the Senate that "the evacuation" had been a "military necessity." He went on to create more scares. "Enemy ships *could* swoop in and shell New York," FDR told a White House press conference. "Enemy planes *could* drop bombs on the war plants in Detroit. Enemy troops *could* attack Alaska." All of this was possible in theory. Yet Japan's battle fleet was 5,000 miles away from the West Coast. And no country had bombers able to fly across oceans without refueling. Anyway, by June 1942, the invasion threat had passed. At the Battle of Midway, U.S. Navy planes had destroyed four of the six aircraft

carriers that attacked Pearl Harbor. From then on, Japan never had a victory, or the United States a defeat, in the Pacific.[64]

A few words from so beloved a leader as Roosevelt would have calmed the public. Several appeals reached the White House, urging him to speak out on behalf of the uprooted. Monroe E. Deutsch, vice president of the University of California at Berkeley, even sent a model fireside chat. It read in part:

> I deeply regret the necessity which prompted the removal of the Japanese nationals and their children from the Pacific Coast area; it seemed a wise precaution. . . . But remember that not a single one of those evacuated had been proved guilty of any crime—of any subversive act or sabotage. . . . Remember [too] that there should be absolutely no stigma upon them; on the contrary their cooperation deserves our approval and calls for our applause.

FDR, however, would say nothing of the sort. To his dying day, he believed what he had written in the 1920s. For him, the Japanese remained "treacherous people" whose leaders had aggression "in the blood."[65]

The uprooting met with scant opposition from the public. There was work to do, and a war to be won, so the plight of a tiny minority counted for little in the grand scheme of things. Only four mildly critical editorials appeared in the *New York Times;* no other major newspaper challenged Executive Order 9066. Magazines aimed at political and religious liberals—*The Nation, The New Republic, The Christian Century, Commonweal*—objected, but they had few readers.[66]

As Asians, Chinese Americans took pains to distinguish themselves from the Japanese. Shopkeepers put signs in their windows announcing THIS IS A CHINESE SHOP. Many also wore I AM CHINESE buttons. The national media pointed out the differences, too. *Life,* the leading picture magazine, and *Time,* the popular newsmagazine, compared Chinese and Japanese racial traits. Though both peoples looked much the same, *Time* noted, there were differences: "The Chinese expression is likely to be more placid, kindly, open; the Japanese more positive, dogmatic, arrogant. Japanese are hesitant, nervous in conversation, laugh out loud at the wrong time." Because China was an ally, Congress in 1943 repealed the Chinese Exclusion Act, but Chinese immigrants still could not apply for naturalization.[67]

Usually sympathetic to the oppressed, the Jewish community said hardly anything about the uprooting. By 1942, the Holocaust, Adolf Hitler's effort to exterminate the Jewish people, was well under way. Across German-occupied Europe, death squads shot Jews, sometimes 30,000 at a time, and tossed their bodies into unmarked graves. Worse yet, they killed millions by pumping poison gas into sealed chambers. Rather than worry about Japanese Americans, Jewish groups threw their energies into ending the slaughter by supporting President Roosevelt and the war effort.[68]

African Americans were sworn enemies of racism. Though the Civil War had ended slavery nearly eighty years before Pearl Harbor, blacks did not have equality with whites. Southern states passed scores of "Jim Crow" laws. (Jim Crow was the name of a character from an old minstrel song who wore blackface and behaved foolishly.) These laws aimed at keeping blacks "in their place" through segregation—that is, forced separation from whites. Jim Crow prevented blacks from voting and put black children into inferior all-black schools. Buses had blacks-only sections in the rear, but riders had to give their seats to whites if asked. Blacks were the last hired and first fired, and "Negro jobs" were heavy, hot, dirty, and low-paid.

The National Association for the Advancement of Colored People, the leading black civil rights group, wanted to bury Jim Crow. And a good place to begin was job discrimination. So when America went to war, NAACP leaders focused on gaining equality in the war industries. But to achieve this, they needed white allies. Opposition to the uprooting, however, would not further this aim, and perhaps would even set it back. President Roosevelt made it clear that he wanted black newspaper editors to avoid "subversive language"—that is, to print no articles critical of Executive Order 9066. FBI agents, too, visited black editors to complain about reporters who exposed the "Jim Crowing" of black soldiers in the South.[69]

Nonetheless, some black editors and reporters stood their ground. On Christmas Day 1943, for example, the *Chicago Defender* published an article titled "A Contagious Disease." The disease, of course, was racism and Jim Crow. "As Americans," it argued, "the Negroes have but one genuine concern for the Japanese of the West Coast, who are today as much victims of racial prejudice as any Negro in the South."[70]

George Schuyler, a hard-hitting reporter, tied blacks' struggle for equality to the plight of the uprooted. By not defending their rights, Schuyler declared, blacks opened themselves to worse discrimination. Already, racists such as Mississippi senator Theodore G. Bilbo had urged Congress to withdraw Nisei citizenship and deport the Nisei to Japan after the war. Schuyler saw the handwriting on the wall. "Once the precedent is established with 70,000 Japanese-American citizens, it will be easy to denationalize millions of Afro-American citizens," he wrote in the *Pittsburgh Courier.* "So whether or not we care anything about the fate of the Japanese-American citizens, we must champion their cause as ours."[71]

Leaders of the American Civil Liberties Union thought otherwise. Founded in 1920, the ACLU aimed to defend civil liberties, chiefly free speech, in federal, state, and local courts. The ACLU was devoted to President Roosevelt; he was its hero because he had rescued the nation from the brink of disaster during the Great Depression. With regard to the uprooted, however, the New York–based group failed to live up to its name. Its national director, Roger Baldwin, even congratulated General DeWitt for carrying out the "evacuation" with so little hardship! Another top official, Alexander Meiklejohn, accepted the White House line at face value. The uprooting, he wrote, was akin to isolating people with an infectious disease. Presumably, "the Japanese citizens, as a group, are dangerous both to themselves and their fellow-citizens." Only the ACLU's Northern California branch condemned the president's action.[72]

Norman Thomas was the most important national figure to oppose the uprooting. A cofounder of the ACLU and six-time Socialist Party candidate for president, Thomas accused the organization of betraying its ideals. At every turn, he denounced Executive Order 9066. He declared that the essence of democracy was the right to defend oneself against all charges in a court of law and that anything less was totalitarianism, a form of government

Norman Thomas, a cofounder of the American Civil Liberties Union and an outspoken critic of the internment camps. (November 15, 1937)

in which a dictator has total control over people's lives.

America was not Hitler's Germany or Imperial Japan, Thomas insisted. "Military necessity" was not just a matter of the president's say-so. Even the nation's highest elected official was obliged to support his case with facts. Thomas charged FDR with basing his decision on rumors and racist myths. The uprooting was "our own brand of totalitarianism and racism," an attack on core principles of American liberty. "No democracy, even in war time," Thomas concluded, "can completely surrender its own principles to war and look for a victory of anything but dictatorship." Arguments such as this did not move the man in the Oval Office. Roosevelt had decided about Japanese people long ago, and probably no one could have persuaded him otherwise.[73]

A TYRANNY OF WORDS

Nations at war are like chains under terrific strain. Just as a chain is only as strong as its weakest link, a nation's strength depends upon its people's willingness to sacrifice for victory. Doubts about a war's conduct and morality can weaken national unity and the will to fight. To maintain unity, therefore, governments try to manage public opinion. Often they do this by hiding unpleasant truths or twisting them to suit the needs of the moment.

As regards the West Coast Japanese, WRA officials faced twin problems. On the one hand, they needed to limit the influence of critics like George Schuyler and Norman Thomas to avoid bad publicity and to keep the calm in the relocation centers. Then again, they sought to convince the American public of the humanity and necessity of the uprooting. These tasks required special methods.

Schools in the centers did more than focus on academic subjects. WRA rules called for teachers to emphasize certain patriotic themes. The core theme for all grades and subjects was "Education for Relocation." Translation: Whenever possible, teachers were to slip the importance of the uprooting into their lessons.[74]

This policy applied especially to history teachers. In the WRA's version of the American experience, "relocation" was the very essence of Americanism. Our country's story, according to the history curriculum, was "one of continuous relocation," which was a key "part of the American heritage." Americans had always been restless folk, forever moving to better their lives. Students, therefore, had no reason to complain. The uprooting was actually a favor granted by a caring government! Furthermore, teachers explained, "far greater dangers confronted the pioneers, who were always moving westward, than confront the [Japanese] people in relocating. The spirit of America is in such pioneering." Teachers neglected to say that pioneering whites had always relocated *voluntarily,* and to wherever they pleased.[75]

The WRA also sought to control what its charges read, and thus what they knew and thought. Strict rules banned just about anything written in the Japanese language except Bibles, hymnbooks, and dictionaries. Letters to people on the outside had to be written in English and dropped unsealed into a letter box. WRA censors blacked out whatever they deemed inappropriate.[76]

Every center had a newspaper, usually made up of three sheets folded in half, with names like *Topaz Times* and *Manzanar Free Press.* Most issues had a tiny section written in Japanese (duly censored), and the rest was in English. Newspaper staffs could write anything they wished, so long as WRA censors approved. Writers were forbidden to discuss war news, politics, and center living conditions. Articles focused instead on gossip, trivia, sports, marriages, births, and official business: new and changed rules and other announcements. No complaint, let alone mention of a guard's shooting anyone, made its way into print. Writers and readers knew the score, and they resented being treated "as if we were a bunch of little kids that need constant watching." Center police also seized Japanese phonograph records, spoken or musical. Nor could meetings, classes, or lectures be conducted in Japanese.[77]

The WRA influenced public opinion by manipulating words; by not calling things by their right names, it used language to obscure and confuse. George Orwell, an English novelist and social critic, wrote a famous 1945 essay about this tactic. In "Politics and the English Language," Orwell says that words matter in ways we may not fully realize. Words have power. They shape our thoughts and feelings. The words that are used to describe an event are critical to how we view and understand the event. According to Orwell, there is a world of difference between everyday language and political language. We use everyday language with each other; it is simple, direct, colorful, and even profane. "Political language," however, "is designed to make lies sound truthful." It does this through the use of euphemism, the substitution of a mild word or phrase for one normally considered blunt, unpleasant, or upsetting.[78]

Used one way, euphemisms can spare another's feelings. After all, the terms *passed away* and *departed* are gentler than saying a loved one *croaked* or *popped off.* Similarly, *lavatory* and *restroom* are not as gross as *crapper,* a traditional term for *toilet. Bathroom tissue* has replaced *toilet paper;* we refer to *senior citizens,* not *old people,* and to the *hearing-impaired,* not the *deaf.* Animal shelters do not *kill* cuddly kittens; they *put them down* or *put them to sleep.* Political language, however, avoids clarity in order to mask the truth—to deceive. In this way, words lose their real meaning. Adolf Hitler's killers were masters of euphemism—experts, Orwell said, at making "murder respectable." Thus, Jews got *special handling* or *special treatment* and were *resettled in the East* to further the *final solution of the Jewish question*—all code for *extermination.*[79]

The WRA used its own euphemisms in pamphlets, press releases, official reports, and informational films. Americans learned that their army had *evacuated* the West Coast Japanese to *assembly centers* and *relocation centers,* terms we are already familiar with. Yet the reality was nothing so benign as what *evacuated* seemed to imply. By definition, *evacuation* means the temporary moving of people away from an imminent danger such as a hurricane or volcanic eruption. The Issei and Nisei, however, were moved not for their own safety but out of fear, economic jealousy, and racial bigotry. More accurate terms are *eviction, ejection, expulsion, forced removal*—and, of course, *uprooting.*

Milton S. Eisenhower, the WRA's first director, described the assembly center in a way designed to hide its real nature. It was, he said, "a convenient gathering point, within the military area, where evacuees live temporarily while awaiting the opportunity for orderly, planned movement to a Relocation Center outside of the military area." Actually, it was a *temporary detention center* or *transit camp,* whose inmates feared the "opportunity" (a favorite WRA word) awaiting them.[80]

A true relocation center is a place where people move to get away from a lasting threat such as a toxic chemical dump. WRA publications described its centers as "pioneer communities" and "wartime communities," where "residents" enjoyed "protective services" supplied by the military. "Colonists" had "comfortable wooden buildings covered with tar paper, bathhouses and showers and plenty of wholesome food." They could cultivate lands "raw, untamed [and] full of opportunity." Again, the glowing description did not match the bleak reality. So-called *residents* were in fact *inmates* (a term we have used) and *prisoners.* As for *protective services,* General DeWitt ordered MPs to arrest anyone trying to leave without permission and to do it by "using such force as is necessary to make the arrest," a euphemism for *shoot to kill.*[81]

General DeWitt, Director Eisenhower, and their underlings banned the term *concentration camp*. It was offensive—not "politically correct," as we might say today. Americans saw such camps as awful places where the Japanese brutalized civilians and Hitler murdered Jews. Nevertheless, President Roosevelt called the centers by their correct name. So did Harold Ickes, the secretary of the interior, a key cabinet official. Ickes admitted that the uprooted "were hurried away to concentration camps in the great American desert. We gave the fancy name of 'relocation centers' to these dust bowls, but they were concentration camps nonetheless." He also declared them "both stupid and cruel." The catalog of the Library of Congress still has the subject heading "Concentration Camps—United States of America." Like FDR and Ickes, we will use this term from now on, because it best describes reality.[82]

Concentration camps were also dubbed "internment camps." School textbooks still call them that, as do some authors of historical articles and books; this wording shows how euphemisms coined in the 1940s have endured for generations. Internment, as we have seen, is part of American and international law, but the term is deceptive when applied to the West Coast Japanese. Except for the community leaders arrested in the days after Pearl Harbor, no other Issei had their cases heard by a special panel and thus were not interned. Nor could their Nisei children be interned, because they were American citizens, not aliens. *Internment camp* is yet another euphemism, like *relocation center,* for *concentration camp.*

IMAGE MAKERS

You've heard the adage "A picture is worth a thousand words." Images, like words, have emotional power. Photos can arouse feelings of approval and loyalty, but also of outrage, shame, disgust, and horror. Thus, to shape public opinion in wartime, governments try to manage the images the public sees. In doing so, they also decide what will appear in tomorrow's history books and on television screens, justifying their actions to future generations.

The WRA relied on government

Toyo Miyatake, a professional photographer, smuggled a camera lens and film into Manzanar and was the only Japanese American to take pictures inside the camps, using a wooden box camera that an interned carpenter help him make. This is a portrait of Miyatake taken by famed nature photographer Ansel Adams. (c. 1943)

photographers to put the best face on concentration camp life. These photographers had strict orders not to shoot barbed-wire fences, guard towers, machine guns, or MPs. They were supposed to take pictures of smiling inmates, baseball games, dances, and youngsters reciting the Pledge of Allegiance—all to hype the merits of camp life.

The uprooted were forbidden to have cameras, because the WRA feared bad publicity, not spies. Toyo Miyatake was the only Japanese American to take pictures inside a concentration camp. A professional photographer based in Los Angeles, he smuggled a camera lens into Manzanar, which he mounted in a wooden box. Miyatake was a man with a mission. "As a photographer," he told his son Archie, "I have a responsibility to record the camp life so this kind of thing will never happen again." Ralph Merritt, the camp's director, was a decent man, but also patronizing toward the inmates, calling them "my children." When Merritt realized what was going on, he allowed Miyatake to set up a small studio and shoot whatever he liked, within reason. Miyatake took hundreds of photos, including of a watchtower and boys peering through a barbed-wire fence (see photo p. 121). These and one other by an anonymous photographer may be the only images that depict such scenes. Miyatake's works are vital historical documents. Unfortunately, the public knew nothing of his work during the war and for a long time afterward. The University of California at Los Angeles first exhibited it in 1978.[83]

The works of two Caucasian photographers deserve close attention: Ansel Adams and Dorothea Lange. Ansel Adams was famous for his dramatic treatments of western landscapes, particularly mountains. In 1943,

Adams visited Manzanar at the invitation of his friend Ralph Merritt. A selection of Adams's photos appeared the following year in a lavish 112-page book titled *Born Free and Equal*. He gladly allowed the Office of War Information, the government's propaganda agency, to use his work to counter Japan's charge of "diabolic savagery" in the camps.

Though no racist, Adams still praised the WRA for "doing a magnificent job" and being "firm and ruthless in their definitions of true loyalty." His photos give an upbeat view of Manzanar. *Born Free and Equal* has a large photo of the main entrance and its sign, MANZANAR WAR RELOCATION CENTER, an evocation of the rustic welcoming signs at national parks. Another sign, posted at the camp's perimeter and addressed to "Persons of Japanese Ancestry," issued a warning: STOP—AREA LIMITS. SENTRY ON DUTY. Adams omitted this menacing sign. Instead, he favored portraits, all posed, of happy inmates, often against the majestic background of the Sierras. Adams described Manzanar as a small-scale version of "an average American metropolis." It was merely

A sign Ansel Adams chose not to include in his collection of images from the concentration camps. (September 28, 1943)

the natural environment served the uprooted as nothing else could. "I believe that the acrid splendor of the desert, ringed with towering mountains, has strengthened the spirit of the people at Manzanar. . . . The huge vistas and the stern realities of sun and wind and space symbolize the immensity and opportunity of America." Some inmates agreed with Adams, though none had sought *this* particular "opportunity."[84]

Dorothea Lange took a different approach. Perhaps America's best documentary photographer, she saw herself as more than an artist with a camera— she was a champion of the underdog. In the 1930s, in the depth of the Great Depression, Lange produced iconic images like *Migrant Mother,* a portrait of a ragged farmworker and her hungry children. To Lange's surprise, the WRA hired her to document the uprooting, while showing it in the best light. She gave her employer more than it bargained for.

Lange demanded a lot from herself. Despite poor health, she put in seventeen-hour days, seven days a week. She hid in tight corners, concealed her camera, and sat atop the roof of her car—anything for a candid shot. The photographer set out to document

"a rocky wartime *detour* on the road to American citizenship . . . a vast expression of a government working to find a suitable haven for its war-dislocated minorities." He neglected to say that most inmates were Nisei—citizens and the only minority forcibly dislocated by the government. Adams also claimed every aspect of the uprooting, from people's normal lives before relocation to life in the so-called assembly and relocation centers. Most of all, she focused on the humanity, and the tragedy, of the uprooted. Her pictures need no explanation; they speak for themselves. For example, Lange caught children reciting the Pledge of Allegiance just days before having to leave school. She photographed a sign in a shopwindow, I AM AN AMERICAN, and billboards telling people when and where to report for evacuation. She dubbed these "savage, savage billboards."[85]

Lange's photos of what she called the "process of processing" show fami-

A portrait of Dorothea Lange holding her camera. (c. 1936)

lies waiting in line to be questioned, registered, searched, examined, and tagged, all under the watchful eyes of the military. Disgusted by the blatant racism, she wrote: "What was horrifying was to do this thing completely on

One of Dorothea Lange's photos of the Tanforan Assembly Center, showing the horse stalls that were converted into living quarters for the detained families. (April 29, 1942)

the basis of what blood may be coursing through a person's veins, nothing else. Nothing to do with your affiliations or friendships or associations. Just blood."[86]

Lange visited Tanforan, the transit camp where Miné Okubo was an inmate, though they never met. She visited the Manzanar concentration camp three times but seems not to have met Toyo Miyatake, either. Upon seeing her friend Ansel Adams's photos of the place, however, she declared them "shameful."[87]

In all, Lange took some 800 pictures. It soon became clear that she was defying WRA policy. Camp police began following her around, declaring certain places off-limits, and generally giving her a hard time. In April 1942, she lost her job and was ordered to hand over all her prints and negatives. These wound up in a file that was labeled "impounded" and closed to the public. A prime visual record of the uprooting, they remained under wraps for the next sixty-four years.[88]

Yet even as Lange packed up to leave Manzanar, the Japanese American community was taking an important role in the war effort. From that community would come some of the most heroic fighters ever to serve under the Stars and Stripes: the Yankee samurai.

CHAPTER 5

YANKEE SAMURAI

We believe we are entitled to share in the good things of democracy just as much as we should share in the sacrifices and the heartaches of our country. . . . Somewhere, on the field of battle, in a baptism of blood, we and our comrades must prove to all who question [our loyalty] that we are ready and willing to die for the one country we know and pledge allegiance to.
—Mike Masaru Masaoka, Nisei community leader (1942)

DISTRUSTED

Passed in September 1940, the Selective Training and Service Act required men between the ages of twenty-one and thirty-five to appear before local draft boards. If the board ruled them fit for military service, they went into the army when called—but not into the Marine Corps or Army Air Corps. These elite services kept out not only draftees (both white and nonwhite) but also nonwhite men who voluntarily enlisted. In the slang of the day, they were "lily-white" until some blacks were

This soldier enlisted in the army in July 1941 but was furloughed in order to help his widowed mother and family prepare for their expulsion. They're posing shortly before evacuation on their family's three-acre strawberry farm, which her children leased so she wouldn't have to work for someone else anymore after years of working in a strawberry-basket factory. (May 11, 1943)

allowed to enlist toward the end of the war. The navy's only African Americans were mess hall "boys," ship stewards, and freight handlers. On the day Japan struck Pearl Harbor, 3,188 Nisei wore army khaki and served at Hawaiian and West Coast bases. Nisei shared the same barracks, ate in the same mess halls, and had the same training as their comrades, for they were American soldiers.[1]

On December 8, 1941, after Congress declared war on Japan, draft boards stopped calling up Nisei. Young men awaiting their notices began receiving postcards changing their classification without giving any reason. From Class 1-A (eligible for service), they went to 4-C (ineligible enemy alien) and 4-F (undesirable).[2]

As for Nisei already in uniform, their world turned upside down. In the hysteria that swept the nation, army brass declared them untrustworthy. Official policy called for their discharge, unless service needs required otherwise. In practice, however, most remained in uniform, though removed from combat units, disarmed, and assigned to menial tasks like cleaning latrines.

The distrust lingered and grew deeper. In April 1942, two months after President Roosevelt signed Executive Order 9066, he visited Fort Riley, Kansas, on an inspection tour. MPs locked down the base hours before he arrived. "That morning," a soldier recalled, "they put us Nisei in a garage, surrounded us with machine guns and armed officers, and kept us there under guard until he left. That's when our morale really went down."[3]

Official distrust, so openly on display, hurt more than a physical blow. The word *haji* (shame) is among the most fearful in the Japanese language. A family's self-respect and standing in the community depended upon its honorable reputation. By shaming oneself, one shamed one's entire family, as well as the spirits of one's ancestors. Parents were forever reminding children of their duty to safeguard the family's good name. No wonder the Japanese American Citizens League, the community's leading civil rights group, begged Washington to reopen the draft to Nisei. Such an opportunity to serve, it knew, would erase any hint of disloyalty.[4]

What league members did not know was among the most closely guarded secrets of the Second World War. Months before the Pearl Harbor disaster, a select group of Nisei had begun work that would shorten the conflict and save countless American lives.

SECRET WARRIORS

During the 1930s, budget cuts and lack of public interest had severely weakened the nation's armed forces. The U.S. Army ranked eighteenth in the world, behind the armies of Spain, Portugal, Switzerland, Holland, and Belgium. But thanks to FDR's leadership and skill at getting Congress to vote the money, by 1940 America was well on its way to becoming the "Arsenal of Democracy." Once its industry hit full stride after Pearl Harbor, the sky was the limit. American factories produced more than half the military equipment of the rest of the world combined. Its auto plants turned out 2.5 million military trucks, 600,000 jeeps, and over 88,410 tanks. Aircraft factories mass-produced 297,000 warplanes of all types. Shipyards launched 141 aircraft carriers and hundreds of other warships.[5]

Yet weapons alone decide nothing. As a Marine Corps officer put it, "To lack intelligence is to be in the ring blindfolded." *Intelligence* is the military term for information. In war, brains are as important as bullets. For without good intelligence, the finest weapons are so much junk, and the bravest armies flailing mobs. Victory requires a steady flow of information about the enemy: his plans, positions, numbers, morale, equipment, and supplies. Such information can best come from the enemy himself. Obviously, one cannot gather intelligence without a command of the enemy's language.[6]

The U.S. military had no trouble with the languages of two of its three likely enemies. Living in America were millions of descendants of German and Italian immigrants, fluent in both English and their native tongues. This was not the case with Japanese. A 1941 survey found a mere sixty whites enrolled in Japanese-language college courses.

Only a handful of army officers knew enough Japanese for intelligence work. They had served as military aides to American ambassadors in Tokyo, where they gathered information on the Japanese military from public sources and spies. Yet with war fast approaching, the army would need thousands of language experts. Though there was little time to train whites in sufficient numbers, army intelligence chiefs believed that most Nisei knew Japanese. They had, after all, grown up in Japanese households and gone to schools that taught Japanese language and culture.[7]

Three officers were ordered to locate Nisei soldiers qualified to serve as linguists. Captain Kai E. Rasmussen, Captain Joseph K. Dickey, and Colonel John Weckerling had all done tours of duty at the Tokyo embassy; Weckerling spent eight years there. From July to October 1941, they interviewed all 1,300 Nisei soldiers stationed on the West Coast. Each was shown a Japanese army manual and asked to read, translate, and explain a few passages.[8]

To their dismay, the officers found that the young Nisei knew little Japanese. The language schools, on which their parents had spent so much money,

had taught them next to nothing. Hardly any could speak a few coherent sentences, let alone read and write, in Japanese. Worse yet, more than 90 percent did not know enough to qualify as trainable. Some even confessed that their parents spoke Japanese when they wished to keep something from them. Clearly, racists who argued Japaneseness lay "in the blood" did not know what they were talking about. Nisei had Japanese facial features. But in their speech and thoughts, habits and outlook, they were Americans.[9]

The officers decided they would have to start from scratch, building on success over time. At the outset, they planned to pick a few of the best candidates and put them through a demanding six-month training course. Upon graduation, most would deploy to army units on bases in the Pacific. However, a select group, the best of the best, would stay behind to train the next class, and so on. Eventually, their Military Intelligence Service Language School would employ scores of instructors.

Everything about MISLS was secret, because the school promised to give America a unique advantage. Germany and Italy assumed that America had plenty of people able to translate captured documents and intercepted radio messages. Therefore, German and Italian forces used complex codes, which they changed regularly, often on a daily basis. Important messages went directly to commanders, but only to those who needed the information to carry out a specific mission. During retreats, headquarters staffs burned documents, files, reports, and codebooks before leaving.

The Pearl Harbor attack showed that Japan's military could make plans in secret and carry them out with stunning effect. Yet, oddly enough, they were lax about routine security. "The Japanese," an American officer noted, "seem to have a mania for putting things down on paper and hanging on to old documents." Nor were they careful about what they did with these. The study of English was also discouraged. Mary Kimoto Tomita, a Nisei student in Japan, told how a man slapped a fellow student across the face, screaming, "How dare you read an English book! Don't you know we are fighting a war and we are going to exterminate America and England!" Japanese schools, Mary added, banned the study of English and punished those "who read the 'language of the enemy.'"[10]

To make matters worse, Japan's military leaders had lulled themselves with their own racial myths. Some commanders—we cannot know the exact number—believed that their language was too complicated for any but a few Americans to understand, and certainly not ordinary combat soldiers. In effect, they saw Japanese itself as a nearly unbreakable code. So they seldom changed codes. Commanders often sent radio messages "in the clear," without putting them into code at all. When retreating or during routine moves, staffs left documents behind, most likely because they thought Americans too stupid to read them. It also seemed a sure bet that American racism would prevent the Nisei from becoming intelligence officers.[11]

On November 1, 1941, five weeks before Japan struck Pearl Harbor, MISLS began work in an old airplane hangar at the Presidio in San Francisco. Its first class had sixty students (fifty-eight Nisei and two whites), taught by four Nisei instructors. John Aiso, the chief of instruction and a Harvard-educated lawyer, set the schedule and course of study. Classes started at 8:00 a.m. and continued, with a short break, until 9:00 p.m., five days a week. Lights-out was at 11:00 p.m., but students went to the barracks' latrine, the only place the lights stayed on all night, to study for Saturday exams. "You cannot study beyond 11 o'clock," one recalled, "but if your [*sic*] on a toilet bowl, nobody [is] going to bother you." Besides learning to speak, they had to master three types of written Japanese: printed, script, and shorthand. In addition, they studied Japanese military vocabulary (an extremely difficult subject), document analysis, map reading, radio communications, and methods of collecting battlefield intelligence.[12]

In May 1942, as the first class neared graduation, MISLS moved to Camp Savage, outside Minneapolis, Minnesota; it later moved to nearby Fort Snelling. Though the move was necessary for tightening secrecy, the main reason for it was the hysteria sweeping the West Coast. Nisei students felt imprisoned in the Presidio, fearing to go into San Francisco. Meanwhile, Executive Order 9066 had set the stage for the uprooting of their families. Minnesota, an instructor explained, "not only had room physically but also had room in the people's hearts." Minnesotans received the strangers warmly but had no idea why they were in their state.[13]

We would love to know what uprooted families thought of their young men's secret duties, but the written record is mum about this. Students were angry—this we know. However, they believed their service would make things better for their families. Bowing to necessity, the army put aside racism to allow MISLS to recruit from concentration camps. Men from behind barbed wire, joined by volunteers from Hawaii, accounted for nearly all the 6,000 Nisei linguists trained during the war.

Upon graduation, most went to the Allied Translator and Interpreter Section in Australia. A joint project—American, Australian, New Zealander—ATIS was the heart of Allied intelligence in the South Pacific. Ultimately, every scrap of captured Japanese paper went there. Papers taken from offices and dead bodies, often soiled by blood and filth, were cleaned, translated, analyzed, and cataloged for future reference. By war's end, Nisei had translated over twenty million pages of Japanese documents. ATIS, too, assigned Nisei linguists to front-line outfits. Called the "eyes and ears" of the combat troops, they saw action in every Pacific campaign. But before following their exploits, we must see where and whom they fought.[14]

The official logo of the Seabees. (Date unknown)

THE PACIFIC THEATER

Based at Pearl Harbor, the American high command in the Pacific planned to smash "the Empire," as it called Japan. The idea was not to seize all of the country's island fortresses; that would take too much time and cost too many lives. Instead, American forces would capture one or two key islands in an area. Army engineers and Seabees (the navy's construction teams) would then build new naval bases and airfields— or improve existing ones—as needed. Having secured a foothold, American forces would "leapfrog" over neighboring islands, leaving their defenders to "wither on the vine" through starvation, disease, and air attacks. Each victory would punch a hole in Japan's defense ring, bringing American forces closer to the home islands.

It was one thing for planners to draw lines on maps, another for those at the "spear-point" to carry out their plans. In many ways, the Pacific theater of operations was unlike any that American fighting men had ever faced. Some islands, like Tarawa in the Gil-

berts, were tiny, treeless coral reefs a few feet above sea level. With no place to hide on islands defended by dug-in Japanese Marines, assault troops fought under the blazing sun. In America, the desert concentration camps were hot, but the temperature fell sharply after sunset, giving several hours of relief. On these islands, in contrast, the porous coral absorbed heat, releasing it at night, so the temperature was only a few degrees less than the daytime high.

Other islands, such as Guadalcanal in the Solomons, a thousand miles north of Australia, were "green hells." Their jungles were so thick that troops had to hack out trails, inch by inch, with machetes. Bloodsucking leeches dropped onto exposed flesh from overhanging branches. Rats swarmed over men in waterlogged foxholes. The high

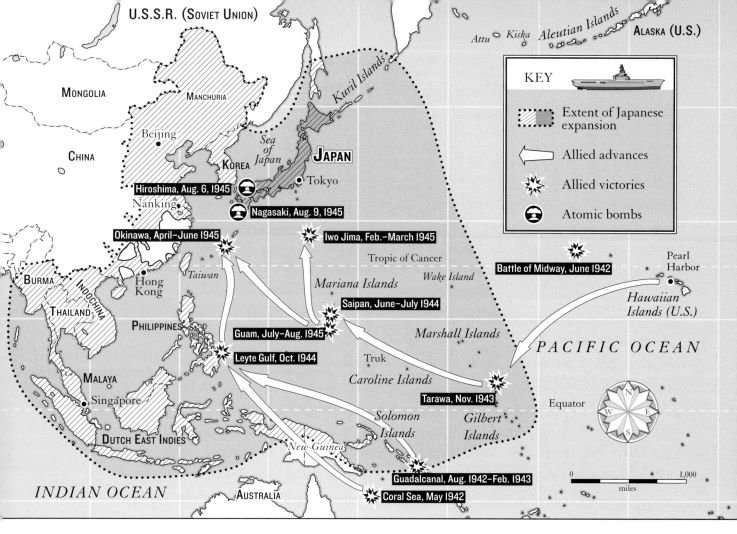

A map of the Pacific theater showing Japanese expansion and key Allied action.

humidity rotted uniforms, covering their wearers' skin with angry rashes, slimy fungal infections, and oozing sores. James Jones, a twenty-one-year-old army private who fought on Guadalcanal, later described conditions there in his 1962 novel, *The Thin Red Line*:

The moist humidity was so overpowering, and hung in the air so heavily, that it seemed more like a material object than a weather condition. It brought the sweat starting from every pore at the slightest exertion....[This] sweat ran down over their bodies soaking everything to saturation. When it had saturated their clothing, it ran down into their shoes, filling them, so that they sloshed along in their own sweat as if they had just come out of wading a river....[The] sun blazed down on them . . . heating their helmets to such temperatures that the steel shells actually burned their hands.[15]

But nature was never as cruel as the human enemy, especially in his treatment of captives. It had not always been so. The Japanese had held different attitudes toward captives at different times in their history. In the wars of old Japan, lords and their samurai had no wish to hold prisoners for long periods. Nor was there any shame in surrendering. After a battle, victors invited the defeated to join their side. The defeated that chose not to relinquished their weapons and went home, having given their word of honor to sit out the rest of the war.[16]

This tradition continued into modern times. Of all nations, Japan had the best reputation for humane treatment of captives. During its first war with China (1894–1895), generals released thousands after they signed "paroles," pledges not to fight Japan again. In the war with Russia (1904–1905), captives praised the "brave Japanese," who tended Russian wounded as they would their own men. President Theodore Roosevelt admired their decency. "The

Japanese soldiers," he said in 1905, "are not only full of valor and of knowledge of military science, but also they are very humane, have self-restraint, and are honest. . . . I have great admiration and respect for them." During the First World War, Japanese guards treated German captives as honored guests, not despised enemies.[17]

In the 1920s, a different mind-set took hold. By then, Japan's military leaders had corrupted the ideals of Bushido, the ancient way of the warrior, to boost their power. Along with employing racism and brutal discipline, they now insisted that nothing worse could happen to a warrior than to be captured, even while wounded or unconscious. The *Field Service Code,* the Japanese soldier's handbook, left no doubt about his duty: "Do not endure the shame of being made a prisoner while alive; die and do not leave behind the sullied name of one who foundered and fell." Save your last bullet for yourself![18]

Fear of shaming explains some odd behavior—odd, that is, to Americans. Japanese airmen wore swords, not parachutes. Captured soldiers who escaped and returned to their units were shot. Survivors of sunken warships swam *away* from American rescuers. Doctors killed the wounded out of "kindness." One explained: "When a Japanese surrenders . . . he commits dishonor. One must forget him completely. His wife and his poor mother and children erase him from their memories. There is no memorial placed for him. It is not that he is dead. It is that he never existed." It followed that enemy captives had also disgraced themselves, were less than men, and deserved to be treated accordingly.[19]

The American military painfully learned what China had known since the Rape of Nanking. On December 10, 1941, Japanese veterans of the China war landed in the Philippine Islands. As they advanced, General Douglas MacArthur, commander of the American and Filipino forces, abandoned Manila and ordered a retreat to the Bataan Peninsula of Luzon, the main island. In the siege that followed, Japanese troops killed Allied wounded, shot medics, and bombed hospitals that had huge red crosses painted on their roofs. Army nurse Juanita Redmond described the horrific result of a raid:

This time they scored a direct hit on the wards. A thousand-pound bomb . . . smashed the tin roofs into flying pieces; iron beds doubled and broke jaggedly like paper matches. . . . Only one small section of my ward remained standing. Part of the roof had been blown into the jungle. There were mangled bodies under the ruins; a blood-stained hand stuck up through a pile of scrap; arms and legs had been ripped off and flung among the rubbish. Some of the mangled torsos were almost impossible to identify. One of the few corpsmen who had survived unhurt climbed a tree to bring down a body blown into the top branches. Blankets, mattresses, pajama tops hung in the shattered trees.[20]

On April 9, 1942, as the Military Intelligence Service Language School prepared to graduate its first class, 76,000 Allied troops surrendered on Bataan. In the States, newspapers announced the event with screaming headlines. "Bataan Collapses! Japs Crush American Defenders," said the *San Francisco Examiner.* Of course, the captives had heard about Japanese

atrocities in China. Yet most were skeptical, dismissing the reports as exaggerations to arouse public opinion and sell newspapers. They had fought bravely and believed the Japanese would treat them decently, out of regard for their courage. "Everything is going to be all right," officers told their men. "Just stick together, and don't worry."[21]

But they had plenty to worry about. The victors mocked their American prisoners as racial inferiors, the filthy dregs of a corrupt nation. "As I gaze upon these crowds of surrendered soldiers," a Japanese reporter wrote, "I feel as if I am watching dirty water running from the sewers of a nation . . . whose pride has been lost. Japanese soldiers look extraordinarily handsome, and I feel proud to belong to their race." Those handsome soldiers made starving, sick, and wounded men walk sixty-five miles to prison camps under the blazing sun. Guards bayoneted, shot, or beheaded their prisoners along the way. Other prisoners received the "oriental sun treatment." William Dyess, a fighter pilot who escaped, wrote:

> The Japs seated us on the scorching ground, exposed to the full glare of the sun. Many of the Americans and Filipinos had no covering to protect their heads. . . . When I thought I could stand the penetrating heat no longer, I was determined to have a sip of the tepid water in my canteen. I had no more than unscrewed the top when the aluminum flask was snatched from my hand. The Jap who had crept up behind me poured the water into a horse's nose-bag, then threw down the canteen. He walked on among the prisoners, taking away their water and

The Japanese controlled the Philippine media, and thus portrayed imperial forces as helpful liberators. This front page of the local *Tribune* claims that Japanese occupation will bring peace and tranquility. (April 24, 1942)

A photograph taken by a Japanese soldier of American prisoners using improvised stretchers to carry their comrades who, from lack of food or water, fell along the road. (c. May 1942)

pouring it into the bag. When he had enough he gave it to his horse.[22]

American soldiers photographed along the Bataan Death March, with hands tied behind their backs. (c. May 1942)

In what became known as the Bataan Death March, some 10,000 men lost their lives, of whom 2,300 were Americans.[23]

To be fair, we should acknowledge that some Japanese soldiers treated some prisoners kindly. "So sorry, so sorry," these men said in broken English as they drove by in trucks. Several offered prisoners drinks from their own canteens. One night, a guard wakened a sleeping American and gave him a cup of hot chocolate; he hadn't had a bite of food or a drop of water in three days. "All through the night he gave me something, because he knew I needed strength," the soldier recalled. "In the morning he was gone." Sadly, such men were so few during that dreadful April.[24]

We cannot exaggerate the importance of the Bataan Death March. Next to Pearl Harbor, it did more to harden American attitudes toward Japan than anything else. Though Tokyo wished to hide the atrocity, too many people knew what had happened. Thousands of Filipino villagers had watched the march from the roadside, offering the wretched men water, which guards usually spilled on the ground before their eyes. What is more, scores of marchers escaped into the jungle. The lucky ones joined bands of Filipino guerrillas—resistance fighters—to begin raids on enemy outposts. U.S. Navy submarines, summoned by the guerrillas' short-wave radios, evacuated a few of these to Australia. Scuttlebutt—repeated stories and rumors—did the rest. Almost instantly, American outfits across the Pacific reacted to the news. "We knew about Bataan," recalled the marine corporal Eugene "Sledgehammer" Sledge years later. "You developed an attitude of no mercy because they had no mercy on us." Vengeance became the watchword, "a no-quarter, savage kind of thing."[25]

A poster created to capitalize on the spirit of vengeance sparked by the atrocities of the Japanese military during the Bataan Death March. (c. 1944)

FROM THE SOLOMON ISLANDS TO BURMA

On August 7, 1942, the 1st Marine Division landed on Guadalcanal. Two months earlier, the Japanese had begun to carve an airfield out of the jungle. The marines had to seize it before they finished the job. Otherwise, enemy planes would be able to cut the sealanes to Australia, threatening the island continent. Because the marines needed linguists, the army sent a team of Nisei. Guadalcanal would provide

The infamous photograph of Japanese officer Yasuno Chikao about to behead Australian sergeant Leonard G. Siffleet, which was found on the body of a Japanese soldier. (October 24, 1943)

warrants for their relatives in Japan. The American marines, however, were the Nisei's most urgent concern. When they saw anyone with a Japanese face, their instinct was to shoot first and ask questions later. To avoid "accidents," officers assigned each Nisei linguist a bodyguard. Some Nisei, doubly cautious, went to various marine units, telling them, "Take a *good* look at me!"[26]

The marines were in no mood to take prisoners. Everyone on Guadalcanal knew that American survivors of an ambush had hidden in the jungle, watching the enemy torture and behead their comrades. Later, a photo found on the body of a Japanese soldier showed a Japanese officer with a raised sword, standing over a bound and blindfolded Australian, who awaited the blow on his knees. When marines saw copies of this dreadful image, their imaginations ran wild. The photo also appeared in Australian newspapers and in *Life* magazine. It left a deep impression not only on fighting men but also on Allied civilians, further demonizing the enemy.[27]

Guadalcanal was not going to be another Bataan. "Kill or Be Killed" became the marines' slogan. Hatred and vengeance became so powerful they

their first chance to prove themselves in a crucial campaign.

The Nisei had a lot on their minds. If the Japanese captured them, they could expect the worst: a slow death by torture, during which the enemy would likely discover their mission and tighten security, costing untold American lives. Capture would also sign death drove some to do terrible things. War correspondent Edgar L. Jones wrote, "We shot prisoners in cold blood, wiped out hospitals, strafed lifeboats, . . . finished off the enemy wounded, tossed the dying into a hole with the dead, and in the Pacific boiled the flesh off enemy skulls to make table ornaments for sweethearts, or carved bones into letter openers." *Life* printed a full-page "Picture of the Week" showing a young woman gazing wistfully at a skull her boyfriend sent as a "memento." Another issue had a picture of a burned Japanese head, openmouthed as if screaming, speared on top of a wrecked enemy tank. President Roosevelt received a letter opener carved from a Japanese soldier's arm bone. He sent it back, saying that he "did not wish to have such an object in his possession." The arm-bone story caused a stir in Japan, too, fueling propaganda about American savagery.[28]

At first, Nisei linguists found it hard to get information, because the marines usually shot "escaping" prisoners, despite orders to the contrary. The solution: For each prisoner brought in alive, reward his captor with a three-day furlough away from the front lines and a pint of ice cream from the supply

The *Life* magazine "Picture of the Week" showing a young war worker gazing at the Japanese skull her soldier boyfriend sent her from New Guinea. (May 22, 1944)

ships offshore. This incentive worked, and interrogation soon became a Nisei specialty.[29]

When questioning German and Italian prisoners, officers might use threats and violence. "A mouthful of knuckles," it was said, loosened tongues quickly. The Nisei, however, made a valuable discovery on Guadalcanal. Life still mattered to Japanese soldiers who had decided not to fight to the death. But by surrendering, they became outcasts, cut off from everyone and everything that bound them to Japan. This realization gave linguists an advantage. Most prisoners, if treated humanely, would cooperate. So before questioning began, a kind word and a cigarette would set the tone. One Nisei offered a mug of coffee and a bag of cookies. "Go ahead," he told the famished prisoner. "Please eat." Then they had a long talk.[30]

A Nisei who shared a personal matter moved captured Japanese lieutenant Kiyofumi Kojima. "He informed me," recalled Kojima, "that his grandmother and grandfather lived in Hiroshima, and asked what I thought of Nisei soldiers. . . . 'You were born in America,' I replied. 'You're fighting for your country, America.' . . . He was like me, and I did the same thing for my country. Then he told me about how Japanese-Americans were horribly ill-treated in America, that they were placed in camps."

Refusal to cooperate would bring a stern warning: American authorities would notify the prisoner's family of his capture through the International Committee of the Red Cross, thereby shaming the family before the community. That threat usually did the trick. Some prisoners not only told what they knew but also pinpointed targets on maps and even flew on bomber missions with their captors.[31]

After a battle, Nisei searched the

A Nisei interpreter interrogating a captured Japanese commanding general in Okinawa. (c. 1945)

pockets and packs of the enemy dead, grisly work because bodies were often mangled and putrid with decay. Diaries, for instance, were extremely valuable. American soldiers were forbidden to keep diaries since they might jot down details best kept quiet. The Japanese, however, had a different view. To them, a diary was as much a part of a soldier's "remains" as his body. The Imperial Army shipped diaries home, along with soldiers' ashes. In his diary, a soldier revealed his innermost feelings, often in sensitive, emotional poems. Often, too, a diary contained tidbits of information that, linked to tidbits from other diaries, formed a larger picture. The writer's unit number, where the unit had been, where it was going, its morale and living conditions: all provided insights about the enemy at a given time.

Occasionally, the Nisei found treasure troves of information. Among these was the Japanese Army List, a register of the names, ranks, and units of 40,000 Japanese officers as of October 15, 1942. Translations of this document allowed American planners to compare the names with those on decoded radio messages and thus form a picture of enemy troop movements throughout the Pacific. Another find was a complete list of Imperial Navy ships, including their radio call signs and those of every Japanese naval fighter squadron. One discovery must have given the linguists a chuckle. It was the schedule of senior officers' visiting hours at a "comfort house" near their headquarters on the island of New Britain. An air strike followed. Afterward, an American report noted, Japanese leadership on New Britain "was never the same."[32]

Little by little, the Nisei earned their comrades' respect. "People are screaming for them," an intelligence officer wrote his superiors. After the army took over from the marines on Guadalcanal, General Alexander M. Patch would go to the transports to personally welcome each fresh group of Nisei. That the families of such men should be in concentration camps in the United States angered their comrades. Robert E. Borchers, a twenty-two-year-old private, wrote to the American Legion: "I am one of the fortunate Marines who have recently returned to this country after serving in the offensive against the Japanese on Guadalcanal.... We find... a condition behind our backs that stuns us. We find that our American citizens, those of Japanese ancestry, are being persecuted, yes, persecuted as though Adolf Hitler himself were in charge. . . . I'm putting it mildly when I say it makes our blood boil. . . . We shall fight this injustice, intolerance and un-Americanism at home! We will not break faith with those who died. . . . We can endure the hell of battle, but we are resolved not to be sold out at home."[33]

Japanese resistance on Guadalcanal ended in February 1943. Two months later, Admiral Yamamoto, mastermind of the Pearl Harbor attack, met his end. Nisei linguists had translated a radio message giving his schedule for an inspection tour of bases in the Solomon Islands. Fighters from Guadalcanal shot his plane down. Later, Japanese searchers found Yamamoto's bullet-riddled body in the wreckage.

As the MISLS graduated more linguists, the army gave them more to do. Several Nisei teams trained and advised Chinese troops. This activity could be more dangerous than frontline combat. The Chinese, like the marines on Guadalcanal, shot at anyone who looked Japanese. One Nisei team, mistakenly captured by a Chinese outfit, desperately used sign language to show they were Americans. Afterward,

the Nisei "remained a pale green for the next three months or more."[34]

Nisei also joined Merrill's Marauders in India. The all-volunteer unit, 3,000 strong and led by a thirty-nine-year-old general named Frank D. Merrill, had a vital mission. Japanese forces had cut the Burma Road, the land route for trucking American supplies into China. Worse yet, the Japanese occupied much of Burma (now Myanmar), from which they planned to invade neighboring India. The Marauders were to operate behind enemy lines in Burma, supplied with equipment and food parachuted in by cargo planes. Moving swiftly, they intended to capture Myitkyina, a key crossroads with an all-weather airfield. Success would pave the way for British troops from India and American and Chinese forces from China to retake Burma.

In February 1944, General Merrill plunged into the Burmese jungle. Though the Marauders were in top physical shape, nothing had prepared them for the ordeal that lay ahead. They climbed hills so steep they practically had to crawl on hands and knees; one said it was "like walking up and down the teeth of a saw!" Every day or so, they had short, savage firefights with enemies hidden in the jungle. The

Japanese tortured captive Marauders horribly; sometimes they cut a man to pieces and then laid the body on a trail, "right out there in the open where you could see it." Even so, some Marauders could not help admiring Japanese courage. Had they been Americans, said Lieutenant Meredith Coldwell, "they'd have got the Congressional Medal of Honor."[35]

The Nisei became all-around soldiers in Burma. They translated documents, questioned prisoners, tapped Japanese field-telephone lines, and fought. Sergeant Roy A. Matsumoto was the team's daredevil. Matsumoto had volunteered for intelligence work while in a concentration camp. He was game for anything, whatever the danger. At night, he would slip close to enemy positions to eavesdrop on officers' conversations. One time, he overheard orders for an attack. At sunrise, the Japanese found the Marauders gone but their fighting positions rigged with booby traps. During another attack, the Japanese began to waver and fall back. Thinking fast, Matsumoto shouted *"Susume!"*—"Advance!" The enemy changed course and rushed ahead into a hail of Marauder bullets.[36]

Another Nisei, Herbert Miyasaki, General Merrill's personal interpreter (he later named his son Merrill), had a knack for getting information out of captured Japanese officers. A simple, and unexpected, act of kindness would go a long way. The first thing Miyasaki did was to give back the officer's samurai sword. "The sword had nothing to do with the Emperor," he explained; "oftentimes, it was a family heirloom and a symbol of the officer's authority." The moment the officer took the sword, he grasped the top of the handle with both hands and propped it under his chin, signaling respect for the weapon and gratitude to his captor. Then he (usually) began to talk freely. "He must have thought," Miyasaki explained, "'Hey, this guy's alright, now that I'm not naked.'"[37]

After the fall of Myitkyina in August, the Marauders, their mission accomplished, disbanded. General Merrill gave the Nisei a large share of the credit for his unit's success. "I couldn't have gotten along without them," he declared. Like the veterans of Guadalcanal, his men learned not to judge people by their appearance or ancestry. "We of the Merrill's Marauders," one said, "wish to boast of the Japanese-Americans fighting in our outfit. . . . Many of the boys, and myself especially, never knew a Japanese-American or

Three of the Marauders: from left to right, Interpreter Herbert Miyasaki, General Frank Merrill, and Interpreter Akiji Yoshimura. (May 1, 1944)

what one was like—now we know and the Marauders want you to know that they are backing the Nisei one hundred percent. It makes the boys and myself raging mad to read about movements against Japanese-Americans by some 4-F'ers back home. We would dare them to say things like they have in front of us."[38]

IMPERIAL SUNSET

American "leapfroggers" also took long strides across the Central Pacific west of Hawaii. Their target was the Mariana Islands, just 1,385 miles south of Tokyo.

Only three islands in this group were large enough to have military value: Saipan and Tinian, seized from Germany after the First World War, and Guam, taken from the United States in the first days of the Second. Because they were keys to Japan's outer defense line, their fall would put American bombers within range of all its major cities.

The U.S. Navy recovered quickly after Pearl Harbor. By the spring of 1944, the nation had built the most powerful fleet the world had ever seen. Its striking arm consisted of aircraft carriers protected by battleships, cruisers, destroyers, and submarines. Carrier planes, in turn, guarded the slow-moving troop transports and hit enemy positions ashore. Nobody aboard the 535-ship task force expected Saipan, its first objective, to be easy. The island's waters teemed with sharks, and its 32,000 defenders were expected to fight to the last man.

On June 13, a Japanese soldier awoke to the cry "The American battle fleet is here!" He later said: "I looked up and saw the sea completely black with them. What looked like a large city had suddenly appeared offshore." Then it began. Ships' guns opened fire and carrier planes zoomed in low, raking the defenders with machine guns and bombs. Marines and army troops landed two days later, with their own teams of Nisei linguists. None of them knew that other Nisei had already helped avert a disaster.[39]

Three months earlier, Japan's naval chiefs had figured the Marianas were likely to be next on the Americans' target list. Secretly, they devised the "Z-Plan," which called for using nearly all of Japan's remaining naval forces to ambush the invasion fleet. By a stroke of Yankee good luck, a plane carrying a Japanese officer with the plan crashed into the sea off the Philippines. Filipino fishermen found a briefcase containing a twenty-two-page document bound in a red cover. It seemed important, so they gave it to Filipino guerrillas. A radio message to Australia brought an American submarine for the mysterious document.

Two Nisei sergeants, Kiyoshi Yamashiro and Yoshikazu Yamada, did the final translation. As expected, when the Saipan landings began, the Japanese triggered their Z-Plan. The American fleet was ready. In the two-day Battle of the Philippine Sea (June 19–20), the Imperial Navy lost three carriers and 475 planes, a disaster from which it never recovered. The United States lost 70 planes, mostly because their fuel ran out, and two small escort vessels. From then on, the U.S. Navy would strike anywhere it pleased.

Ashore, Saipan's defenders steadily gave ground. As had happened on so many other islands, the Japanese soldiers made all-out suicide attacks when facing defeat; even the wounded clad in bandages staggered into American fire. *Tenno heika banzai!* they cried— "Long live the emperor!" Yet that was just the beginning. Some 35,000 Japanese civilians also lived on Saipan, and

Tokyo had brainwashed them with hate propaganda for years. It was true that America put people of Japanese ancestry into concentration camps. But it was an absurd lie that marines were cannibals drafted from asylums for the criminally insane.[40]

The civilians panicked, often choosing death over capture by "cannibals." Dreadful scenes took place. Children begged their parents to kill them, or they sat in circles, tossing live grenades from hand to hand until they exploded. At Marpi Point, a sheer 220-foot cliff at the northern tip of the island, families held hands and jumped onto the jagged coral below. Mothers leaped with infants in their arms. Horrified marines tried to shorten the children's agony in the only way they knew. "I

used to shoot the children as they went down," Michael Witowich recalled, "so they wouldn't suffer when they hit the coral. I used to think in my dreams whether it was right for me to do that, so they wouldn't have to suffer when they went down. 'Cos when they hit the coral they'd still be alive and have a horrible death, so it was like shooting a horse that breaks its leg—and this is a human being."[41]

Nisei linguists pleaded over loudspeakers, but the mayhem continued. One linguist, however, rescued a large group of civilians single-handedly. Born in Hawaii, Hoichi "Bob" Kubo had been an army medical technician when the Japanese struck Pearl Harbor. As the attackers machine-gunned fleeing men, Kubo rushed to aid the wounded. Afterward, he volunteered as a linguist, rising to the rank of sergeant.

Kubo was patrolling near Marpi Point when two civilians suddenly appeared. They stood on the edge of a cliff, motionless, their hands raised above their heads. Under questioning, they revealed they were not natives of Saipan but construction workers from Okinawa, an island on mainland Japan's very doorstep. Eight Japanese soldiers, they said, were holed up in a

Sergeant Hoichi "Bob" Kubo, the most decorated Nisei linguist of the Second World War, comforts a Japanese child in Saipan. (c. 1944)

cave at the base of the cliff with scores of men, women, and children. The two men wanted to live; they had climbed to the top on a rope. The people in the cave were jumpy; unless something was done quickly, they might commit suicide, or the soldiers would kill them and then themselves.

"I'm going down!" Kubo told Lieutenant Roger Pyre, the patrol leader. Slipping a pistol and some K rations (dried meals for combat troops) under his shirt, he rappelled down the cliff on the rope the workers had used.

Kubo came face to face with the soldiers at the cave's mouth. Each aimed his rifle at Kubo's head. Luckily, nobody fired; probably the sight of a "Japanese" in an American uniform caught them by surprise. Kubo took off his helmet and started a conversation.

"You're a spy!" a soldier shouted.

"I am an American!" Kubo shouted back, louder. And, he added, his grandfathers had served with the Japanese army during the Russo-Japanese War, in the famous 5th and 6th Divisions. Impressed, the soldiers invited Kubo into the cave. Then they sat cross-legged on the ground, sharing rations and getting to know each other.

Kubo appealed to their sense of honor, invoking the ancient code of Bushido. Americans did not fight civilians, he said. If these men wanted to kill themselves, that was their business, but he asked them to spare the civilians. "You are the sons of Japanese parents. You were born in Japan and fight for your country, Japan. I am also the son of Japanese parents, but I was born in the United States. The United States is my country and I fight for it. The United States has honored me by making me a sergeant." At these words, the soldiers, all privates, bowed their heads.

Kubo then recited a traditional Japanese saying: "If I am filial, I cannot serve the emperor. If I serve the emperor, I cannot be filial." That did the trick. In one sense, being filial means respecting and obeying one's parents. But it also means that one's loyalty must always go to the higher authority. Thus, as an American, a Nisei must serve the land of his birth, the United States, not his ancestral land, Imperial Japan. It would be shameful to do otherwise.[42]

Two hours later, the soldiers led 122 civilians out of the cave. After they climbed to safety, a sniper shot Lieutenant Pyre, the force of the bullet sending his body rolling down the cliff. Kubo was furious. He lined the Japanese up, shouting, "Someone shot that man who saved all of your lives! Is there not a samurai among you?" Overcome by shame, the soldiers fought with each other to climb down the cliff and retrieve Pyre's body. Kubo, the real hero, received the Distinguished Service Cross, making him the most decorated Nisei linguist of the Second World War.[43]

America had 3,426 killed or missing in action on Saipan. Of the 32,000 Japanese troops, 1,000 survived; more than 20,000 civilians lost their lives, chiefly by suicide. When Tokyo learned of the island's fall, Admiral Osami Nagano, Emperor Hirohito's chief naval adviser, moaned, "All hell is on us." So it was.[44]

American forces drew closer to the Japanese homeland. In the Central Pacific, construction crews turned the Marianas into bases for the newly developed B-29 Superfortress. The world's most advanced bomber, it could fly 5,800 miles round-trip without refueling. On February 19, 1945, the third anniversary of Executive Order 9066, marines landed on Iwo Jima, a volcanic island 775 miles from Tokyo. Two months later, they leapfrogged to Okinawa, a mere 350 miles from the Japanese capital.

Meanwhile, in the fall of 1944, General Douglas MacArthur, now commanding American forces in the South Pacific, struck south, retaking the Philippine Islands by the following spring. Survivors of the Bataan Death March greeted MacArthur's troops with hoarse cheers, for by then all were little more than living skeletons. Starving army and navy nurses, held in a fenced-off area at the University of Santo Tomas in Manila, were astonished. Their rescuers were pictures of health, thanks to the stream of supplies that flowed from American farms and factories. Bertha Dworsky said they "looked like giants to us because we were so emaciated and thin." The troops, another nurse recalled, "were like from another planet. They were so young, healthy-looking, pink cheeks filled out, you know, all of them. I felt as high as a kite."[45]

Nothing the Japanese did seemed able to slow the American advance. Fleets of B-29s struck one city after another. On the night of March 9–10, 1945, bombers turned 15.8 square miles of Tokyo to ashes. A police officer, Ishikawa Koyo, described the streets as "rivers of fire [with] flaming pieces of furniture exploding in the heat, while the people themselves blazed like 'matchsticks' as their wood and paper homes exploded in flames." Around

A B-29 Superfortress drops bombs on a mission to Osaka. (June 1, 1945)

97,800 people died that night, 41,000 were injured, and over one million were left homeless. Moreover, U.S. submarines sank nearly every oil tanker and cargo ship flying the Rising Sun flag. To meet the desperate food shortage, the government of Japan gave out recipes for preparing meals from acorns, sawdust, grasshoppers, and rats.[46]

The Nisei linguists did their part. In each campaign, they questioned prisoners, translated documents, and decoded radio messages. Some flew in B-29s, listening through earphones while jotting down air-to-ground messages from Japanese fighter pilots. Now and then, they struck pure gold. On Saipan, they found a book listing the quantity, condition, and location of all major Japanese weapons, including artillery and tanks. In the Philippines, navy divers gave them papers recovered from a sunken warship. The amazed linguists spent weeks on what turned out to be a complete library of all plans and orders issued by Imperial

Navy headquarters since 1941. Other prizes included military maps and maps of minefields at the entrances to Japanese harbors.[47]

Though defeat loomed, Japan's military rulers refused to give up. Instead, they devised what was, in reality, a plan for national suicide. Besides 2.5 million troops, they still had some 2,000 planes and the pilots willing to crash them into American ships. Every male between the ages of fifteen and sixty, and every female from seventeen to forty-five, was drafted and armed with knives and bamboo spears. Younger teenagers were taught to strap dynamite to their bodies and throw themselves under American tanks or blow themselves up while charging American soldiers. "Due to the nationwide food shortage and the imminent invasion of the home islands," declared a senior army officer, "it will be necessary to kill all the infirm old people, the very young, and the sick. We cannot allow Japan to perish because of them."[48]

If the invasion had gone ahead as planned, countless Americans and Japanese would have faced certain death. Yet this did not happen, because the United States used the atomic bomb, a weapon its scientists had secretly developed.

The development of and debate over the morality of using this terrible weapon were important subjects, but the troops in the field and their commanders were not involved in such discussions. On August 6, 1945, a lone B-29 dropped the new weapon on Hiroshima; had Germany not surrendered in May, the bomb would probably have been used there as well. The blast and fire killed 125,000 people outright; radiation poisoning killed thousands more in the raid's immediate aftermath and in the years to come. Nagasaki, where Europeans had first landed four centuries earlier, was next. An atomic bomb incinerated the city on August 9, killing another 40,000 civilians. Japanese, however, were not the only ones to suffer. Both cities held Allied prisoners in local jails—twelve American airmen in Hiroshima and nine British and Dutch soldiers in Nagasaki. They, too, perished in the explosions. Though some fanatical officers wanted to fight to the last, Emperor Hirohito refused to back them. Japan, he told the people in a nationwide radio broadcast, must "endure the unendurable"—surrender.

On September 2, representatives of the Japanese government and military signed the surrender document aboard the battleship *Missouri* in Tokyo Bay. Among the flags flown from the *Mis-*

The atomic bomb's mushroom cloud over Nagasaki, seen from nearby Koyagi-jima. (August 9, 1945)

souri was the same Old Glory that had flown over the White House on December 7, 1941. Beside it fluttered a flag with thirty-one stars; it had flown from the mainmast of Commodore Perry's "black ship," the *Powhatan,* in 1853.

Americans held in prison camps in Japan's home islands, including survivors of the Bataan Death March, had worked as slaves on various building projects. Free at last, they boarded trains that would take them to ships bound for the United States. During the journey, they passed through towns struck by B-29s, each a wilderness of

rubble. On the first day, Private John Falconer recalled, "We cheered. We could look from one edge of a town to the other and see not one thing standing. Just flat areas of ashes, like a beach bonfire that burns all the way out. Here and there a pathetic figure might be seen searching for anything of use." After a while, they stopped cheering. "The devastation was so total that it overpowered our senses. . . . By the second day we said little, but just stared out the windows. I had come to loathe and despise these people, but this was almost too much. I began to feel sorry

Shattered religious figures
sit among the rubble of
a temple in Nagasaki six
weeks after the atomic
bomb was dropped there.
(September 24, 1945)

Shattered religious figures sit among the rubble of a temple in Nagasaki six weeks after the atomic bomb was dropped there. (September 24, 1945)

for them. I still wanted to kill them, but a feeling of sympathy crept in alongside the hatred." Already the thirst for vengeance had begun to subside.[49]

General MacArthur led the army of occupation. Not only did he disarm Japan's remaining forces, but he set out to change the country in basic ways. Some 4,000 Nisei linguists aided him, helping Japan rebuild its economy and create a democratic government. Nisei also played a role in tracking down war criminals. General Masaharu Homma, commander of the troops who carried out the Bataan Death March, was tried, convicted, and executed by an American firing squad. More than 500 Nisei women, volunteers who had left the concentration camps to train at the Military Intelligence Service Language School, became linguists, teachers, office workers, and medical professionals. So did Nisei students trapped in Japan after Pearl Harbor, among them Mary Kimoto Tomita, the keen young letter writer. She and other Nisei had not been imprisoned during the war but had been required to take low-paying jobs and regularly report to the police.[50]

General Charles Willoughby deserves to have the last word here. As intelligence chief to General MacArthur, he had come to rely on the Nisei linguists. Willoughby declared that "the use of these Japanese Americans shortened the Pacific war by at least two years and saved hundreds of thousands of American casualties."[51]

The war in the Pacific, however, was only one chapter in the saga of the Yankee samurai. The European chapter was filled with bitterness and glory.

BITTERNESS

After Pearl Harbor, Nisei had become ineligible for the draft, and those already in the service were discharged or given menial jobs. But the political climate was changing, even if Secretary of War Henry L. Stimson's distrust of the Japanese "race" was not. Japan's criticism of America's concentration camps was damaging America's image in Asia. How, Chinese and others asked, could America claim to be waging a moral war overseas while oppressing minorities at home? To show the virtues of American democracy, Stimson decided

Japanese officers lay down their samurai swords in surrender at Kuala Lumpur, Malaysia. (c. 1945)

to form an all-Nisei combat outfit led by white officers. It would face not the Japanese in the Pacific but the Germans in Europe because, Stimson felt, it would be more "trustworthy" there.

President Roosevelt, ever the politician, approved Stimson's plan. On February 1, 1943, he issued a statement. "No loyal citizen of the United States," FDR declared, "should be denied the democratic right to exercise the responsibilities of his citizenship, regardless of his ancestry. . . . Americanism is a matter of mind and heart; Americanism is not, and never was, a matter of race or ancestry." These were fine words and true, though in saying them, the president ignored or "forgot" his own actions. For he spoke almost a year to the day after signing Executive Order 9066, allowing the uprooting of innocents because of their race and ancestry, an action he did not regret.[52]

Stimson planned to have Nisei men from the concentration camps volunteer. Failing a good turnout, he would have them drafted. To clear volunteers for service, the army had first to register them. The War Relocation Authority saw the plan as a way to advance its own aims. WRA director Dillon S. Myer, formerly a federal farming expert, be-

lieved the camps harmed inmates, and he wanted to release as many as possible. His agency would encourage them to leave in small batches, while helping them start over in places far from the West Coast. Thus, it allowed hundreds of high school graduates to attend colleges in the midwestern and eastern states. Myer hoped they would eventually forget Japanese customs, culture, and ways and finally become "Americans." President Roosevelt agreed entirely. So as not to "discombobulate" (his term) whites, he wished to scatter "Japanese people from Japan who are citizens" throughout the country. Though Nisei were citizens, in FDR's eyes they remained American-born *Japanese*.[53]

Myer persuaded the War Department to register all camp inmates at once, claiming this would save time and money. To register for the army, male Nisei had to answer a four-page questionnaire. The WRA form was titled "Application for Leave Clearance." Modeled on the army form, it was meant for Nisei women and all Issei age seventeen and over.

Most of the thirty questions on both forms were routine, covering the inmate's family, interests, education, and job history. Two questions, however, were anything but routine. On the army form, Question 27 asked, "Are you willing to serve in the armed forces of the United States on combat duty, wherever ordered?" Question 28 asked, "Will you swear unqualified allegiance to the United States and forswear [reject] any form of allegiance or obedience to the Japanese emperor?" On the WRA form, Question 27 asked Nisei women if they were willing to volunteer for the Army Nurse Corps or the Women's Auxiliary Army Corps, which performed support duties to free men up for combat duty. And Question 28 asked if Issei rejected allegiance or obedience to the Japanese emperor.[54]

Both questions sparked Nisei anger, Issei fears, and family quarrels. Neither question went over well among Nisei men. Answering "yes" to Question 27 meant you were volunteering for the army. A "no" answer branded you "disloyal." As for Question 28, Nisei asked why they were the only American citizens required to take a loyalty oath. Besides, as U.S. citizens, they had never sworn allegiance to the emperor. Jack Tono, an inmate at the Heart Mountain concentration camp, was furious at FDR. "I said to myself, here's a Presi-

dent saying that we have to go out and preserve democracy. You start thinking, where the hell is the democracy we learned in school?" Other Nisei bristled at the idea of serving in a segregated outfit—of being "Jap Crowed" like Jim Crowed blacks in the South.[55]

Question 28 on the WRA form terrified the Issei. It seemed like a trick designed to entrap them. Though they had spent decades in the United States, they remained citizens of Japan because of a racist naturalization law. If they denied allegiance to the emperor, they might be giving up Japanese citizenship and become "stateless aliens," people without a country. WRA officials saw the problem and rewrote the question. The new version omitted reference to the emperor, asking only that Issei promise to abide by the laws of the United States. The title of the form was changed to "Information for Leave Clearance." This new wording was to indicate that any information Issei gave would be used only if they asked to leave the camps to work or resettle away from the West Coast.[56]

Although Issei welcomed these changes, for many they came too late; the damage had already been done. These individuals thought it foolish to trust the government. After all, it had uprooted them, herded them behind barbed wire, ruined their careers, and impoverished them. Now they felt too old, too tired, and too emotionally drained to start over. At least the camps offered a place to live—such as it was—food, and companionship. "Leave clearance" struck them as Washington sweet talk, a euphemism for scattering them among strangers.

Yet the vast majority tried to make the best of the situation. Despite their doubts, they grudgingly answered "yes" to both questions, thus their nickname "Yes-Yeses." Of the 75,000 Issei and Nisei who filled out forms, 7,600 answered "no," thus their nickname "No-Noes." Some 1,200 Nisei from the concentration camps volunteered for the army. In Hawaii, where there were no camps, proud parents urged their sons to enlist. Though, for starters, the army wanted only 1,500 from the islands, nearly 10,000 volunteered. When leaving day came, thousands saw them off at dockside with cheers, songs, and flowers. The mainland, however, saw yet another uprooting. The WRA labeled No-Noes "disloyal," then shipped 9,000 people—individuals and families—to Tule Lake. To make room

there, it sent "loyals" to other camps—under armed guard, as usual.[57]

The order to move again struck like a hammer blow. Aging Issei expected their children's loyalty and help; it was their duty. Yet, for many Nisei, respect for parents clashed with their American identity. Mary Tsukamoto, an inmate in an Arkansas camp, later wrote: "People walked the roads, tears streaming down their troubled faces, silent and suffering. There were young people stunned and dazed. The little apartments were not big enough for the tremendous battle that raged in practically every room: between parents and children, between America and Japan, between those who were hurt and frustrated, but desperately trying to keep faith in America and those who were tired and hurt and disillusioned.... The outside world seemed hostile; we were falling apart within, with nowhere to turn."[58]

Whatever choice one made, it was likely to bring pain to loved ones or to oneself. In some families, disagreements ran so deep that members did not speak to each other for years, if ever again. Some Nisei broke under the stress. A fourteen-year-old boy, for example, held out against his en-

tire family, all of whom chose exile to
Tule Lake. A week after they left, he
suffered a nervous breakdown. Other
holdouts simply said, "I am an American," and enlisted.[59]

Tule Lake, officially termed a "segregation center," felt like salt rubbed
into raw wounds. Rejected by America, hundreds of "No-No boys," who'd
never said a bad word against their
country, turned pro-Japanese. Defi-
ant crowds gathered to demand "Japanization," a program to promote all
things Japanese. Hundreds gathered to
wave homemade Rising Sun flags and
shout *"Banzai!"* Groups of "pressure
boys" formed, extremists bent on forcing Japanization on everyone. "This is
Japan," they chanted. "Who dares to
speak English here?"[60]

In November 1943, pressure boys
rioted, threatening WRA staff, setting fires, and clubbing anyone who
disagreed with them. It took a battalion of troops in full battle gear, backed
by six tanks, to restore order at Tule
Lake. MPs arrested the "hard cases"
and hauled them to the newly built
stockade, a high-security prison within
the camp. Anyone who stepped out of
line there got a beating and time in the
"hole," a windowless cell.

Members of a pro-Japanese
group gather at Tule Lake,
Northern California.
(c. June 1945)

President Roosevelt was upset. Very
upset. He demanded harsh measures at
Tule Lake, and "it did not make any difference what the Japs in Japan thought
about it," he told a White House meeting. However, Vice President Henry A.
Wallace thought of the American prisoners of war. "Wait a minute, Mr. President," Wallace interrupted. "It makes
a lot of difference to the Americans
whom the Japs have in the camps in
the Philippine Islands." FDR changed
the subject. But in the wake of the riot,
6,882 Nisei renounced their citizenship,
asking to be sent to Japan after the war.
Congress then passed the Renunciation
Act of 1944, allowing citizens to give
up their citizenship in wartime. Unoffi-
cially known as the "Denationalization
Act," this law enabled the army to keep
"troublemakers" and would-be "traitors" locked away, without trial, for the
duration of the conflict.[61]

Since so few Nisei had volunteered,

Secretary Stimson ordered them drafted into the army. There was another outcry, but from a different group. While No-No boys rejected any military service, draft resisters felt it their duty to serve, but only as free citizens. Fight for democracy? Fight for Old Glory and the American way? Return my rights, and I will gladly fight! One resister, Mits Koshiyama, had a simple answer: "You can't draft me to fight for something that you're taking away from me."[62]

Resistance groups formed in most camps. The best known was the Fair Play Committee at Heart Mountain. When ordered to report for physicals, sixty-three of its members refused, not out of cowardice or malice but out of loyalty to democratic values. "We have defied an immoral law," a leaflet declared, "IN ORDER TO CONTEST THE ISSUE." In other words, the committee was picking a *peaceful* fight.[63]

This was the method Martin Luther King Jr. would adopt a generation later. In 1963, police in Birmingham, Alabama, arrested the civil rights leader while he was protesting Jim Crow laws. King turned the tables, using his jail cell as a podium from which to ad-

dress the nation. In his "Letter from Birmingham Jail," King argued, "An unjust law is no law at all." People of conscience, he said, had to get others to think about the wrong they were doing. And the way to confront them was "to create such a crisis" that the issue could not be ignored. Violence, however, would only confirm opponents in their wrong beliefs. King insisted that nonviolent disobedience, and the willingness to accept punishment, would ultimately change minds.[64]

The Nisei draft resisters wound up behind bars. In June 1944, as fighting raged on Saipan, they contested the issue in a court of law—and lost. The judge, in ruling against them, declared that they had violated the draft law by refusing to take physical exams. Even if the government had violated their rights, he continued, "one may not refuse a lawful call of his government merely because in another way it may have injured him." Translation: Though Washington has wronged you, you must obey the law anyhow. All sixty-three resisters received three-year sentences in a federal penitentiary. Later, seven leaders of the Fair Play Committee went on trial for exercising the right of free speech. A law dating from the First World War made it a crime, punishable by a heavy fine and twenty years in prison, to advise draft resistance. The leaders were "lucky" to get a three-year sentence.[65]

GLORY

Nisei volunteers and draftees served in Europe not as linguists but as soldiers on the front line. They belonged to two separate and racially segregated outfits: the 100th Infantry Battalion (Separate) and the 442nd Regimental Combat Team.

The 1,432 Hawaiian-born Nisei in the 100th had served in the Hawaiian National Guard before the war began. Though disarmed right after Pearl Harbor, in the spring of 1942 their National Guard regiments were reorganized into a racially segregated unit named the 100th Infantry Battalion (Separate). Members of the 100th prided themselves on their raring-to-go spirit. The battalion flag bore the motto "Remember Pearl Harbor." Its members said, "We'll *never* forget Pearl Harbor. We were there. We saw our country being bombed." They called themselves AJAs (Americans of Japanese ancestry). It was not wise to call

them "Japs." And those who did were in for trouble.[66]

The second outfit, the 442nd Regimental Combat Team, started with 3,886 men—2,686 Hawaiians and 1,200 mainlanders drafted from the concentration camps. It was activated in January 1943. The shoulder patch of the 442nd showed a hand holding a torch of liberty against a red, white, and blue background. "Go for Broke," the regiment's motto, was a pidgin Hawaiian phrase popularized by gamblers for "shoot the works." Daniel Inouye, a member of the 442nd, explained its meaning this way: "To give everything we did, everything we had; to jab every bayonet dummy as if it were a living, breathing [Hitler soldier]; to scramble over an obstacle course as if our lives depended on it; to march quick-time until we were ready to drop, and then to break into a trot."[67]

Both units underwent intensive training at Camp Shelby, Mississippi. Their arrival outraged southern racists, and none more than Representative John Rankin, whom we have already met. Camp Shelby, he yelled, was "teeming with spies and trouble makers." He thought the army should use "these brutal apes," as well as all black recruits, as laborers, not fighting men.

Like fellow racists, Rankin also linked "Japs" and blacks in another, more sinister way: their blood.[68]

Charles R. Drew, an African American physician and medical researcher, had recently developed the method of preserving blood plasma still used today. Blood is blood, biologically the same regardless of the donor's race. Giving transfusions to the wounded saved lives. It did so without affect-

ing the genes, the parts of cells passed from parents to children that determine physical traits. Yet racists, in their ignorance, claimed otherwise. Rankin insisted that "to pump Negro blood or Japanese blood into the veins of a white man" would "mongrelize this nation," poisoning the superior race. Hitler's soldiers, too, believed in "race-poisoning" through transfusions; wounded Germans died rather than accept blood

Members of the 442nd Regimental Combat Team looking at an anti-tank gun during training at Camp Shelby, Mississippi. (c. June 1943)

from Russians. We do not know if Secretary of War Stimson believed such rubbish; his writings are silent on the subject of transfusions. But to quiet noisy bigots, his War Department had blood plasma segregated according to the race of the donor, a practice that continued until 1950.[69]

The 100th and 442nd saw Jim Crow in all its ugliness. Army training camps located in the South followed Jim Crow rules. Barracks, showers, mess halls, canteens, water fountains, and latrines were strictly segregated. Black soldiers dared not visit nearby towns on their days off. In Gordon, Arkansas, for instance, bigots threatened: "If we catch you niggers here in town after sundown, you are going to hang." Black civilians lived in fear, too. "Uppity" blacks, those who gave offense in any way, like talking back to a white person, might get a visit from the Ku Klux Klan, a racist group whose members wore pointy hoods and long white gowns to hide their identity. A KKK visit was likely to bring, in escalating order, a warning, a whipping, a hanging, or a "Negro barbecue"—burning alive.[70]

To avoid trouble, commanders wanted Nisei soldiers to keep their distance from black people. Though having a Japanese great-grandparent meant being uprooted, in the South the army classified Nisei as whites. An officer informed Daniel Inouye's company: "I have been instructed to tell you that during your time in this state, you will be treated by its people as white men." Thus, Nisei became "honorary whites," just as Hitler termed his Japanese allies honorary members of the German *Herrenvolk* (master race).[71]

Army policy angered the Nisei, particularly the Hawaiians. There was no Jim Crow in their islands, and they defied him in Mississippi. "We were not afraid of the white man," recalled Hideo Nakamine. "We from Hawaii don't tolerate abuse." When riding a bus, Nisei, as "whites," were not supposed to sit in the back with black passengers. They did anyhow. If a driver ordered them to the front, they refused to move—and not very politely. When a driver pushed an elderly black lady to the ground, they taught him manners. "I grabbed the bus driver by the shirt and dragged him off the bus," a Nisei recalled. "Six of us kicked the hell out of him for knocking that poor black woman down."[72]

While the 100th and 442nd trained

in Mississippi, American and British leaders drew up a master plan to win the war in Europe. It had several parts, each starting at a different time but, like pieces of a jigsaw puzzle, designed to fit together. Allied armies would invade Hitler's ally Italy and German-occupied France from the south. Several months later, another, far larger force based in England would invade northern France from across the English Channel. As the invaders cleared German troops from Italy and France, then drove into Germany itself, Russian armies would roll in from the east.

The men of the 100th saw action first. In September 1943, they landed near Salerno, in southern Italy, as part of a massive operation. Hitler sent reinforcements, battle-tested veterans from Germany. Nevertheless, the Allies advanced up the Italian "boot," sometimes fifteen miles a day, until they came to Monte Cassino in February 1944. Monte Cassino was a Roman Catholic monastery perched atop a 1,500-foot hill of the same name. A natural fortress, the monastery had ten-foot-thick walls and commanded the road to Rome, Italy's capital, to the north. German troops had taken over the building, strengthening their position with steel-lined dugouts, barbed-wire entanglements, and minefields.

For forty-three days and nights, the Battle of Monte Cassino raged. American and British bombers, hundreds at a time, blasted the monastery to rubble. Yet the Germans hung on. During the fighting, other units hailed the soldiers of the 100th as "the little iron men." The 100th also earned the nickname "Purple Heart Battalion." Nearly every member suffered a wound of some kind. Even so, if the wounded could still walk, they could not tolerate being safe in a hospital bed. "Da boys need me," the men would say as they "deserted" from the hospital to return to the front line, bandages and all. Nisei never went AWOL. Being absent without leave would have brought *haji* (shame) to the entire battalion. Nobody wanted to have *that* on his conscience.[73]

The 100th was so badly mauled at Monte Cassino that only 521 of its original 1,432 men were fit for duty when the battalion was pulled out of combat. Finally, after more rounds of desperate fighting, Polish troops stormed the ruined monastery. After Monte Cassino, men from the 442nd joined the 100th

Members of the 100th Infantry Battalion receive grenade training. (c. 1943)

to fill the gaps left by the battle. Thus, the two units became a single outfit, known as the 100/442.[74]

In America's concentration camps, inmates read about Nisei exploits with mixed feelings. Yukio Ota was proud and hopeful. In a poem titled "Faith," the teenager wrote:

My heart is proud,
My soul is glorious and free.
You, young Nisei, are fighting for
our lives, our country, our future,
and everything we stand for.

We are right behind you.
You are proving that we are loyal
in Italy and wherever you go.

Casualties suffered by the 100/442 also stirred camp inmates, as evidenced by Ota's poem "Worry":

Trembling hand
As the mother opens
The V-mail.[75]

Parents who'd never learned to write in English did so now. A mother explained: "I want to be able to write my son a letter. I'm always asking other people to write for me. When he's in service and worried, I want him to know I'm all right. I want him to understand from my own letter that I care for him and that I'm okay."[76]

The Allied advance continued. Rome fell on June 4, 1944. Though the 100/442 did not take part in the victory parade, Italian civilians welcomed its members wherever they went. Private First Class Ernest Uno wrote his sister Mae: "Being part of front line troops, we are usually the first to march thru the towns which have cost so much blood

and sweat to liberate. But the people are grateful. They know that when we come, the war is over for them. As soon as we enter, we are showered with all they have to spare. What they have to give is simple, but when you're tired and worn out from fighting you accept their gifts with a lump in your throat."[77]

D-Day came on June 6, two days after the fall of Rome. In the largest seaborne invasion in history, American, British, and Canadian armies crossed the English Channel to Normandy, on the northern coast of France. Just then, the 100/442 sailed from Italy, bound for southern France, along the Mediter-

An autographed photograph of a son in battle, among other mementos in the Yonemitsu home in the Manzanar War Relocation Center. (c. 1943)

ranean coast. Again part of a massive invasion force, the Seventh Army, the 100/442 moved inland. The Seventh Army had orders to advance up the Rhône Valley, then cross into Germany. During five days of heavy fighting, the Nisei set out to rescue the "Lost Battalion," 300 Texans trapped behind enemy lines. The Germans had vowed that they would take no prisoners and would kill the Texans in battle or when they surrendered. On October 30, the fifth day, the Nisei broke the siege. In saving the remaining 211 Texans, they suffered 800 dead or wounded. "We were never so glad to see anyone as those fighting Japanese Americans," the Texans roared. "We love them!"[78]

German troops did not love them. Everything about the Nisei was puzzling. When monitoring radio signals, Germans might hear, "*Hama hama* Tommy gun *boltsu, hayaku,* eh? And *ammo mote kite kudasai.*" The baffling language was pidgin Hawaiian, a dialect that combines native Hawaiian, English, Japanese, and Tagalog (Filipino) words. This message meant: "Rush order on a Tommy gun bolt and please bring up some more ammo."[79]

Like the Japanese soldiers Hoichi Kubo faced in that Saipan cave, the Germans wondered about Nisei loyalty to the country that had uprooted their families. Stanley Akita gave the usual answer. After his capture, the twenty-one-year-old found himself in a prison camp in Germany.

"How come you're fighting for America?" a German officer asked.

"Because I'm an American," Akita replied.

"What makes you feel like an American?"

"Because I was born in America."

Germans feared the Nisei more than they feared other American soldiers "because they never give up" and kept plugging away until killed, wounded, or forced to surrender.[80]

Attacked from the west and east, on land and from the sky, Germany tottered toward collapse. Events moved with dizzying speed. On April 12, 1945, President Roosevelt died and Vice President Harry S. Truman took his place. On April 30, Hitler shot himself as Russian troops neared his underground shelter in Berlin. The day before the tyrant's suicide, Americans reached the heart of darkness: Dachau concentration camp.

Hitler's concentration camps were nothing like those in America. In the

States, the uprooted, whatever they might feel, knew they would not be murdered. Hitler's camps, however, were meant to torture, enslave, starve, and ultimately kill. Several camps, like Auschwitz and Treblinka in occupied Poland, were industrial-scale death factories where millions of Jews and other so-called *Untermenschen* (sub-humans) died in gas chambers. Others, like Dachau, had various purposes. The main camp was located ten miles northwest of Munich, Germany's third-largest city. It also had 240 sub-camps for Hitler's political foes, slaves assigned to various work projects, and people awaiting execution.

It is ironic that a Nisei patrol found a Dachau sub-camp on April 29. Spring had come late, and snow still lay on the ground. The soldiers knew something was wrong when they found ragged men lying by the roadside, blue-lipped, all "skin and bones." Within an hour, the patrol entered the camp through a gate. The guards were fleeing, leaving behind the dead and dying, singly and in heaps. "Here I was kneeling down," a Nisei recalled. "In my arms sat an inmate of Dachau, and all I could do was hold him as he said, 'Please help me.' As his body went limp, all I could do was cry. I had to think. What the heck am I doing here? My family was still behind barbed wire in Wyoming . . . [and] here I was in Germany liberating people from camps."[81]

In another part of the camp, Yanina Cywinska, a Polish Catholic, stood with a group of blindfolded women, waiting to be shot. Her "crime" was helping Jews escape from the Warsaw Ghetto, most of whose population of 400,000 the Nazis murdered in gas chambers. A light snow was falling. The women shivered from the cold or, more likely, from fear. Suddenly they heard a heavy mechanical sound, followed by crunching and bullets whipping through the air. They could not see the American tank smash into a section of barbed-wire fence, toppling and rolling over it.

After the shooting stopped, Cywinska felt someone tugging at her blindfold. "He tugged this way and that way, and then he jumped up because he was short and pulled it off. I saw him and thought, Oh, now the *Japanese* are going to kill us. . . . I said, 'Just kill us, get it over with.'" The soldier tried to convince her that he was an American and had no intention of harming her. She did not believe him. "I said, 'Oh, no, you're Japanese and you're going to kill us.' We went back and forth, and finally he landed on his knees, crying, with his hands over his face, and he said, 'You are free now. We are *American* Japanese. You are free.'" She touched him, crying, too. Cywinska later became a ballet dancer, moved to America, and set up a ballet school in Fairfield, California. "To this day," she said in 1991, "if anyone says the word 'Jap,' I become a vicious woman. I adore Japanese people for giving me the chance to live."[82]

Three days after Cywinska's rescue, on May 2, another patrol approached the main camp at Dachau. Clarence Matsumura and three other Nisei were riding in a jeep when they began finding people along the roadside. "All of them were wearing black and white striped uniforms," Matsumura recalled. "They couldn't speak. Most of them were lying on the ground." Prisoners on a "death march" to another camp, they had been abandoned the night before by their guards. Many had already died from starvation and exposure.

Solly Ganor, a sixteen-year-old slave laborer from Kaunas, Lithuania, was stunned. He wrote years later:

I closed my eyes, waiting for a bullet to put me out of my misery. Then I heard someone speaking English. When I opened my eyes, four men in khaki uniforms were approaching. They looked unshaven and tired. Their oriental features astonished me. . . . Japanese? . . . My throat constricted. I dared not think, and could not speak.

One of the men [Matsumura] came up and knelt in front of me. He gently touched me on the shoulder and said, "You are free, boy. You're free now," he said, and then smiled. That smile has been with me ever since. It wreathed his whole face and made his eyes nearly disappear. . . .

I was groping for my English, actually wanting to fall on my knees and kiss his feet. "Who . . . are you?" I whispered. . . .

"Americans. Americans," the angel said, "Nisei, Japanese Americans. My name is Clarence," he added. "What's yours?"

Matsumura and his comrades brought the handful of survivors to a nearby village, where they made them comfortable and gave them water and chocolate bars for quick nourishment. Then they radioed for medics to take over and went on their way. After the war, Ganor moved to Israel, where he later lectured schoolchildren on the Holocaust and the Nisei "angels" who gave him back his life.[83]

Germany surrendered on May 7, four months before Japan. By then, the 100/442 had become the most decorated outfit in American history. It suffered 9,486 casualties, including 600 killed, and earned 3,600 Purple Hearts for wounds. Its members also received 18,143 individual decorations, among them 52 Distinguished Service Crosses, 560 Silver Stars, and 4,000 Bronze Stars.[84]

Sadao S. Munemori, who had been recruited from Manzanar, received the Medal of Honor, the nation's highest award for valor, the only Japanese American to be so recognized during the war. While he was fighting in Italy, German machine-gun fire pinned him and two companions down in a shell crater. The twenty-one-year-old private first class crawled out and destroyed the machine-gun nest. But as he made his way back, a grenade struck his helmet, bounced off, and rolled into the crater. Munemori dove onto the grenade before it exploded, dying to save the others. No tributes have ever been so well deserved, or so nobly earned, as those given Munemori and his fellow Yankee samurai.[85]

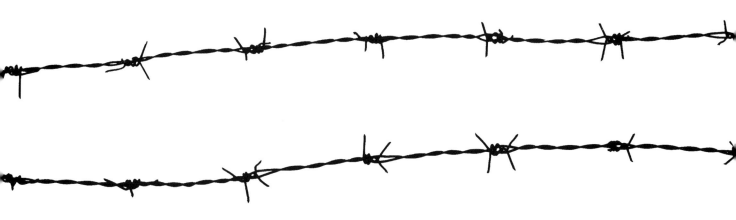

CHAPTER 6

THE WHEELS OF JUSTICE

The wheels of justice turn slowly, but grind exceedingly fine.
— TRADITIONAL PROVERB

NINE WISE MEN

It was a scene played out in every American concentration camp. As part of the "Education for Relocation" program, a history teacher would announce to the class: "Today we will study the Constitution." And the class would laugh and titter, as if it were a bad joke. Or, like eighth grader Tetsuko Morita at Tule Lake, students muttered, "Who cares! I had just started to learn about the Constitution, and I knew they were doing a wrong thing." Today most Americans would agree about the "wrong thing"—uprooting people without charges or trial and based solely on their ancestry. During the war, however, this conclusion was not so clear, even to the nine justices of the U.S. Supreme Court.[1]

The Founders, who set up our system of government, distrusted human nature. James Madison, the "Father of the Constitution," wrote, "If men were angels, no government would be necessary." But men are not angels. Human beings, Madison knew from history, act out of self-interest and use political power for their own advantage. Though government is necessary to keep order, it has to be checked. Therefore, the Founders devised the "separation of powers." According to the U.S. Constitution, Congress makes federal laws, but the president enforces them, so that neither can control the entire government. As a further check, the Founders created the Supreme Court. Only it can decide if a law or a presidential action agrees with the Constitution—is "constitutional." At least that is the way it is supposed to be. The real test comes in wartime.[2]

In 1943, civil rights attorney Wayne M. Collins observed, "In wartime, judges wear epaulets under their robes." Epaulets are ornaments worn on the shoulders of military officers' uniforms. What Collins meant was that Supreme Court justices are, above all, patriots—in effect, citizen-soldiers. Since war is a life-or-death struggle, they are inclined to see things through the government's eyes while the danger lasts. For "the war power of the national government is the power to wage war successfully," and by any means necessary. Nor are justices, being people and not demigods, immune from the prejudices of their time.[3]

Hundreds of Nisei resisted the draft. Yet only four challenged the legality of the uprooting before the U.S. Supreme Court. Minoru Yasui, the first challenger, was a lawyer from Portland, Oregon. In March 1942, when General DeWitt ordered a curfew for those of Japanese descent, Yasui refused to obey, and U.S. marshals arrested him. Tried and convicted in a federal district court, he received the maximum penalty of a

Portland lawyer Minoru Yasui became the first challenger of the legality of uprooting after disputing a jail sentence for being out after a curfew imposed on those of Japanese descent. (Date unknown)

year in jail and a fine of $5,000. Yasui and his legal team decided to appeal to a higher court. The Justice Department sent the case directly to the Supreme Court.

In May 1942, Gordon Hirabayashi, a senior at the University of Washington and a devout Christian, disobeyed the curfew, too. Moreover, he visited the FBI office in Seattle, saying he also intended to violate the order to register for "evacuation" and then to test the legality of his arrest. In a four-page statement titled "Why I Refuse to Register for Evacuation," Hirabayashi explained:

University of Washington student Gordon Hirabayashi also defied the curfew and refused to register for evacuation. (Date unknown)

This order for the mass evacuation of persons of Japanese descent denies them the right to live. It forces thousands of energetic, law-abiding individuals to exist in a miserable psychological and a horrible physical atmosphere. . . . It kills the desire for a higher life. Hope for the future is exterminated. Human personalities are poisoned. . . . If I were to register and cooperate under these circumstances, I would be giving helpless consent to the denial of practically all the things which give me incentive to live. I must retain my Christian principles. I consider it my duty to maintain the democratic standards for which this nation lives. Therefore, I must refuse this order of evacuation.[4]

Police officers arrested Hirabayashi. A jury convicted him, and a federal district court judge sentenced him to three months in jail. His lawyers decided to appeal. Again, the Justice Department sent the case to the Supreme Court.

On June 21, 1943, the court ruled on the *Yasui* and *Hirabayashi* cases together. In these and later cases, it ruled on the narrowest grounds it could.

This strategy allowed the justices to deal only with specific violations of law, without having to consider key questions or overrule the government. Did a true crisis exist on the West Coast after Pearl Harbor? Was the uprooting justified by military necessity? Had the "evacuees," including infants and toddlers, been deprived of their constitutional rights? The justices simply ignored these issues.

By a unanimous decision, they found both men guilty of violating lawful curfew and evacuation orders. In his written opinion, Chief Justice Harlan Fiske Stone said the court could not second-guess the military or question "the wisdom of their action." Stone added that the army's claim of military necessity was reasonable and that "in time of war" people of "[certain] ethnic affiliations . . . may be a greater source of danger than those of a different ancestry." Since Japan threatened the West Coast more than Germany or Italy did, it followed that the military "may place citizens of one ancestry in a different category from others . . . [and] set these citizens apart from others who have no particular associations with Japan." Put simply, because people of Japanese ancestry looked like the enemy, they could be uprooted without being charged with any crime.[5]

Justice Frank Murphy sided with his colleagues on the specific points of law, but he felt uneasy. The decision as a whole smelled of racism. "Today is the first time," he wrote in a separate opinion, "that we have sustained a substantial restriction of the personal liberty of citizens of the United States based upon the accident of race or ancestry." Just then, he noted, the hateful Hitler was doing the very same thing. "In a sense," Murphy continued, the court's decision "bears a melancholy resemblance to the treatment of the Jewish race in Germany and in other parts of Europe." Yet the ruling stood. Yasui and Hirabayashi were guilty as charged.[6]

Another Nisei, Fred Korematsu, wanted to avoid the uprooting for private reasons, not to become a symbol of resistance to injustice. In May 1942, his Japanese-born parents reported to Tanforan, joining Miné Okubo and thousands of others in the transit camp. Korematsu, an unemployed shipyard welder, stayed behind. He was in love and wanted to be with his Italian American girlfriend. To conceal his identity, he had plastic surgery to his eyelids to make himself look less Japanese, changed his name to Clyde Sarah, and claimed to be of Spanish and Hawaiian ancestry. The FBI nabbed him anyhow.

While in a San Francisco jail awaiting trial, Korematsu had a visitor: Ernest Besig, the director of the Northern California branch of the American Civil Liberties Union. Unlike the ACLU's main office, it was protesting the uprooting, and Besig asked Korematsu to test the constitutionality of the evacuation orders. He agreed. "I didn't feel guilty because I didn't do anything wrong," he told the *New York Times* forty years later. "Every day in school, we said the pledge to the flag, 'with liberty and justice for all,' and I believed all that. I was an American citizen, and I had as many rights as anyone else." Besig assigned Wayne M. Collins to handle the case. But Korematsu was found guilty by a federal district court, sentenced to five years' probation, and sent to the Topaz concentration camp in Utah. Collins appealed to the Supreme Court.[7]

On December 18, 1944, it ruled against Korematsu by a vote of six to three. Justice Hugo L. Black wrote the majority opinion. The army had not ex-

Fred Korematsu resisted internment so he could stay with his Italian American girlfriend. (Date unknown)

cluded Korematsu from a military zone "because of hostility to him or his race," said Black. It was because America and the Japanese Empire were at war, and the military, which knew the situation best, "feared an invasion of our West Coast." Black had no regrets about his decision. In 1967, he told the *New York Times* that he would "do precisely the same thing today." After all, "they all look alike to a person not a Jap. Had [Japan] attacked our shores, you'd have a large number of them fighting with the Japanese troops." How the learned justice knew this remains a mystery.[8]

Three justices disagreed with the majority—strongly. In separate written opinions, they put race prejudice at the heart of the *Korematsu* case. Justice Murphy said that expelling "all persons of Japanese ancestry" from the West Coast "falls into the ugly abyss of racism." Justice Owen J. Roberts agreed, arguing that imprisoning a person "in a concentration camp, based on his ancestry, and solely because of his ancestry," was "a clear violation of constitutional rights." There is, moreover, no such thing as "group disloyalty." For "under our system of law, individual guilt is the sole basis for deprivation of rights."[9]

Justice Robert H. Jackson took a different tack. Upholding Korematsu's conviction, he feared, involved far more than this individual. A military order, though it may be unconstitutional, has a natural life span; it expires with the end of the crisis that gave it birth. However, once the Supreme Court stamps its approval "on the principle of racial discrimination," its ruling threatens the future of America. Jackson warned: "The principle then lies about *like a loaded weapon,* ready for the hand of any authority that can bring forward a plausible claim of an urgent need. . . . If the people ever let command of the war power fall into irresponsible and unscrupulous hands, the courts [will then] wield no power equal to its restraint." The nation will have become a lawless tyranny.[10]

The Supreme Court's ruling in the fourth case opened the gates of the concentration camps. Known as *Ex parte Endo*—legalese for "in the absence of Endo"—this involved a twenty-two-year-old woman named Mitsuye Endo. A clerical worker for the State of California, Endo and other Nisei had lost their jobs when the uprooting began. Supposedly, they showed "failure of good behavior," could read and write Japanese, and belonged to "certain Japanese organizations." Endo was sent to Topaz.[11]

Meanwhile, the Japanese American Citizens League asked James C. Purcell to try another approach. A well-known

Clerical worker Mitsuye Endo won her case for being wrongfully detained. (Date unknown)

San Francisco civil rights attorney, Purcell decided it would be a waste of time to challenge the curfew and exclusion orders again. Instead, he would claim the government denied camp inmates habeas corpus, the right to a court hearing in which charges must be stated or the accused set free. Endo's seemed the ideal test case. No matter what officials said, she had a fine work record, spoke no Japanese, and belonged to no Japanese organization. Better yet, she had a brother in the U.S. Army. Purcell asked Endo to allow him to appeal in her name. He would do everything, and she need not appear in court.

The Supreme Court ruled on *Ex parte Endo* on December 18, 1944, the same day as the *Korematsu* decision. Unanimously, it declared in the young woman's favor. Justice William O. Douglas delivered the court's opinion. Endo had never been charged with a crime, he wrote. Nor had she given the slightest hint of disloyalty. Yet "she is confined in the Relocation Center under armed guard and held there against her will. . . . Mitsuye Endo is entitled to an unconditional release by the War Relocation Authority." Justice Murphy added that Endo's confinement was but another example of the "racism inherent in the entire evacuation program." By freeing her, the court also freed all others not charged with a specific crime. Each had already spent around 900 days in captivity.[12]

The justices did not, however, question the uprooting itself. This was no oversight. Their conclusions, as Justice Black wrote, deliberately avoided "the underlying constitutional issues." In plain English, the court ignored the much larger questions raised by the uprooting. Instead, it ruled on the narrowest grounds, on only specific matters. Bottom line: The uprooting might be racist and wrong, but it was legal.

LEAVING

Within hours of the *Endo* decision, the army and the WRA announced that the concentration camps would close within six months to a year. All people of Japanese ancestry could return to the West Coast or go anywhere they wished—that is, anywhere that would accept them.

Not everyone looked forward to leaving. One inmate spoke for many of the Issei: "We are told and encouraged to relocate again into the world as a stranger in strange communities! We now have lost all security. . . . Where shall we go? What shall we do at the twilight of the evening of our lives?" Younger people also worried about the future. Rui Kameo, the mother of two daughters, wrote from the concentration camp in Poston, Arizona: "So back to California we go, just where we started from! . . . We have no home. . . . I'm not sure where we will locate yet. . . . Well, I am really lost right now, but will trust to luck and my God to take care of us."[13]

"Education for relocation" and "pioneering" was no longer a WRA goal. Now the agency set out to ease the transition to "normal" life. Despite its good intentions, many inmates found the WRA patronizing, as if it were stooping to the level of inferiors. Camps gave courses in "life-skills"; presumably, inmates had not yet learned to cope with real-life problems. In Topaz, for example, Miné Okubo attended seminars called "How to Make Friends" and "How to Behave in the Outside World." Some camps hired social workers whose aim, a supervisor explained in the best professional jargon, was "to work with families, thus giving them the opportunities to discuss individual attitudes, fears, and needs."[14]

The WRA was in as great a hurry to empty the camps as it had been to fill them. Once the process slid into high gear, inmates left at a rate of 2,000 a week. On their last day, they turned in blankets, filled out forms, and had a quick medical exam. In the camp director's office, each received, courtesy of Uncle Sam, a train ticket and $25 in cash, plus $3 a day for meals while traveling. As she boarded the bus that would take her to the train, Miné Okubo was handed a booklet titled "When You Leave the Relocation Center" and told to read it carefully. The bus pulled away, and the camp gradually faded into the distance. "There was only the desert now. My thoughts shifted from the past to the future."[15]

It did not go easily for the aged and the fearful. Steadily, the WRA squeezed them out. As ever more inmates left, it cut services. Schools, clubs, newspapers, clinics—all closed. As barracks emptied, workers disconnected water faucets, toilets, and electricity. Block mess halls closed, forcing holdouts to eat with strangers in the few blocks that still served food. An observer wrote: "People began to feel that the substance of block life was disintegrating. . . . There was a feeling of decay and decline in the air that weighed more and more on people. . . . As the blocks crumbled, the relocation centers began to disintegrate before people's eyes and under their feet." Camp police grabbed the last holdouts, packed their bags, and physically carried them to the buses. Tule Lake, the last concentration camp, closed on March 20, 1946. The War Relocation Authority dissolved on June 30, 1946.[16]

REACTIONS

News of the camps' closing angered usually anti-Japanese groups. West Coast chapters of the American Legion, the nation's leading war veterans' organization, declared returnees liable to cause "another Pearl Harbor." Farmers' groups and labor unions feared competition from returnees. The Teamsters union was particularly irate. Japanese American truck drivers threatened jobs, union officials declared. "The Teamsters," according to a press release, "are campaigning to banish Japanese from the entire Pacific Coast." The Native Sons of the Golden West again fueled anxieties over "our daughters" and "blood-poisoning," the supposedly inevitable result of "race-mixing." As

A Japanese American family returns to Seattle from the concentration camps to find their garage vandalized with racist graffiti and broken windows. (May 10, 1945)

ever, it claimed the West as "white-man's country" and warned that "the white race wants to survive."[17]

Old-line organizations worked with dozens of newly formed groups. These had sinister names: Remember Pearl Harbor League, Pacific Coast Japanese Problem League, and No Japs Incorporated. A handbill of the Home Front Commandos of Sacramento, California, summarized these groups' outlook and program: "Lend your help to Deport the Japs—If you can't trust a Jap, you won't want him as a neighbor—Any good man can become an American citizen, but a Jap is and always will be a Stabber-in-the-Back gangster; rebel. After the war, ship them back to their Rising Sun Empire." Various groups posted signs proclaiming WE DON'T WANT ANY JAPS BACK HERE—EVER![18]

Anti-Japanese groups also had influential political friends. Among these was Henry "Scoop" Jackson, a U.S. representative (and later senator) from Washington State, who had praised the uprooting. Now he was dead set against its victims' return. Japanese forces had used "infiltration tactics" on Bataan, Jackson wrote. And they had been quietly infiltrating America since their arrival in the 1880s—"infiltration into the vitals of our economic, political, and domestic structure." Even when Nisei soldiers visited their former West Coast homes on furlough, their uniform was not proof enough of their loyalty, for Jackson. Across the continent, New York mayor Fiorello La Guardia blasted "deceitful Jap monkeys" and asked Washington to prevent them from invading his city.[19]

Words inspired deeds. Newspapers reported more than forty incidents of threats or violence against returnees. Night riders shot into their houses or into houses in which they found temporary shelter. A group of white Californians torched a house near San Jose, then shot at the occupants as they tried to douse the flames. When Wilson Makabe of the 442nd returned, minus his right leg, he called his brother George, only to learn that hoodlums had burned the family home in Loomis, California. "Oh, you can't describe the feeling," he recalled years later. "I remember the pain and the hurt, the suffering in the hospitals in Italy—that was nothing compared to this. I cried for the first time. All that time in the hospital I don't remember shedding a tear, but I cried that night. You wonder if it was worth going through all that. It wasn't much of a house, but my dad had built the thing, with some of the other people helping."[20]

Nisei veterans suffered indignities, each perhaps small in itself but doubly hurtful to men who had endured so much. In Los Angeles, graffiti chalked on sidewalks warned JAPS, WE DO NOT WANT YOU. A highway sign outside a small town in the San Joaquin Valley announced NO MORE JAPS WANTED HERE. Passersby spit on Nisei veterans in the street. Two soldiers were stoned while driving through Parker, California, on their way to visit family at the Poston, Arizona, concentration camp. Daniel Inouye, now a captain, had lost his right arm in combat in Italy. On his way back to Hawaii, a Purple Heart pinned to his uniform, his empty sleeve pinned to his shirt, Inouye stopped for a haircut in San Francisco. The barber refused to touch his hair, growling, "We don't serve Japs here."[21]

We should note that Jim Crow treated black veterans far worse in the South. Newspapers printed dozens of articles about brutality. Apparently, racists feared blacks might not "know their place" when they got back home.

Captain Daniel Inouye, who served in the 442nd Regimental Combat Team, received a Purple Heart after the war but was met with prejudice upon his return to the U.S. (Date unknown)

The result, for lack of a better word, was terrorism. The masked thugs of the Ku Klux Klan threatened, beat, burned, and shot those who "stepped out of line." So did those responsible for public safety. Drivers still in uniform were stopped by highway patrol officers and arrested or beaten senseless for some infraction—or for none at all. In Aiken, South Carolina, police dragged Sergeant Isaac Woodward off a bus and clubbed him about the head, blinding him. Near Monroe, Georgia, a mob literally shot to pieces two veterans and their wives. Local authorities did nothing.[22]

Yet for African Americans, change was in the air. The modern civil rights movement was born in the aftermath of the Second World War. Growing numbers of veterans joined organizations like the National Association for the Advancement of Colored People, energizing them and renewing their determination to gain equal rights. Similarly, the public began to see Japanese Americans in a different light.

OUR BETTER ANGELS

Signs of change often come in small but telling ways. These are marvelous examples of what Abraham Lincoln called the "better angels of our nature," the human capacity to grow by learning, thinking, and admitting mistakes. Wilson Makabe, who had lost his leg in the war, recalled a man who had found his better angel. One day, Makabe pulled up to a local gas station. When the owner saw him struggling to get out of the car to fill the tank, he came out of the office. "I'd like to talk to you," he said. Makabe told him to get in, and they drove off. The owner sat silently, then after a while said, " 'Y'know, I was one bastard. I had signs on my service station saying No Jap trade wanted.

Now, when I see you come back like that [minus a leg], I feel so small.' And he was crying."[23]

Prominent military figures spoke out in ways sure to catch the public's attention. My favorite example involves Sergeant Kazuo Masuda. While fighting at Monte Cassino, Masuda deliberately gave his life so his men could escape with vital information. After the victory in Europe, his family returned to their home in Talbert, California, from the Gila River, Arizona, concentration camp. Scarcely had they unpacked their things when men came to the door, warning that they'd better leave—or else. The Masudas did leave, but returned six months later, in December 1945. Kazuo had been awarded the Distinguished Service Cross, and army brass had decided to present his family with the medal in a ceremony covered by the press. General Joseph W. Stilwell would do the honors.[24]

Nicknamed "Vinegar Joe" because of his sour temper, Stilwell had led American forces in China and Burma; Merrill's Marauders served under his orders. He also knew General DeWitt, whom he described as a "jackass," a bigot given to snap judgments and emotional outbursts. Vinegar Joe had already sounded off about the Nisei as soldiers. "The Nisei," he declared, "bought an awful big chunk of America with their blood. You're damn right those Nisei boys have a place in the American heart, now and forever.... We cannot allow a single injustice to be done to the Nisei without defeating the purposes for which we fought."[25]

Stilwell led the guests to the Masudas' front porch, where the family stood waiting. Facing the hero's sister, Mary, he said: "The Distinguished Service Cross in itself is a small thing, but since it stands for gallantry in action, I hope you and your family will remember that Sergeant Masuda, in winning it, has also won the respect and admiration of all real Americans." The general then motioned for the representative of the American Veterans Committee, a young actor and army captain named Ronald Reagan, to step forward. In the name of "the family of Americans," Reagan said, "I want to say for what your son Kazuo did—Thanks."[26]

The commander in chief, President Harry S. Truman, had more influence

Sergeant Kazuo Masuda's sister, Mary, receiving the Distinguished Service Cross on her brother's behalf. (c. December 1945)

than any general or actor. Though he came out of a racist background—his ancestors had owned slaves, and he used slurs like *nigger* and *coon* in private—Truman believed everyone should be treated fairly. In that spirit, he criticized Executive Order 9066 and the camps it authorized. "They were concentration camps," Truman told an interviewer. "They called it reloca-tion, but they put them in concentra-tion camps, and I was against it. . . . It was one place where I never went along with Roosevelt. He never should have allowed it."[27]

"Give 'Em Hell Harry," as friends called Truman, had served as an army captain in the First World War. He knew about combat and courage. Though the president despised the "Jap" enemy—"savages, ruthless, mer-ciless and fanatic"—he admired Nisei heroism. The bigotry of the West Coast states, particularly California, infuri-ated him. Such disgraceful behavior by the Californians, he snapped, "almost make[s] you believe that a lot of Ameri-cans have a streak of Nazi in them."[28]

Truman let the country know how he felt. On July 15, 1946, he awarded the 100/442 a Presidential Unit Citation. The troops paraded down Constitution Avenue to the Ellipse, a park located just south of the White House. After reviewing them, and giving a snappy salute, the old soldier spoke briefly. "You are now on your way home," Truman said. "You fought not only the enemy, but you fought prejudice—and you have won. Keep up the fight, and we will continue to win—to make this great Republic stand for just what the Constitution says it stands for: the welfare of all the people all the time." These were fine words, but they also held a promise, unspoken but real: Tru-man meant to live up to the American ideal of fair play under the rule of law.[29]

California, too, heard its better an-gels. In November 1946, Proposition 15 came before the voters. If passed, this measure would have made it impossible for people of Japanese descent ever to own land in the Golden State. Proposi-tion supporters rehashed the timeworn charges of Japanese "disloyalty." By then, however, Nisei courage had cap-tured the moral high ground, aided by Truman's praise of the 100/442. More-over, the horrors of the Holocaust hit home. A survivor explained: "In Ger-many, the Jews . . . have been victims of race bigotry and cruelty. In our own South, persons of black skin are victims of discrimination and even lynching, and now California is . . . making the

President Truman salutes the 100th Infantry Battalion and the 442nd Regimental Combat Team during the presentation of the seventh Presidential Unit Citation, awarded for outstanding accomplishments in combat. (July 15, 1946)

Japanese the butt of discrimination and prejudice." Voters understood. For the first time, Californians rejected an anti-Asian measure.[30]

STARTING OVER

Readjusting to freedom was nearly as hard as adjusting to the uprooting had been. Economically, returnees had suffered huge losses. Many of the household items they'd stored or left with neighbors had been stolen, vandalized, or ruined by neglect. Sumi Seo's experience was not unusual. She asked a former friend about her furniture, only to be told, "I don't have your furniture. It was stolen. Get off my porch. Go away!" The Federal Reserve Bank of San Francisco estimated that Japanese Americans lost $400 million in property during the initial "evacuation": houses, farms, hotels, shops, businesses, fishing boats, automobiles. The same items that amount of money bought in 1942 would cost $5.8 billion in 2015. Added to that total were lost earnings and profits, a sum impossible to calculate.[31]

Finding a place to live was a daunting task. Some returnees, the lucky ones, moved back to their old homes.

At first, however, most relied on hostels set up by church and community groups. They also found shelter in parish halls, vacant army barracks, and trailer camps once used by workers in the war industries. Organizations like the Salvation Army gave cots, bedding, cooking utensils, and food. Better-off Japanese people helped, too. Daniel I. Okimoto of San Diego told what happened when his family worried about where their next meal would come from. Often, at night, they'd hear a knock at the door. Upon opening it, they'd find bags of groceries, even hot meals, on the porch. His mother believed these came directly from God. "If so, the agents of delivery were undoubtedly big-hearted Japanese friends who knew our plight and did not want to embarrass us with what might be regarded as handouts or charitable offerings."[32]

Returnees tried to find jobs quickly. A few with special skills found excellent jobs on the East Coast. For example, high-class magazines like *Fortune* hired Miné Okubo as an artist, and museums put on exhibitions of her drawings. New York fashion houses sought returnees with expertise in the needle trades. Charles James, a top Madison Avenue designer, put them to work on his "most important bigger clothes, ball dresses, and such." Japanese women, James added, had "a special quality of precision," an attention to detail he found lacking in the typical New York garment worker. Most returnees, however, took up their former occupations. Professionals picked up where they left off in 1942, as doctors, dentists, and lawyers reopened their practices. Others opened small restaurants and shops or worked as hired hands until they could save enough to buy or rent farmland. Gradually, they settled down with their memories.[33]

OF MEMORY AND PAIN

Not all wounds bleed. Experiences of extreme danger, fear, and hardship are wounds to the mind and spirit. Invisible as these wounds are, they can be as painful as those to flesh and bone. Nor do they vanish when the bad time passes, and they may last a lifetime. Today we use a dry scientific term to describe this mental condition: *posttraumatic stress disorder*. Among the symptoms of PTSD are feelings of anger, hopelessness, guilt, and shame.

Though returnees rebuilt their lives, their time in the concentration camps had been a great trauma, the worst thing they had ever experienced. Left emotionally scarred, many felt humiliated, as if they had done wrong, even though they hadn't. Others could not bear to talk about their ordeal. Jeanne Wakatsuki Houston, who with her husband wrote the classic memoir *Farewell to Manzanar* (1973), was a child when the uprooting began. Still, it left its mark. "You know," her husband said years later, "every time Jeanne starts talking about Manzanar she bursts into tears and starts crying."[34]

We also read of parents who closed off part of themselves to protect their children. For them, love commanded silence. "I was afraid that if I started talking about it, I would cry," recalled eighty-seven-year-old Mary Matsude Gruenewald. "And I didn't want to cry in front of my children, so I kept it all in." Though some parents never spoke of the camps, their children understood, and loved them all the more for what they had suffered. In "Questions," poet Ann Muto, born in 1944 in the Poston concentration camp, tells of its sad legacy:

Our parents hid
Their history from us
They swallowed
Their pain

They didn't want us to lose our way
In bitterness or anger.

Yet silence built an invisible wall between mother and daughter, as Muto tells us in "Regret":

My sorrow is that we never talked:
How it was for her,
How it was for me.[35]

Muto's mother and others had become very focused. They did their best to bury bad memories by immersing themselves in the routines of everyday life. Like Jewish Holocaust survivors, they did not make pilgrimages to former concentration camps or describe their ordeals in public statements. Nor did they form organizations to correct the injustices done to them. For years, Miné Okubo's book, *Citizen 13660,* published in 1946, was the only account of camp life by an inmate. Still, nothing ever stays the same. Change is the way of the world, and America had unfinished business.

JUSTICE

The wheels of justice began to turn slowly. With the end of the war, anxiety over the Japanese American "threat" faded. This made it easier for President Truman to act. In 1947, he gave all Nisei wartime draft resisters full pardons because they had acted out of conscience, not cowardice or ill will. The following year, he issued Executive Order 9981 to desegregate the armed forces, and he signed the Japanese American Evacuation Claims Act into law. Though this law provided a mere $28 million for economic losses due to the uprooting, it recognized that innocent people had suffered at the hands of their government.

At Truman's urging, in 1952 Congress passed the Immigration and Nationality Act, which declared that the country could not deny citizenship because of race. As a result, Issei began studying for their citizenship exams. "And in time," wrote historian Bill Hosokawa, "tiny old ladies bent by toil, gray-haired old men gnarled by a lifetime of labor, men and women in their sixties and seventies and eighties . . . stood before federal judges and took the oath of allegiance as America's newest citizens. It was a privilege and an honor that had been a long time coming."[36]

Meanwhile, civil rights attorney Wayne M. Collins began a lengthy struggle. Of the 6,882 Nisei imprisoned at Tule Lake after renouncing their citizenship, 1,116 boarded ships for Japan in February 1946. The authorities allowed the other 5,766 to remain, though only as resident aliens, since they posed no threat to national security. By then, however, most regretted their action. With all its faults, America was still their country. They wanted to get back their citizenship. The government said they could, provided appeal boards ruled on each case separately. Collins vowed to help them. The uprooting, he declared, was "the foulest goddam crime the United States has ever committed against a wonderful people." For twenty-nine years, until his death in an airplane crash in 1974, he argued that official abuse had goaded loyal Americans into renouncing their birthright. Largely through his tireless efforts, nearly all eventually regained their citizenship.[37]

While Collins argued, Earl Warren became a better man. After serving three terms as California's governor, he was named chief justice of the United States by President Dwight D. Eisenhower in 1953. The following year, Warren led the court in its landmark *Brown v. Board of Education* decision, striking down racial segregation in the public schools. In 1967, he went further, writing the court's unanimous decision overturning all laws against racial intermarriage as unconstitutional. Citing the court's wartime *Hirabayashi* and *Korematsu* decisions as warnings against judging people "solely because of their ancestry," the chief justice declared, "Marriage is one of the 'basic civil rights of man,' fundamental to our very existence and survival. To deny this fundamental freedom on so unsupportable a basis as [race] is surely to deprive . . . citizens of liberty without due process of law."[38]

The court's decision affected marriage discrimination laws in fifteen states: Alabama, Arkansas, Delaware, Florida, Kentucky, Louisiana, Mississippi, Missouri, North Carolina, Oklahoma, South Carolina, Tennessee, Texas, Virginia, and West Virginia.

Warren's championing of racial equality surprised those who knew his attitude toward Japanese Americans. Yet his action showed that people can change. For the chief justice had come to realize that racial prejudice arose from the same poisonous myth that America's concentration camps had. Having supported the uprooting, he confessed, made him ashamed; it was "one of the worst things I ever did." In his autobiography, Warren said he "deeply regretted the removal order," and his role in promoting it, "because it was not in keeping with our American concept of freedom and the rights of citizens." The reason, however, was not merely legal but intensely personal for this father of six. "Whenever I thought of the innocent little children who were torn from home, school friends, and congenial surroundings, I was conscience-stricken." In the final analysis, he believed, "it was wrong to react so impulsively, without positive evidence of disloyalty" on the part of the uprooted.[39]

Most *Sansei* (pronounced *SAHN-say*), the "third generation" of Japanese in America, had not yet been born or were very young during the uprooting. Sansei entered college in the late 1960s and early 1970s. These years were another time of turmoil in America. Protests against Jim Crow erupted, led by Martin Luther King Jr. and others, as did a mass movement to end America's role in the Vietnamese civil war. Amid this uproar, and having studied the Second World War in college, Sansei began to question their parents and grandparents. What has been called the "silent years" finally ended. Tearfully, the story of the uprooting poured out, and with it long-repressed rage.[40]

Aided by Sansei activists, several former camp inmates, inspired in part by the Holocaust, began the so-called redress movement. Clifford Uyeda, one of its leaders, explained: "German Jews were systematically murdered en masse—that did not happen to Japanese Americans, but the point is that both Germany and the United States persecuted their own citizens based on ancestry." Like Germany, our country needed to admit its wrongdoing and pay reparations to—compensate financially—those it had injured.[41]

Reparations, however, were really not about money, much less a handout or payoff. The idea behind them stems from an age-old principle: The law must "make whole" the victims of wrong by requiring the wrongdoer to bear responsibility. It cannot put a price tag on wrong, for human dignity has no cash value. How much are broken lives, lost childhoods, or the tears of innocents worth? "The issue," Uyeda explained, "is to acknowledge the mistake by providing proper redress to the victims of injustice, and thereby make such injustices less likely to recur."[42]

Although racism was still widespread, by the late 1970s it carried the stigma of ignorance, bigotry, and un-Americanism. Therefore, President Gerald R. Ford felt free to wipe Executive Order 9066 off the books with a presidential proclamation. He chose the date deliberately: February 19, 1976, exactly thirty-four years after FDR had signed his infamous order. Congress then repealed Public Law 503, which had made violating Executive Order 9066 a federal offense.

The wheels of justice kept turning. In 1980, Congress created the Commission on Wartime Relocation and Internment of Civilians to investigate the uprooting. The CWRIC held hearings in which 750 witnesses—former inmates, camp staff, War Department officials—testified. Three years later, the commission issued a report. Titled *Personal Justice Denied,* it dealt with the uprooting from every angle and remains a valuable source for historians. Its conclusion was a slap at President Roosevelt, Secretary of War Stimson, General DeWitt, and the system they created:

Executive Order 9066 was not justified by military necessity, and the decisions which followed from it . . . were not driven by analysis of military conditions. The broad historical causes which shaped these decisions were race prejudice, war hysteria and *a failure of political leadership.* Widespread ignorance of Japanese Americans contributed to a policy conceived in haste and executed in an atmosphere of fear and anger at Japan. A grave injustice was done to American citizens and resident aliens of Japanese ancestry who, without individual review or any probative [provable] evidence against them, were excluded, removed and detained by the United States during World War II.[43]

Harsh as this judgment was, worse followed. In the early 1980s, legal scholar Peter Irons uncovered what he called "a legal scandal without precedent in the history of American law." While researching legal aspects of the uprooting, Irons found certain files in the archives of the solicitor general of the United States, the official who represents the government in Supreme Court cases. In making their ruling in the *Korematsu* case, the justices had relied on "evidence" submitted by the so-

licitor general's office. Irons proved that officials had lied to the highest court in the land. Deliberately, they withheld, changed, and destroyed evidence that Japanese Americans had not threatened national security. This evidence consisted of reports (already discussed here) that were kept secret: reports from the FBI, the Office of Naval Intelligence, and Curtis B. Munson.[44]

Irons's findings sped up the wheels of justice. Aided by teams of volunteer lawyers, Fred Korematsu, Minoru Yasui, and Gordon Hirabayashi had their cases reopened. By 1984, appeals courts overturned their convictions, finally clearing their names. In vindicating Korematsu, Judge Marilyn Hall Patel of the U.S. District Court in San Francisco said his case should serve as

Fred Korematsu, Minoru Yasui, and Gordon Hirabayashi around the time their cases were reopened. (c. 1986)

a warning: "It stands as a constant caution that in times of war or declared military necessity . . . [we] must be prepared to protect all citizens from the petty fears and prejudices that are so easily aroused."[45]

Judge Patel said something else, too: "*Korematsu* remains on the pages of our legal and political history." In other words, she had ruled narrowly, on the facts of a specific case. She had not, and could not, erase the Supreme Court's decision; only the court itself can do that. The original 1944 decision has never been overturned. It remains, dangerous as ever. To repeat Justice Robert Jackson's words, it "lies about *like a loaded weapon*, ready for the hand

of any authority that can bring forward a plausible claim of an urgent need."[46]

All the same, President Ronald Reagan took the next step. After much debate, he signed the Civil Liberties Act of 1988 into law. It formally apologized to the Japanese American community for the uprooting and granted each survivor $20,000, tax-free, as redress for the injustice done to them. "No payment," Reagan said at the signing ceremony, "can make up for those three lost years. So what is most important in this bill has less to do with property than with honor. For here we admit a wrong. Here we reaffirm our commitment as a nation to equal justice under the law." As the president signed, Senator Daniel Inouye stood to his right, proudly looking on.[47]

On June 21, 2000, President Bill Clinton awarded Medals of Honor to twenty-one members of the 100/442, whose heroism, "above and beyond the call of duty," finally received the recognition it deserved. Senator Inouye was among the recipients. "Rarely has a nation been so well served by a people it has so ill-treated," said the president.[48]

On May 29, 2004, President George W. Bush dedicated the World War II Memorial on the National Mall in

Captain Daniel Inouye, then a senator from Hawaii, receiving the Congressional Medal of Honor from President Clinton. (June 21, 2000)

Washington, D.C. The memorial honors the sixteen million who served in the armed forces and the more than 400,000 who lost their lives. In his remarks, Bush also paid tribute to the minorities who resisted homegrown racism: "America gained strength because African Americans and Japanese Americans and others fought for their country, which wasn't always fair to them. In time, these contributions became expectations of equality, and the advances for justice in post-war America made us a better country."[49]

It took sixty-two years for the wheels of justice to grind out this conclusion. But the story is not over, because time does not stand still.

CHAPTER 7

REMEMBERING THE PAST

Those who cannot remember the past are condemned to repeat it.
—GEORGE SANTAYANA, *The Life of Reason* (1905)

On September 11, 2001, hijackers crashed four airliners: into the Pentagon in Arlington, Virginia, the nation's military nerve center; the twin towers of the World Trade Center in New York City; and a field in rural Pennsylvania. While 2,343 American servicemen died at Pearl Harbor, some 3,200 civilians lost their lives in the worst terrorist act in our nation's history. The nineteen hijackers belonged to al-Qaeda, an extremist Muslim group led by a Saudi Arabian renegade named Osama bin Laden. For bin Laden and his followers, the attack was a godly action against those they called the "Party of Satan." As bin Laden said, "Killing Americans and their allies—both civilians and military personnel—is a commandment for every individual Muslim who can do this, in any country in which he can do this." Another al-Qaeda leader added, "Muslims are religiously entitled to use chemical and biological weapons against the U.S."—thereby sanctioning the killing of tens of millions of civilians.[1]

Within days of the attack, President George W. Bush did what President Franklin Roosevelt failed to do after Pearl Harbor. FDR never drew a clear line between people of Japanese ancestry and the Imperial Japanese enemy. Bush, however, explained how mainstream Muslims, the vast majority, differed from fanatics who used religion as a pretext for murder. "The terrorists," he told the nation, "are traitors to their own faith, trying, in effect, to hijack Islam itself. The enemy of America is not our many Muslim friends; it is not our Arab friends. Our enemy is the radical network of terrorists and every government that supports them."[2]

Bush was right. Though Muslims may fight in self-defense, the Prophet Muhammad preached that they must do so in the right way, within limits. "Fight in the cause of Allah against those who fight you, but do not transgress limits," says a verse in the Qur'an (Koran), the Muslim holy book. In other words, do not become an aggressor. Moreover, the Qur'an teaches, no-

The front page of the *New York Times* announcing the September 11, 2001, terrorist attacks. (September 12, 2001)

body should be forced to accept Islam, because "there is no compulsion in religion." When the Prophet died in 632, his follower Abu Bakr became caliph, the Muslim community's religious and military leader. He set out formal rules for warriors. These said that Islam never permits wanton killing—a hell-deserving sin—and least of all the killing of innocents. The caliph decreed: "Neither kill a child, nor a woman, nor an aged man. Bring no harm to the trees, nor burn them with fire, especially those that are fruitful. Slay not any of the enemy's flock, save for your food." Nor does Islam permit suicide, because God is the Creator of Life, and none may defile God's creation.[3]

The terrorist attacks stunned moderate Muslims. In Cairo, Egypt, the head of Al-Azhar University, perhaps the greatest center of learning in the Muslim world, declared: "Attacking innocent people is not courageous; it is stupid and will be punished on the Day of Judgment." In the United States, Muslim organizations issued a joint statement: "American Muslims utterly condemn the vicious and cowardly attacks of terrorism against innocent civilians. . . . No political cause could ever be assisted by such immoral means." However, in the wake of September 11, 2001, as after December 7, 1941, hysteria often overcame truth and reason.[4]

An Iranian woman and her mother light a candle in honor of those lost in the September 11, 2001, terrorist attacks in the United States. (c. September 2001)

For some Americans, religious bigotry replaced racial bigotry. They branded all Muslims as extremists based on the fact that the terrorists were Muslim. Supposedly, their religion made Muslims uniquely prone to violence. Political commentator Ann Coulter claimed, "Not all Muslims may be terrorists, but all terrorists are Muslims—at least all terrorists capable of assembling a murderous plot against America." Yet history tells a very different story. No human group is immune to hatred and the violence it can inspire. In the 1940s, for example, members of the Stern Gang, a radical Jewish group, assassinated dozens of British army officers. Their goal was to drive British forces from Palestine, clearing the way for the creation of the State of Israel. In April 1995, Timothy McVeigh, a lapsed Catholic, blew up a federal building in Oklahoma City, Oklahoma, killing 168 innocent people, including children in a nursery school, out of hatred for the U.S. government, not from religious motives.[5]

After September 11, 2001, incidents of Muslim bashing multiplied. Some shops and restaurants displayed signs reading NO MUSLIMS INSIDE and NEVER TRUST A MAN NAMED MOHAMAD. Passersby called Muslims "camel jockeys," telling American citizens to "go back where you came from." There were claims that Islam could not be protected by the First Amendment to the Constitution because the religion was inherently hostile to free speech and thus anti-American. A group calling itself the American Family Association demanded a halt to Muslim immigration to "protect our national security and preserve our national identity, culture, ideals and values." This blame game touched children, too. "I was walking and a lady called me a terrorist

and made killing signs," a ten-year-old girl recalled. An eleven-year-old girl was asked, "How can you be here if you just dropped the twin towers?" The charge hurt deeply, she said, because "it makes me sad that I am being blamed for something I didn't do."[6]

In the wake of the attacks, according to news reports, Attorney General Alberto Gonzales "stated that as commander in chief, the president has the authority to override the laws passed by Congress if he is acting in the name of 'national security.'" In October 2001, Congress passed, and the president signed, the Patriot Act. Aimed at tightening security, the law allowed federal agencies to do a host of things based solely on suspicion. Agencies could search homes and businesses without the owners' consent or knowledge; seize telephone, Internet, and email records without a court order; and even take library records to track borrowers' interests. The government could also arrest aliens and secretly hold them without pressing charges or allowing them lawyers or court hearings.[7]

Critics saw similarities between reactions to Muslim Americans after 9/11 and to Japanese Americans sixty years earlier. As author David Cole argues,

A poster announcing a Day of Remembrance held on the sixtieth anniversary of Executive Order 9066. The event encouraged Americans to recall the mistreatment of Japanese Americans after the Pearl Harbor attacks when considering Muslim citizens after the September 11 attacks. (c. February 2002)

"The post-9/11 response constitutes a reprise of some of the worst mistakes of the past." By targeting Muslims because of their religious identity, the government repeated "the fundamental error of the Japanese internment." However, the fact that there were seven million Muslim Americans made a replay of that tragedy impossible.[8]

Japanese Americans were keenly aware of how a crisis could generate an atmosphere of hysteria, endangering civil liberties. They had a special obligation, as Gordon Hirabayashi saw it, to teach that "ancestry is not a crime." All Americans are responsible, before the law, not for *who* they are but for *what* they do. In that spirit, activists denounced the Patriot Act. Yet we must also consider this fact: The Japanese American threat was entirely invented, but radical Muslims have carried out several terrorist attacks in the United States, and the authorities have thwarted many other serious plots since 9/11. The Boston Marathon bombing of April 15, 2013, for example, took the lives of six innocent people and wounded 264 others.[9]

Regardless, the big questions remain:

How do we balance liberty with security? Can we have both? If we cannot, which is more important? What do Americans gain, or lose, by choosing one over the other in dangerous times? The answers are still fiercely debated, and probably always will be—or at least until people become angels.

A further question: Can another uprooting happen? The short answer: Yes. Early in 2014, while discussing this dark chapter in our history, Supreme Court justice Antonin Scalia was brutally frank. "It was wrong," he said, "but I would not be surprised to see it happen again, in time of war. It is no justification, but it is reality." Scalia knew that in wartime military necessity and national security should not be used to shield government actions from scrutiny. Yet he also knew that Supreme Court justices still "wear epaulets under their robes." For good or ill, the high court bows to military and political leaders when it comes to crises in national security.[10]

There is a bright side, too. Of all forms of government, democracy is the strongest. Its greatest strength is that it operates under the rule of law, which enables it to correct mistakes peacefully. This correction may not happen quickly or easily, but time is on the side of justice. Given enough time, tempers cool and bitterness subsides. New facts emerge, changing minds. That is why the study of history is so important. History is not destiny; it describes the past but does not decide the future. Yet it is a constant reminder of tragedies like the uprooting, and a warning against repeating them. Human beings can learn from experience. And therein lies hope. As Maya Angelou put it so movingly in her 1993 poem "On the Pulse of Morning":

History, despite its wrenching pain,
Cannot be unlived, and if faced
With courage, need not be lived
again.[11]

NOTES

PROLOGUE: DAY OF INFAMY

1. Mark Selden, "A Forgotten Holocaust: U.S. Bombing Strategy, the Destruction of Japanese Cities and the American Way of War from World War II to Iraq," *Asia-Pacific Journal: Japan Focus,* www.japanfocus.org/-Mark-Selden/2414/article.html.

2. Paul Fussell, *Wartime: Understanding and Behavior in the Second World War* (New York: Oxford University Press, 1989), 281.

3. E. B. Sledge, *With the Old Breed at Peleliu and Okinawa* (New York: Oxford University Press, 1990), 260; Studs Terkel, *"The Good War": An Oral History of World War II* (New York: Pantheon Books, 1984), 60, 62, 64.

4. John W. Dower, *Japan in War and Peace: Essays on History, Culture and Race* (London: Fontana, 1996), 259.

I: THE PACIFIC AGE

1. Joshua Hammer, *Yokohama Burning: The Deadly 1923 Earthquake and Fire That Helped Forge the Path to World War II* (New York: Free Press, 2006), 243.

2. John Gunther, *Inside Asia* (New York: Harper & Brothers, 1939), 24.

3. Meirion Harries and Susie Harries, *Soldiers of the Sun: The Rise and Fall of the Imperial Japanese Army* (New York: Random House, 1991), 24.

4. Inazo Nitobe, *Bushido: The Soul of Japan; An Exposition of Japanese Thought* (Tokyo: Charles E. Tuttle Company, 1969), 30–31.

5. Noel Perrin, *Giving Up the Gun: Japan's Reversion to the Sword, 1543–1879* (Boulder, CO: Shambhala, 1980), 11, 36.

6. Harries and Harries, *Soldiers of the Sun,* 24; Nitobe, *Bushido,* 30.

7. Perrin, *Giving Up the Gun,* 8–9.

8. John W. Dower, *War Without Mercy: Race and Power in the Pacific War* (New York: Pantheon Books, 1986), 239, 244.

9. Perrin, *Giving Up the Gun,* 10.

10. John King Fairbank, *The United States and China,* 4th ed. (Cambridge, MA: Harvard University Press, 1983), 163; Christopher Hibbert, *The Dragon Wakes: China and the West, 1793–1911* (New York: Harper & Row, 1970), 3–4.

11. Peter Ward Fay, *The Opium War, 1840–1842* (Chapel Hill: University of North Carolina Press, 1975), 17.

12. "Qian Long: Letter to George III, 1793," Internet Modern History Sourcebook, ed. Paul Halsall, www.fordham.edu/halsall/mod/1793qianlong.asp.

13. Julia Lovell, "Opium and China," chap. 1 in *The Opium War* (London: Pan Macmillan, 2011), 21, http://theorwellprize.co-uk/wp-content/files_mf/chapteroneoftheopiumwar.pdf.

14. These countries had concessions in China: Austria-Hungary, Belgium, Brazil, Denmark, France, Germany, Great Britain, Italy, Japan, Mexico, the Netherlands, Norway, Peru, Portugal, Russia, Spain, Sweden, and the United States.

15. "The Plant of Joy," www.opiates.net; Lovell, "Opium and China," 33.

16. Samuel Merwin, *Drugging a Nation: The Story of China and the Opium Curse* (New York: Fleming H. Revell Company, 1908), 67.

17. "Lords of Opium," Amoy Magic, www.amoymagic.com/OpiumWar.htm; "'Opium Financed British Rule in India,'" BBC News, http://news.bbc.co.uk/2/hi/south_asia/7460682.stm.

18. "French Indochina: The Friendly Neighborhood Opium Den," Akha Heritage Foundation, www.akha.org/content/drugwar/mccoy/21.htm.

19. Gerald Horne, *Race War: White Supremacy and the Japanese Attack on the British Empire* (New York: New York University Press, 2004), 20, 21, 22.

20. V. G. Kiernan, *The Lords of Human Kind: European Attitudes Towards the Outside World in the Imperial Age* (London: Weidenfeld and Nicolson, 1969), 156.

21. Roger Pélissier, *The Awakening of China, 1793–1949,* ed. and trans. Martin Kieffer (New York: Putnam, 1967), 34; Jacques M. Downs, "Fair Game: Exploitive Myths and the American Opium Trade," *Pacific Historical Review,* 41, no. 2 (May 1972), 146–147; Steven M. Rothstein, "A School Built by Abolitionists—and a Slaver," *Boston Globe,* January 14, 2014; Oswald Garrison Villard, *John Brown, 1800–1859: A Biography Fifty Years After* (London: Constable, 1910), 398; "Were Kerry's Ancestors Drug Runners?," Free Republic, October 11, 2004, www.freerepublic.com/focus/f-news/1242224/posts.

22. Mexico surrendered all or part of what became the states of Texas, New Mexico, Colorado, Utah, Nevada, Arizona, Wyoming, and California.

23. William L. Neumann, *America Encounters Japan: From Perry to MacArthur* (Baltimore: Johns Hopkins Press, 1963), 22, 24, 25, 30.

24. Samuel Eliot Morison, *"Old Bruin": Commodore Matthew C. Perry, 1794–1858* (Boston: Little, Brown, 1967), 319.

25. Ibid., 371–372.

26. Kiernan, *Lords of Human Kind,* 177.

27. Neumann, *America Encounters Japan,* 85; David Scott, "Diplomats and Poets: 'Power and Perceptions' in American Encounters with Japan, 1860," *Journal of World History,* 17, no. 3 (September 2006), 316–317.

28. Scott, "Diplomats and Poets," 317.

29. Kiernan, *Lords of Human Kind,* 183.

30. Laurence Rees, *Horror in the East: Japan and the Atrocities of World War II* (New York: Da Capo Press, 2002), 19.

31. Harries and Harries, *Soldiers of the Sun,* 121.

32. Ronald H. Spector, *Eagle Against the Sun: The American War with Japan* (New York: Free Press, 1985), 36.

33. Saburo Ienaga, *The Pacific War, 1931–1945: A Critical Perspective on Japan's Role in World War II* (New York: Pantheon Books, 1978), 98–99. For details of the Peace Preservation Act, see www.willamette.edu/~rloftus/peacepres.html.

34. Ienaga, *Pacific War,* 105.

35. Ibid., 25, 105.

36. Rees, *Horror in the East,* 17; Gordon H. Chang, "'Superman Is About to Visit the Relocation Centers' and the Limits of Wartime Liberalism," *Amerasia Journal,* 19, no. 1 (1993), 37.

37. Saul K. Padover, "Japanese Race Propaganda," *Public Opinion Quarterly,* 7, no. 2 (Summer 1943), 195; Dower, *War Without Mercy,* 7, 9; Ronald T. Takaki, *Hiroshima: Why America Dropped the Atomic Bomb* (Boston: Little, Brown, 1995), 72.

38. Ienaga, *The Pacific War,* 8, 23; Anthony V. Navarro, "A Critical Comparison Between Japanese and American Propaganda During World War II," Michigan State University, www.msu.edu/~navarro6/srop.html.

39. Takaki, *Hiroshima,* 72; Padover, "Japanese Race Propaganda," 194–195.

40. Dick Wilson, *When Tigers Fight: The Story of the Sino-Japanese War, 1937–1945* (New York: Viking, 1982), 8.

41. Harries and Harries, *Soldiers of the Sun,* 483.

42. Haruko Taya Cook and Theodore F. Cook, *Japan at War: An Oral History* (New York: New Press, 1992), 131; Michael Norman and Elizabeth M. Norman, *Tears in the Darkness: The Story of the Bataan Death March and Its Aftermath* (New York: Farrar, Straus and Giroux, 2009), 79; Rees, *Horror in the East,* 24–25.

43. Dower, *War Without Mercy,* 38.

44. Bob Tadashi Wakabayashi, "The Nanking 100-Man Killing Contest Debate: War Guilt amid Fabricated Illusions, 1971–75," *Journal of Japanese Studies,* 26, no. 2 (Summer 2002), 310–311; Kate Heneroty, "Japanese Court Rules Newspaper Didn't Fabricate 1937 Chinese Killing Game," Jurist, http://jurist.org/paperchase/2005/08/japanese-court-rules-newspaper-didn't.php.

45. Quoted in Iris Chang, *The Rape of Nanking: The Forgotten Holocaust of World War II* (New York: Basic Books, 1997), 59.

46. Quoted in E. F. L. Russell (Baron Russell of Liverpool), *Knights of Bushido: A Short History of Japanese War Crimes* (London: Cassell, 1958), 259.

47. Rees, *Horror in the East,* 28–29; Wilson, *When Tigers Fight,* 80; "Japanese Director Documents Accounts of Nanjing Massacre," *China Post,* March 30, 2010, www.chinapost.com.tw /print/250412.htm; Chang, *Rape of Nanking,* 100–101.

48. Gart Evans, "The Nanking Atrocity: Still and Moving Images, 1937–1944," *Media and Communications,* 2, no. 2 (2014), 55–71.

49. George Hicks, *The Comfort Women: Japan's Brutal Regime of Enforced Prostitution in the Second World War* (New York: Norton, 1995), 17, 59, 149; Wilson, *When Tigers Fight,* 76; Yuki Tanaka, *Hidden Horrors: Japanese War Crimes in World War II* (Boulder, CO: Westview Press, 1996), 94, 99; Rees, *Horror in the East,* 35.

50. Cook and Cook, *Japan at War,* 164, 165; Harries and Harries, *Soldiers of the Sun,* 359–361; Sheldon H. Harris, *Factories of Death: Japanese Biological Warfare, 1932–1945, and the American Cover-up* (London: Routledge, 1994), 190–223.

51. Harries and Harries, *Soldiers of the Sun,* 260.

52. "Japan Shortens Matches, Tans Rat Skins in Vast Effort to Conserve Raw Materials," *New York Times,* July 31, 1938.

53. Mary Kimoto Tomita, *Dear Miye: Letters Home from Japan, 1939–1946* (Stanford, CA: Stanford University Press, 1995), 29; Harumi Shidehara Furuya, "Nazi Racism Toward the Japanese," Universität Hamburg, www2.uni-hamburg.de/oag/noag/noag1995_2.pdf.

54. Neumann, *America Encounters Japan,* 279.

55. Robert Leckie, *Delivered from Evil: The Saga of World War II* (New York: Harper & Row, 1987), 312; Gunther, *Inside Asia,* 30.

56. Hiroyuki Agawa, *The Reluctant Admiral: Yamamoto and the Imperial Navy,* trans. John Bester (Tokyo: Kodansha International, 1979), 232.

57. Denis Warner and Peggy Warner, *Sacred Warriors: Japan's Suicide Legions* (New York: Van Nostrand Reinhold, 1982), 52; Nancy Brcak and John R. Pavia, "Racism in Japanese and U.S. Wartime Propaganda," *Historian,* 56, no. 4 (June 22, 1994), 672, 675; Max Hastings, *Retribution: The Battle for Japan, 1944–45* (New York: Knopf, 2008), 6, 55; Page Smith, *Democracy on Trial: The Japanese American Evacuation and Relocation in World War II* (New York: Simon & Schuster, 1995), 67; Joel V. Berreman, "Assumptions About America in Japanese War Propaganda to the United States," *American Journal of Sociology,* 54, no. 2 (September 1948), 112; Ian Buruma, *Year Zero: A History of 1945* (New York: Penguin Press, 2013), 40.

58. Rotem Kowner, "'Lighter Than Yellow, but Not Enough': Western Discourse on the Japanese 'Race,' 1854–1904," *Historical Journal,* 43, no. 1 (March 2000), 130.

59. Rees, *Horror in the East,* 54; Dower, *War Without Mercy,* 106; William Manchester, *American Caesar: Douglas MacArthur, 1880–1964* (Boston: Little, Brown, 1978), 171.

II: DREAMS OF FORTUNE

1. The poet, little known today, was Thomas Bailey Aldrich, and the title of his poem is "Unguarded Gates." See Stan Steiner, *Fusang: The Chinese Who Built America* (New York: Harper & Row, 1979), 182.

2. "John Winthrop's City upon a Hill, 1630," Mt. Holyoke College, www.mtholyoke.edu/acad /intrel/winthrop.htm; Perry Miller, *Errand into the Wilderness* (Cambridge, MA: Harvard University Press, 1956), 4–6.

3. Benjamin Franklin, *Writings* (New York: Library of America, 1987), 374.

4. U.S. Congress, "An Act to Establish an Uniform Rule of Naturalization (March 26, 1790)," Indiana University, www.indiana.edu/~kdhist/H105-documents-web/week08/naturalization1790.html.

5. Quoted in David Brion Davis, *Inhuman Bondage: The Rise and Fall of Slavery in the New World* (New York: Oxford University Press, 2006), 75.

6. Thomas Jefferson, *Writings* (New York: Library of America, 1984), 265, 1345.

7. Roy P. Basler, ed., *The Collected Works of Abraham Lincoln,* 9 vols. (New Brunswick, NJ: Rutgers University Press, 1953–1955), 2: 249, 276, 281, 363, 461; 3: 16, 222, 235.

8. Edwin Black, *War Against the Weak: Eugenics and America's Campaign to Create a Master Race* (New York: Four Walls Eight Windows, 2003), 166, 167.

9. Charles Howard Shinn, *Mining Camps: A Study in American Frontier Government* (1884; repr., Whitefish, MT: Kessinger, 2010), 180.

10. David E. Stannard, *American Holocaust: Columbus and the Conquest of the New World* (New York: Oxford University Press, 1992), 145.

11. "'Exterminate Them!' California's History of Genocide and Prejudice," Facebook, www.facebook.com/notes/cindy/-butow/exterminate-them-californias-history-of-genocide-and-prejudice/10150610433512077. See also Brendan C. Lindsay, *Murder State: California's Native Genocide, 1846–1873* (Lincoln: University of Nebraska Press, 2012).

12. Robert F. Heizer, ed., *The Destruction of California Indians: A Collection of Documents from the Period 1847 to 1865* (1974; repr., Lincoln: University of Nebraska Press, 1993), 252; Stannard, *American Holocaust,* 142, 144; "The Great California Genocide," *Daily Kos,* August 14, 2008, www.dailykos.com/story/2008/08/14/567667/-The-Great-California-Genocide#; "An Introduction to California's Native People: American Period," Cabrillo College, www.cabrillo.edu/~crsmith/anth6_americanperiod.html.

13. Ronald T. Takaki, *Strangers from a Different Shore: A History of Asian Americans* (Boston: Little, Brown, 1989), 34.

14. Ibid., 35.

15. Ibid., 84, 85; Monique Keiran, "Victoria Was Once the Opium Capital," *Times Colonist,* August 10, 2013, www.timescolonist.com/opinion.columnists/monique-keiran-victoria-was-once-the-opium-capital-1.574430.

16. Takaki, *Strangers,* 88.

17. Takaki, *Hiroshima,* 79; Roger Daniels, *The Politics of Prejudice: The Anti-Japanese Movement in California and the Struggle for Japanese Exclusion,* 2nd ed. (Berkeley: University of California Press, 1977), 17; Takaki, *Strangers,* 115.

18. Steiner, *Fusang,* 81, 163, 180, 181.

19. James Bradley, *The Imperial Cruise: A Secret History of Empire and War* (Boston: Little, Brown, 2009), 281; Takaki, *Strangers,* 111.

20. Carey McWilliams, *Prejudice: Japanese-Americans, Symbol of Racial Intolerance* (Boston: Little, Brown, 1944), 75; Takaki, *Strangers,* 46, 180; Yosaburo Yoshida, "Sources and Causes

of Japanese Emigration," *Annals of the American Academy of Political and Social Science,* 34, no. 2 (September 1909), 163; Raymond Leslie Buell, "The Development of the Anti-Japanese Agitation in the United States," *Political Science Quarterly,* 37, no. 4 (December 1922), 606.

21. Takaki, *Strangers,* 183–184.

22. Robert A. Wilson and Bill Hosokawa, *East to America: A History of the Japanese in the United States* (New York: Quill, 1982), 59.

23. Alison Dundes Renteln, "A Psychohistorical Analysis of the Japanese American Internment," *Human Rights Quarterly,* 17, no. 4 (November 1995), 625.

24. Wilson and Hosokawa, *East to America,* 123; Raymond Leslie Buell, "Again the Yellow Peril," *Foreign Affairs,* December 15, 1923, 307.

25. McWilliams, *Prejudice,* 22–23; Takaki, *Strangers,* 204.

26. Renteln, "A Psychohistorical Analysis of the Japanese American Internment," 634; Takaki, *Strangers,* 201; Geoffrey Hodgson, *The Colonel: The Life and Times of Henry Stimson, 1867–1950* (New York: Knopf, 1990), 251–252.

27. Daniels, *The Politics of Prejudice,* 70.

28. Ibid., 25, 70–71; Neumann, *America Encounters Japan,* 145.

29. Buell, "The Development of the Anti-Japanese Agitation in the United States," 202; Audrie Girdner and Anne Loftis, *The Great Betrayal: The Evacuation of the Japanese-Americans During World War II* (New York: Macmillan, 1969), 50.

30. Buell, "Again the Yellow Peril," 304; Gilbert P. Gia, "States' Rights, T.R., and Japanese Children, 1907," www.gilbertgia.com/hist_articles/civRights/statesrights_tr_japanese _children_1907_%20v1_ci.pdf.

31. Bradley, *Imperial Cruise,* 285; Takaki, *Strangers,* 202.

32. Nathan Miller, *Theodore Roosevelt: A Life* (New York: HarperCollins, 1994), 479; "Theodore Roosevelt: The Threat of Japan," Mt. Holyoke College, www.mtholyoke.edu/acad/intrel /trjapan.htm.

33. Brian Niiya, ed., *Encyclopedia of Japanese American History,* updated ed. (New York: Facts on File, 2001), 335.

34. Takaki, *Strangers,* 52.

35. Ibid., 68, 70.

36. Eileen Sunada Sarasohn, ed., *The Issei, Portrait of a Pioneer: An Oral History* (Palo Alto, CA: Pacific Books, 1983), 52–53.

37. Ibid., 59.

38. Kazuo Ito, *Issei: A History of Japanese Immigrants in North America* (Seattle: Japanese Community Service, 1973), 249.

39. Wilson and Hosokawa, *East to America,* 126; Takaki, *Strangers,* 190, 191.

40. Smith, *Democracy on Trial,* 55, 57.

41. Carey McWilliams, *Brothers Under the Skin* (Boston: Little, Brown, 1943), 169; Takaki, *Strangers,* 215.

42. Yoshiko Uchida, *Desert Exile: The Uprooting of a Japanese American Family* (Seattle: University of Washington Press, 1982), 42; Girdner and Loftis, *The Great Betrayal,* 77.

43. Joseph D. Harrington, *Yankee Samurai: The Secret Role of Nisei in America's Pacific Victory* (Detroit: Pettigrew Enterprises, 1979), 10; Takaki, *Strangers,* 213.

44. Daniel K. Inouye, *Journey to Washington* (Englewood Cliffs, NJ: Prentice-Hall, 1967), 36–37.

45. Takaki, *Strangers,* 217.

46. Girdner and Loftis, *The Great Betrayal,* 95; Ronald T. Takaki, *A Different Mirror: A History of Multicultural America* (Boston: Little, Brown, 1993), 275.

47. Neumann, *America Encounters Japan,* 132.

48. Doug Blair, "The 1920 Anti-Japanese Crusade and Congressional Hearings," http://depts .washington.edu/civilr/Japanese_restriction.htm; Allan R. Bosworth, *America's Concentration Camps* (New York: Norton, 1967), 35; Buell, "Again the Yellow Peril," 300, 303; Smith, *Democracy on Trial,* 43.

49. Speech by Ellison DuRant Smith, April 9, 1924, *Congressional Record,* 68th Congress, 1st Session (Washington, DC: Government Printing Office, 1924), 65: 5961–5962, http://historymatters.gmu.edu/d/5080.

50. Michio Kitahara, *Children of the Sun: The Japanese and the Outside World* (New York: St. Martin's Press, 1989), 71; "The Senate's Declaration of War," *Japan Times and Mail,* April 19, 1924, http://historymatters.gmu.edu/d/5077; Warner and Warner, *Sacred Warriors,* 40–41.

51. Tomita, *Dear Miye,* 49, 53.

52. Ibid., 29, 95.

53. Ibid., 54, 72.

54. Ibid., 28, 30, 31, 66, 69.

55. Ibid., 143.

III: THE PATH TO THE DARK SIDE

1. Cook and Cook, *Japan at War,* 49, 71–72; Ienaga, *The Pacific War,* 142; Donald Keene, "Japanese Writers and the Greater East Asia War," *Journal of Asian Studies,* 23, no. 2 (February 1964), 210, 211, 213.

2. Ienaga, *The Pacific War,* 141, 222; Warner and Warner, *Sacred Warriors,* 53.

3. Michael F. Reilly, *Reilly of the White House* (New York: Simon & Schuster, 1947), 5. Roosevelt's ancestors on his father's side originally came from Holland.

4. Takaki, *Strangers,* 379; Girdner and Loftis, *The Great Betrayal,* 2.

5. Lawson Fusao Inada, ed., *Only What We Could Carry: The Japanese American Internment Experience* (Berkeley, CA: Heyday Books, 2000), 12–13.

6. Girdner and Loftis, *The Great Betrayal,* 10, 12.

7. James C. McNaughton, *Nisei Linguists: Japanese Americans in the Military Intelligence Service During World War II* (Washington, DC: Department of the Army, 2006), 338; Gary Y. Okihiro, *Cane Fires: The Anti-Japanese Movement in Hawaii, 1865–1945* (Philadelphia: Temple University Press, 1991), 157; Inouye, *Journey to Washington,* 56.

8. Miné Okubo, *Citizen 13660* (1946; repr., Seattle: University of Washington Press, 2014), 4; Bosworth, *America's Concentration Camps,* 43.

9. McWilliams, *Prejudice,* 113; Geoffrey Perrett, *Days of Sadness, Years of Triumph: The American People, 1939–1945* (New York: Coward, McCann & Geoghegan, 1973), 204–205.

10. Okihiro, *Cane Fires,* 62, 69.

11. Stephen C. Fox, "Taken into Custody: The Internment of German and Italian Americans During World War II," *Yearbook of German-American Studies* (1997), 117–142; Mitchell Yockelson, "The War Department: Keeper of Our Nation's Enemy Aliens During World War I," April 1998, Great War Primary Documents Archive, www.gwpda.org/comment /yockel.htm.

12. Fox, "Taken into Custody"; Bob Kumamoto, "The Search for Spies: American Counterintelligence and the Japanese-American Community, 1931–1941," *Amerasia Journal,* 6, no. 2 (1979), 69.

13. Kumamoto, "The Search for Spies," 46–47.

14. Yuji Ichioka, "Japanese Immigrant Nationalism: The Issei and the Sino-Japanese War, 1937–1941," *California History,* 69, no. 3 (Fall 1990), 260.

15. Girdner and Loftis, *The Great Betrayal,* 55.

16. Terkel, *"The Good War,"* 112; Ellen Levine, *A Fence Away from Freedom: Japanese Americans and World War II* (New York: Putnam, 1995), 18; Deborah Gesensway and Mindy Roseman, *Beyond Words: Images from America's Concentration Camps* (Ithaca, NY: Cornell University Press, 1987), 139.

17. Gesensway and Roseman, *Beyond Words,* 139; Terkel, *"The Good War,"* 33; Levine, *A Fence Away from Freedom,* 15.

18. Quoted in Terkel, *"The Good War,"* 33–34.

19. Quoted ibid., 28–29.

20. Fox, "Taken into Custody."

21. Quoted in Donald Keene, "Japanese Writers and the Greater East Asia War," 214; Rees, *Horror in the East,* 68.

22. Rees, *Horror in the East,* 71.

23. David McCullough, *Truman* (New York: Simon & Schuster, 1992), 271; Lee Kennett, *For the Duration . . . : The United States Goes to War, Pearl Harbor—1942* (New York: Scribner, 1985), 35, 51–52; Ed Cray, *Chief Justice: A Biography of Earl Warren* (New York: Simon & Schuster, 1997), 114.

24. Commission on Wartime Relocation and Internment of Civilians, *Personal Justice Denied* (Washington, DC: Civil Liberties Public Education Fund; Seattle: University of Washington Press, 1997), 55 (cited hereafter as *Personal Justice Denied*); Cray, *Chief Justice,* 116.

25. Sumi K. Cho, "Redeeming Whiteness in the Shadow of Internment: Earl Warren, *Brown, and a Theory of Racial Redemption,*" *Boston College Third World Law Journal,* 19, no. 1 (1998), 90–91; "Japanese Spies Showed the Way for Raid on Vital Areas in Hawaii," *New York Times,* December 31, 1941.

26. Harrington, *Yankee Samurai,* 13.

27. Takeo Yoshikawa, "Top Secret Assignment," *United States Naval Institute Proceedings,* vol. 86/12/694 (December 1960), www.usni.org/magazines/proceedings/1960-12/top-secret -assignment.

28. Richard R. Lingeman, *Don't You Know There's a War On? The American Home Front, 1941–1945* (New York: Putnam, 1970), 335; Kennett, *For the Duration,* 57, 74.

29. Quoted in Takaki, *Strangers,* 389.

30. Quoted in Jacobus tenBroek, Edward N. Barnhart, and Floyd W. Matson, *Prejudice, War and the Constitution* (1954; repr., Berkeley: University of California Press, 1975), 75.

31. André Schiffrin, *Dr. Seuss & Co. Go to War: The World War II Editorial Cartoons of America's Leading Comic Artists* (New York: New Press, 2009), 17; Roger Daniels, "Words Do Matter: A Note on Inappropriate Terminology and the Incarceration of the Japanese Americans," in Louis Fiset and Gail Nomura, eds., *Nikkei in the Pacific Northwest: Japanese Americans and Japanese Canadians in the Twentieth Century* (Seattle: University of Washington Press, 2005), 183–207.

32. Clayton R. Koppes and Gregory D. Black, *Hollywood Goes to War: How Politics, Profits, and Propaganda Shaped World War II Movies* (New York: Free Press, 1990), 72, 78.

33. Cho, "Redeeming Whiteness," 127n97.

34. Lingeman, *Don't You Know There's a War On?,* 336; Jason Morgan Ward, "'No Jap Crow': Japanese Americans Encounter the World War II South," *Journal of Southern History,* 73, no. 1 (February 2007), 91; John Howard, *Concentration Camps on the Home Front: Japanese Americans in the House of Jim Crow* (Chicago: University of Chicago Press, 2008), 46, 63; "John Rankin: Wartime Stance Against Japanese Americans," *Densho Encyclopedia,* http://encyclopedia.densho.org/John%20Rankin/.

35. Curtis B. Munson, "Japanese on the West Coast," www.home.comcast.net/~eo9066/1941/41 -11/Munson.html.

36. "Ringle Report on Japanese Internment," Naval History and Heritage Command, www.history.navy.mil/library/online/jap%20intern.htm.

37. Kennett, *For the Duration,* 67; Bosworth, *America's Concentration Camps,* 58.

38. John Armor and Peter Wright, *Manzanar* (New York: Times Books, 1988), 22.

39. Joseph Persico, *Roosevelt's Secret War: FDR and World War II Espionage* (New York: Random House, 2001), 168.

40. "FDR and Japanese American Internment," www.fdrlibrary.marist.edu/archives/pdfs /internment.pdf.

41. Barbara W. Tuchman, *Stilwell and the American Experience in China, 1911–45* (New York: Macmillan, 1971), 174; William L. Neumann, "Franklin D. Roosevelt and Japan, 1913–1933," *Pacific Historical Review,* 22, no. 2 (1953), 143–144.

42. Rafael Medoff, "Antisemitism in the White House," www.par2.com/jlinks/Antisemitism _White%20House%203-13.14.pdf.20.

43. Geoffrey C. Ward, *A First-Class Temperament: The Emergence of Franklin Roosevelt* (New York: Harper & Row, 1989), 726n12; Ted Morgan, *FDR: A Biography* (New York: Simon & Schuster, 1985), 275–276; Robinson, *By Order of the President,* 38.

44. Quoted in Robinson, *By Order of the President,* 120. A collection of FDR's articles for the *Macon Telegraph* can be found at "Franklin D. Roosevelt's Editorials for the *Macon Telegraph,*" http://georgiainfo.galileo.asg.edu/.

45. R. J. C. Butow, "The FDR Tapes: Secret Recordings Made in the Oval Office of the President in the Autumn of 1940," *American Heritage,* February/March 1982, 12; "President Roosevelt's Statement Condemning War Crimes," March 24, 1944, History Place: Holocaust Timeline, www.historyplace.com.worldwar2/holocaust/h-roos-statement.htm; Richard Drinnon, *Keeper of the Concentration Camps: Dillon S. Myer and American Racism* (Berkeley: University of California Press, 1987), 255.

46. Drinnon, *Keeper of the Concentration Camps,* 255; Robinson, *By Order of the President,* 120.

47. James McGregor Burns, *Roosevelt: The Soldier of Freedom* (New York: Harcourt Brace Jovanovich, 1970), 214; Franklin D. Roosevelt, "State of the Union Address," January 6, 1942, American Presidency Project, www.presidency.ucsb.edu/ws/?pid=16253.

48. Francis Biddle, *In Brief Authority* (Garden City, NY: Doubleday, 1962), 219, 226.

49. Robinson, *By Order of the President,* 56.

50. Eugene V. Rostow, "The Japanese American Cases—a Disaster," *Yale Law Journal,* 54, no. 3 (June 1945), 494; McWilliams, *Prejudice,* 142; Takaki, *Strangers,* 380.

51. Takaki, *Strangers,* 382; Robinson, *By Order of the President,* 155; Linda Gordon and Gary Y. Okihiro, eds., *Impounded: Dorothea Lange and the Censored Images of Japanese American Internment* (New York: Norton, 2006), 56.

52. John J. Pershing, *My Experiences in the World War,* 2 vols. (New York: Frederick A. Stokes Company, 1931), 2: 327.

53. Perrett, *Days of Sadness,* 216.

54. Robinson, *By Order of the President,* 89; Gerald Stanley, "Justice Deferred: A Fifty-Year Perspective on Japanese-Internment Historiography," *Southern California Quarterly,* 14, no. 2 (Summer 1992), 181; Wilson and Hosokawa, *East to America,* 234.

55. Hodgson, *The Colonel,* 172; Richard D. Dalfiume, "The 'Forgotten Years' of the Negro Revolution," *Journal of American History,* 55, no. 1 (June 1968), 105; Ronald Steel, *Walter Lippmann and the American Century* (Boston: Little, Brown, 1980), 394.

56. Robinson, *By Order of the President,* 106.

57. "Executive Order 9066, February 19, 1942," National Archives and Records Administration, www.archives.gov/historical-docs/todays-doc/?dod-date=219.

58. Biddle, *In Brief Authority,* 212.

IV: SORROWFUL DAYS

1. Harrington, *Yankee Samurai*, 29.

2. "California in World War II: The Battle of Los Angeles," California Military History, http://californiamilitaryhistory.org/BattleofLA.html.

3. Biddle, *In Brief Authority*, 207; Stephen C. Fox, "General John DeWitt and the Proposed Internment of German and Italian Aliens During World War II," *Pacific Historical Review*, 51, no. 4 (November 1988), 434, 438.

4. Tim Newark, *Lucky Luciano: The Real and the Fake Gangster* (New York: Thomas Dunne Books, 2010), 151–157. Lucky Luciano did not serve his full jail term. When the war ended, his sentence was commuted and he was deported to his native Italy because he was not a U.S. citizen.

5. WW2 Cartoons, http://ww2cartoons.org/wp-content/uploads.2012/05/Dec.-42-Japanese -internment1.jpg; Girdner and Loftis, *The Great Betrayal*, 216.

6. Girdner and Loftis, *The Great Betrayal*, 115, 116; Perrett, *Days of Sadness*, 223.

7. McWilliams, *Prejudice*, 193; Takashi Fujitani, "Right to Kill, Right to Make Live: Koreans as Japanese and Japanese as Americans During WWII," *Representations*, 99 (Summer 2007), 31.

8. Yoosun Park, "Facilitating Injustice: Tracing the Role of Social Workers in the World War II Internment of Japanese Americans," *Social Service Review*, 82, no. 3 (September 2008), 474.

9. Bosworth, *America's Concentration Camps*, 112–113.

10. Girdner and Loftis, *The Great Betrayal*, 123; Michi Weglyn, *Years of Infamy: The Untold History of America's Concentration Camps* (New York: Morrow, 1976), 77.

11. Paul R. Spickard, "Injustice Compounded: Amerasians and Non-Japanese Americans in World War II Concentration Camps," *Journal of American Ethnic History*, 5, no. 2 (Spring 1986), 14.

12. Perrett, *Days of Sadness*, 225.

13. Spickard, "Injustice Compounded," 6; Renteln, "A Psychohistorical Analysis of the Japanese American Internment," 645.

14. Park, "Facilitating Injustice," 465–467; Spickard, "Injustice Compounded," 6–7.

15. Robinson, *By Order of the President*, 142.

16. Girdner and Loftis, *The Great Betrayal*, 133.

17. *Personal Justice Denied*, 108, 128; Girdner and Loftis, *The Great Betrayal*, 107; Weglyn, *Years of Infamy*, 77.

18. Jeanne Wakatsuki Houston and James D. Houston, *Farewell to Manzanar: A True Story of Japanese American Experience During and After the World War II Internment* (Boston: Houghton Mifflin, 1973), 13; *Personal Justice Denied*, 123.

19. Judith Fryer Davidov, "'The Color of My Skin, the Shape of My Eyes': Photographs of the Japanese-American Internment by Dorothea Lange, Ansel Adams, and Toyo Miyatake," *Yale Journal of Criticism*, 9, no. 2 (Fall 1996), 223–244; *Personal Justice Denied*, 126.

20. Howard, *Concentration Camps on the Home Front*, 66; Girdner and Loftis, *The Great Betrayal*, 103, 138, 140, 142; Terkel, *"The Good War,"* 29; Takaki, *Strangers*, 393.

21. William Manchester, *The Glory and the Dream: A Narrative History of America, 1932–1972* (Boston: Little, Brown, 1974), 366; Levine, *A Fence Away from Freedom,* 38, 39, 40.

22. *Personal Justice Denied,* 136.

23. McWilliams, *Prejudice,* 133.

24. Brian Thornton, "Heroic Editors in Short Supply During Japanese Internments," *Newspaper Research Journal,* 23, nos. 2/3 (Spring 2002), 106; "S.F. Clear of All but 6 Sick Japs," *San Francisco Chronicle,* May 21, 1942, www.sfmuseum.org/hist8/evac19.html.

25. *Personal Justice Denied,* 136; Caleb Foote, *Outcasts! The Story of America's Treatment of Her Japanese-American Minority* (New York: Fellowship of Reconciliation, 1943), 10, 11.

26. Okubo, *Citizen 13660,* 35, 68.

27. Ibid., 89.

28. Ibid., 74, 76.

29. Ibid., 47.

30. *Personal Justice Denied,* 143; Linda Gordon, *Dorothea Lange: A Life Beyond Limits* (New York: Norton, 2009), 31; Weglyn, *Years of Infamy,* 81.

31. Gesensway and Roseman, *Beyond Words,* 71; Uchida, *Desert Exile,* 96.

32. *Personal Justice Denied,* 156–157.

33. "Toyo Miyatake," Japanese-American Internment Memories, www.japaneseinternment memories.wordpress.com/2012/02/24-toyo-miyatake/; Yosuke Kitazawa, "Toyo Miyatake: Preserving History Through a Lens," KCET, August 1, 2012, www.kcet.org/social /departures/little-tokyo/toyo-miyatake.html; Gerald H. Robinson, *Elusive Truth: Four Photographers at Manzanar: Ansel Adams, Clem Albers, Dorothea Lange, Toyo Miyatake* (Nevada City, CA: Carl Mautz Publishing, 2002), 11.

34. Girdner and Loftis, *The Great Betrayal,* 19; "Japanese Canadian Internment," www.lib .washington.edu.subject/Canada/internment/intro.html; "Japanese Internment: British Columbia Wages War Against Japanese Canadians," *Canada: A People's History,* CBC Learning, www.cbc.ca/history/EPISCONTENTSE1EP14CH3PA3LE.html. See also Patricia Roll, *Mutual Hostages: Canadians and Japanese During the Second World War* (Toronto: University of Toronto Press, 1990).

35. *Personal Justice Denied,* 162.

36. Girdner and Loftis, *The Great Betrayal,* 218, 236; Okubo, *Citizen 13660,* 146–147; Eric L. Muller, *Free to Die for Their Country: The Story of the Japanese American Draft Resisters in World War II* (Chicago: University of Chicago Press, 2001), 35.

37. Gordon, *Dorothea Lange,* 212–213.

38. Gesensway and Roseman, *Beyond Words,* 91.

39. Ronald T. Takaki, *Double Victory: A Multicultural History of America in World War II* (Boston: Little, Brown, 2000), 156; Muller, *Free to Die for Their Country,* 36; Okubo, *Citizen 13660,* 136.

40. McWilliams, *Prejudice,* 209; Drinnon, *Keeper of the Concentration Camps,* 47.

41. Levine, *A Fence Away from Freedom,* 53; Wilson and Hosokawa, *East to America,* 213.

42. Hui Wu, "Writing and Teaching Behind Barbed Wire: An Exiled Composition Class in a Japanese-American Internment Camp," *College Composition and Communication,* 59, no. 2 (December 2007), 241.

43. "Poetry Written by Children in the Japanese Internment Camps," World War II Poetry, www.sccs.swarthmore.edu/users/04/sorelle/poetry/wwii/poetry.html.

44. "WRA Brochure 'Wartime Communities for Wartime Evacuees,'" Studying Poston, www.poston.web.unc.edu/2014/04/11/wra-brochure-relocation-communities-for-wartime -evacuees/; Malvern Hall Tillitt, "Army-Navy Pay Tops Most Civilians'," *Barron's,* April 24, 1944, www.usmm.org/barrons.html.

45. Wilson and Hosokawa, *East to America,* 213.

46. Weglyn, *Years of Infamy,* 97–98; Girdner and Loftis, *The Great Betrayal,* 342.

47. Houston and Houston, *Farewell to Manzanar,* 89.

48. Okubo, *Citizen 13660,* 92, 170, 171.

49. Smith, *Democracy on Trial,* 196.

50. Okubo, *Citizen 13660,* 60; Girdner and Loftis, *The Great Betrayal,* 177.

51. Weglyn, *Years of Infamy,* 91; Raymond Y. Okamura, "The American Concentration Camps: A Cover-up Through Euphemistic Terminology," *Journal of Ethnic Studies,* 10, no. 3 (Fall 1982), 104.

52. "That Damned Fence," War Relocation Authority Camps in Arizona, 1942–1946, http://parentseyes.arizona.edu/wracamps/thatdamnedfence.html.

53. Levine, *A Fence Away from Freedom,* 64; Takaki, *Strangers,* 396; "Children of the Camps: Health Impact," PBS, www.pbs.org/childofcamp/history/health.html.

54. "'Diabolic Savagery,' Tokio Calls East Coast Evacuation of Japanese," *San Francisco News,* March 5, 1942, www.sfmuseum.org/hist8/tokio.html.

55. Bernice Archer, *The Internment of Western Civilians Under the Japanese, 1941–1945* (London: Routledge, 2004), 5.

56. Dr. P. G. Bekkering, "The Japanese Internment Camps—Not a Thing of the Past," http://japaneseburgerkampen.org/vjb/files/6f/16234_bekkering_and_m.pdf, 4; Frances B. Cogan, *Captured: The Internment of American Civilians in the Philippines, 1941–1945* (Athens: University of Georgia Press, 2000), 193, 206.

57. Archer, *The Internment of Western Civilians,* 305.

58. Natsu Taylor Saito, "Justice Held Hostage: U.S. Disregard for International Law in World War II Internment of Japanese Peruvians—a Case Study," *Boston College Third World Law Journal,* 19, no. 1 (1998), 275–292, www.lawdigitalcommons.bc.edu/twlj/vol19/iss1/9; Weglyn, *Years of Infamy,* 55–56. Bolivia, Colombia, Costa Rica, the Dominican Republic, Ecuador, El Salvador, Guatemala, Haiti, Honduras, Nicaragua, Panama, and Peru conducted roundups and deportations at the request of the U.S. government. Argentina, Brazil, Chile, and Mexico did not.

59. "Japanese Latin Americans," *Densho Encyclopedia,* http://encyclopedia.densho.org /Japanese%20Latin%20Americans/; Levine, *A Fence Away from Freedom,* 99, 102.

60. Levine, *A Fence Away from Freedom,* 103.

61. Saito, "Justice Held Hostage," 294. See also Harvey C. Gardiner, *Pawns in a Triangle of Hate: The Peruvian Japanese and the United States* (Seattle: University of Washington Press, 1981); Seiichi Higashide, *Adios to Tears: The Memoirs of a Japanese-Peruvian Internee in U.S. Concentration Camps* (Seattle: University of Washington Press, 2000).

62. Hodgson, *The Colonel,* 259.

63. Allida M. Black, "Confronting the Vital Center: Civil Liberties in War and Peace," chap. 5 in *Casting Her Own Shadow: Eleanor Roosevelt and the Shaping of Postwar Liberalism* (New York: Columbia University Press, 1996), www.thirdworldtraveler.com/Roosevelt_Eleanor /CastingOwnShadow_ER.html; Doris Kearns Goodwin, *No Ordinary Time: Franklin and Eleanor Roosevelt: The Home Front in World War II* (New York: Simon & Schuster, 1994), 323.

64. Foote, *Outcasts!,* 20; Perrett, *Days of Sadness,* 226. Italics added.

65. Weglyn, *Years of Infamy,* 109.

66. Thornton, "Heroic Editors in Short Supply During Japanese Internments," 107.

67. Takaki, *Strangers,* 271; "How to Tell Your Friends from the Japs," *Time,* December 22, 1941; "How to Tell Japs from the Chinese," *Life,* December 22, 1941.

68. Cheryl Greenberg, "Black and Jewish Responses to Japanese Internment," *Journal of American Ethnic History,* 14, no. 2 (Winter 1995), 20–21.

69. Ibid., 23; Richard Polenberg, "The Good War? A Reappraisal of How World War II Affected American Society," *Virginia Magazine of History and Biography,* 100, no. 3 (July 1992), 306–307.

70. Ward, " 'No Jap Crow,' " 95.

71. Foote, *Outcasts!,* 18; Gerald Horne, *Race War! White Supremacy and the Japanese Attack on the British Empire* (New York: New York University Press, 2004), 27.

72. Polenberg, "The Good War?," 304–305.

73. Norman Thomas, *Democracy and Japanese Americans* (New York: Post-War World Council, 1942), 32; Norman Thomas, "The Fate of the Japanese in North America and Hawaii," *Public Affairs,* 16 (March 1943), 95; Greg Robinson, "Norman Thomas and the Struggle Against Internment," *Prospects: An Annual of American Cultural Studies,* 29 (2005), 423.

74. Wu, "Writing and Teaching Behind Barbed Wire," 238, 242.

75. Ibid., 245.

76. Okamura, "The American Concentration Camps," 105.

77. Takeya Mizuno, "Journalism Under Military Guards and Searchlights: Newspaper Censorship at Japanese Assembly Camps During World War II," *Journalism History,* 29, no. 3 (Fall 2003), 99, 101; Perrett, *Days of Sadness,* 225; Weglyn, *Years of Infamy,* 83.

78. George Orwell, "Politics and the English Language," in George Orwell, *Essays* (New York: Alfred A. Knopf, 2002), 967.

79. Ibid.

80. *The War Relocation Work Corps: A Circular of Information for Enlistees and Their Families* (Washington, DC: War Relocation Authority, 1943). See also Okamura, "The American

Concentration Camps"; Daniels, "Words Do Matter"; Japanese American Citizens League, *Power of Words Handbook: A Guide to Language About Japanese Americans in World War II* (2012), https://jacl.org/wordpress/wp-content/uploads/2015/08/Power-of-Words-Rev .-Term.—Handbook.pdf; Edward Schumacher-Matos and Lori Grisham, "Euphemisms, Concentration Camps and the Japanese Internment," NPR Ombudsman, February 10, 2012, www.npr.org/ombudsman/2012/02/10/146691773/euphemisms-concentration-camps-and-the -japanese-internment.

81. *War Relocation Work Corps; Japanese Relocation* (1942), WRA film narrated by Milton S. Eisenhower, www.lib.berkeley.edu/. . ./inter . . . ; Okamura, "The American Concentration Camps," 101. See also "*Japanese Relocation* (1942 film)," https://en.wikipedia.org/wiki /Japanese_Relocation_ (1942 film).

82. Ted Morgan, *FDR: A Biography* (New York: Simon & Schuster, 1985), 629; Schumacher-Matos and Grisham, "Euphemisms, Concentration Camps and the Japanese Internment"; Daniels, "Words Do Matter."

83. Gordon, *Dorothea Lange,* 20.

84. Ibid.; Ansel Adams, *Born Free and Equal: Photographs of the Loyal Japanese-Americans at Manzanar Relocation Center, Inyo County, California* (New York: U.S. Camera, 1944), 9, 25.

85. Elizabeth Partridge, ed., *Dorothea Lange: A Visual Life* (Washington, DC: Smithsonian Institution Press, 1994), 118.

86. Dorothea Lange, *The Making of a Documentary Photographer* (Berkeley: University of California, Regional Oral History Office, Bancroft Library, 1968), 192.

87. Davidov, " 'The Color of My Skin, the Shape of My Eyes.' "

88. After the war, Lange's photos wound up in the National Archives. Over the years, a few appeared in print. Only in 2006 was the veil lifted, when a wide selection of her pictures appeared in *Impounded,* a book edited by Linda Gordon and Gary Y. Okihiro.

V: YANKEE SAMURAI

1. Wilson and Hosokawa, *East to America,* 223. After Pearl Harbor, Congress changed the draft age, making men between eighteen and forty-five years of age eligible for military service. In all, some twelve million men were drafted during the Second World War.

2. Levine, *A Fence Away from Freedom,* 115.

3. McWilliams, *Prejudice,* 218; Muller, *Free to Die for Their Country,* 42.

4. Harrington, *Yankee Samurai,* 85; Wilson and Hosokawa, *East to America,* 224.

5. On U.S. war production, see Maury Klein, *A Call to Arms: Mobilizing America for World War II* (New York: Bloomsbury Press, 2013). This is the bible for the economic side of history's greatest conflict. Arthur Herman's *Freedom's Forge: How American Business Produced Victory in World War II* (New York: Random House, 2012) is also a key work.

6. General David M. Shoup, January 2, 1960, in Robert Debs Heinl Jr., *Dictionary of Military and Naval Quotations* (Annapolis, MD: United States Naval Institute, 2013), 161.

7. McNaughton, *Nisei Linguists,* 24.

8. Tomoko Ozawa, "Nisei Interpreters/ Translators of the U.S. Military," www.jomm.jp/kiyo /pdf/pdf3/kiyou200903.pdf.

9. *Encyclopedia of Japanese American History,* 274.

10. McNaughton, *Nisei Linguists,* 72; Tomita, *Dear Miye,* 148.

11. Masaharu Ano, "Loyal Linguists: Nisei of World War II Learned Japanese in Minnesota," *Minnesota History,* 45, no. 7 (Fall 1977), 285; Harrington, *Yankee Samurai,* 5; Max Everest-Phillips, "The Pre-War Fear of Japanese Espionage and Its Impact and Legacy," *Journal of Contemporary History,* April 2007, 260; Dower, *War Without Mercy,* 261.

12. Harrington, *Yankee Samurai,* 84; Ano, "Loyal Linguists," 281; Roland Kotani, "A Kibei in the Burma Jungle," 100th Infantry Battalion Veterans Education Center, www.100thbattalion .org/archives/puka-puka-parades/mainland-training/secret-missions/mis/a-kibei-in-the -burma-jungle/.

13. Ano, "Loyal Linguists," 278.

14. Ibid., 287.

15. Quoted in John Ellis, *The Sharp End: The Fighting Man in World War II* (New York: Scribner, 1980), 33.

16. Karl F. Friday, "Bushido or Bull? A Medieval Historian's Perspective on the Imperial Army and the Japanese Warrior Tradition," *History Teacher,* 27, no. 3 (May 1994), 339–349.

17. Harries and Harries, *Soldiers of the Sun,* 96; Smith, *Democracy on Trial,* 43; Tanaka, *Hidden Horrors,* 73.

18. Friday, "Bushido or Bull?"

19. Ienaga, *The Pacific War,* 49–50; Gerald F. Linderman, *The World Within War: America's Combat Experience in World War II* (New York: Free Press, 1997), 150, 151.

20. Quoted in Elizabeth M. Norman, *We Band of Angels: The Untold Story of the American Nurses Trapped on Bataan by the Japanese* (New York: Random House, 1999), 80.

21. Norman and Norman, *Tears in the Darkness,* 161.

22. "The Bataan Death March, 1942," EyeWitness to History, www.eyewitnesstohistory.com /bataandeathmarch.htm.

23. Hastings, *Retribution,* 348.

24. John Toland, *But Not in Shame: The Six Months After Pearl Harbor* (New York: Random House, 1961), 337, 339; Donald Knox, *Death March: The Survivors of Bataan* (New York: Harcourt Brace Jovanovich, 1981), 137.

25. Terkel, *"The Good War,"* 60, 61.

26. McNaughton, *Nisei Linguists,* 337–338, 243.

27. Ibid., 69; Mark Felton, "A Culture of Cruelty," *Military History,* 21, no. 5 (January 2011), 33.

28. Dower, *War Without Mercy,* 64; *Life,* May 22, 1944; *Life,* February 1, 1943; "Roosevelt Rejects Gift Made of Japanese Bone," *New York Times,* August 10, 1944.

29. McNaughton, *Nisei Linguists,* 71.

30. Ibid., 339.

31. Ibid., 76, 339.

32. Lyn Crost, *Honor by Fire: Japanese Americans at War in Europe and the Pacific* (Novato, CA: Presidio Press, 1994), 52; *Personal Justice Denied,* 255; McNaughton, *Nisei Linguists,* 246.

33. McNaughton, *Nisei Linguists,* 291, 292; *"What We're Fighting For": Statements by United States Servicemen About Americans of Japanese Descent* (Washington, DC: Department of the Interior, 1944), 1, www.oac.cdlib.org/ark:/13030/hb3489plzl/.

34. McNaughton, *Nisei Linguists,* 282.

35. Harrington, *Yankee Samurai,* 136; Linderman, *The World Within War,* 159; Richard Holmes, *Acts of War: The Behavior of Men in Battle* (New York: Free Press, 1986), 375.

36. Crost, *Honor by Fire,* 119; McNaughton, *Nisei Linguists,* 279–280.

37. Kotani, "A Kibei in the Burma Jungle."

38. McNaughton, *Nisei Linguists,* 282, 285.

39. Cook and Cook, *Japan at War,* 283.

40. Linderman, *The World Within War,* 153.

41. Rees, *Horror in the East,* 108.

42. McNaughton, *Nisei Linguists,* 269, 282, 285; Harrington, *Yankee Samurai,* 147–148.

43. McNaughton, *Nisei Linguists,* 270, 282, 285.

44. Warner and Warner, *Sacred Warriors,* 34.

45. Norman, *We Band of Angels,* 204–205.

46. Selden, "A Forgotten Holocaust"; Ian Buruma, *Year Zero: A History of 1945* (New York: Penguin Press, 2013), 61.

47. McNaughton, *Nisei Linguists,* 270, 282, 285, 339.

48. McCullough, *Truman,* 438; Ienaga, *The Pacific War,* 182.

49. Quoted in Knox, *Death March,* 451–452.

50. On Nisei women during the Second World War, see Brenda L. Moore, *Serving Our Country: Japanese American Women in the Military During World War II* (New Brunswick, NJ: Rutgers University Press, 2003).

51. Bosworth, *America's Concentration Camps,* 18.

52. Robinson, *By Order of the President,* 170.

53. President Franklin D. Roosevelt, "Press and Radio Conference No. 982," November 21, 1944, Press Conferences of President Franklin D. Roosevelt, 1933–1945, Franklin D. Roosevelt Presidential Library and Museum, www.fdrlibrary.marist.edu/archives/collections/franklin/?p=collections/findingaid&id-508.

54. Inada, *Only What We Could Carry,* 313.

55. John Tateishi, *And Justice for All: An Oral History of the Japanese American Detention Camps* (New York: Random House, 1984), 170.

56. McWilliams, *Prejudice,* 182; Smith, *Democracy on Trial,* 293.

57. Weglyn, *Years of Infamy,* 143; McWilliams, *Prejudice,* 187.

58. Quoted in McWilliams, *Prejudice,* 202–203.

59. Ibid., 185, 203.

60. Smith, *Democracy on Trial,* 324.

61. Morgan, *FDR,* 629; Wilson and Hosokawa, *East to America,* 232.

62. Levine, *A Fence Away from Freedom,* 134–135.

63. "Fair Play Committee Bulletin #3," March 1, 1944, Conscience and the Constitution, PBS, www.pbs.org/conscience/resistance/we_hereby_refuse.

64. "Martin Luther King's 'Letter from Birmingham Jail,'" *Atlantic,* April 16, 2013, http://theatlantic.com/politics/archives/2013/04/martin_luther_kings_letter_from_birmingham_jail/274668.

65. Muller, *Free to Die for Their Country,* 114; William H. Rehnquist, *All the Laws but One: Civil Liberties in Wartime* (New York: Knopf, 1998), 173.

66. Crost, *Honor by Fire,* 15, 19, 68.

67. Ibid., 63; Daniel S. Davis, *Behind Barbed Wire: The Imprisonment of Japanese Americans During World War II* (New York: Dutton, 1982), 103–104.

68. Ward, "'No Jap Crow,'" 93; "Protests Against the Formation of 442nd," 442nd Regimental Combat Team, www.the442.org/protestsagainst442nd.html.

69. McWilliams, *Brothers Under the Skin,* 39–40; Polenberg, "The Good War?," 321. The American Red Cross blood bank came out of Charles Drew's work. On German soldiers refusing blood transfusions, see Vasily Grossman, *A Writer at War: Vasily Grossman with the Red Army, 1941–1945,* ed. and trans. Antony Beevor and Luba Vinogradova (New York: Vintage Books, 2005), 102.

70. McWilliams, *Brothers Under the Skin,* 32; Howard, *Concentration Camps on the Home Front,* 48.

71. Inouye, *Journey to Washington,* 96.

72. Ward, "'No Jap Crow,'" 97; Levine, *A Fence Away from Freedom,* 125.

73. Crost, *Honor by Fire,* 78, 115.

74. Ibid., 116.

75. "Poetry Written by Children in the Japanese Internment Camps."

76. Smith, *Democracy on Trial,* 191, 348. V-mail (Victory Mail) was the primary means of correspondence during the Second World War with soldiers stationed abroad.

77. "Pfc. Ernest Uno Writes to His Sister Mae, WWII (Read by Mike Hagiwara)," *American Experience,* "Transcript: War Letters," PBS, www.pbs.org/wgbh/americanexperience/features/transcript/warletters-transcript/.

78. Crost, *Honor by Fire,* 185; Bosworth, *America's Concentration Camps,* 15; Takaki, *Strangers,* 401.

79. Crost, *Honor by Fire,* 78.

80. Ibid., 183; Girdner and Loftis, *The Great Betrayal,* 331.

81. Linda K. Menton, "Research Report: Nisei Soldiers at Dachau, Spring 1945," *Holocaust and Genocide Studies,* 8, no. 2 (Fall 1994), 262; Levine, *A Fence Away from Freedom,* 126.

82. Peggy Orenstein, "Reunion," Talk of the Town, *New Yorker,* November 11, 1991, 33; Levine, *A Fence Away from Freedom,* 127.

83. Solly Ganor, "Essays by Holocaust Survivor Solly Ganor," 36–37, http://chgs.umn.edu /histories/armenian/sollyganor.pdf; "An Interview with Solly Ganor," PBS, www.pbs.org .wgbh/sugihara/readings.ganor.html.

84. Takaki, *Strangers,* 401–402.

85. Crost, *Honor by Fire,* 253–256.

VI: THE WHEELS OF JUSTICE

1. McWilliams, *Prejudice,* 209; Levine, *A Fence Away from Freedom,* 49.

2. *The Federalist No. 51,* in James Madison, *Writings* (New York: Library of America, 1999), 295.

3. Girdner and Loftis, *The Great Betrayal,* 481; Rehnquist, *All the Laws but One,* 199.

4. Peter Irons, "Scenes from the Struggles of a Courageous American: Recollections of Peter Irons About the Life of Gordon Hirabayashi," *Seattle Journal for Social Justice,* 11, no. 11, article 2 (2012), 19–26, http://digitalcommons.law.seattleu.edu/sjsj/vol11/iss1/2.

5. "*Hirabayashi v. United States* by Harlan F. Stone: Opinion of the Court," Wikisource, http://en.wikisource.org/wiki/Hirabayashi_v._United_States/Opinion_of_the_Court.

6. Peter Irons, ed., *Justice Delayed: The Record of the Japanese Internment Cases* (Middletown, CT: Wesleyan University Press, 1989), 69.

7. "Fred Korematsu, 86, Dies: Lost Key Suit on Internment," *New York Times,* April 1, 2005.

8. Roger Daniels, "The Japanese American Cases, 1942–2004: A Social History," *Law and Contemporary Problems,* 68 (Spring 2005), 159–171, http://scholarship.law.duke.edu/cgi /viewcontentcgi?article=1355&content=lcp; "*Korematsu v. United States,*" Cornell University Law School, www.law.cornell.edu/supremecourt/text/323/214; "*Korematsu v. United States,*" *Densho Encyclopedia,* http://encyclopedia.densho.org/Korematsu_v._United_States/.

9. "*Korematsu v. United States,*" Cornell University Law School.

10. Ibid. Italics added.

11. "*Ex parte Endo*":323 U.S. 2f3 (1944): Justice U.S. Supreme . . . https://supreme.justice.com /cases/. . ./case.html.

12. "*Ex parte Mitsuye Endo,* 1944," Fred T. Korematsu Institute, www.korematsuinstitute.org /institute/aboutfred/internmentcases/ex-parte-mitsuye-endo; Timothy P. Maga, "Ronald

Reagan and Redress for the Japanese-American Internment, 1983–88," *Presidential Studies Quarterly,* 28, no. 3 (Summer 1998), 607.

13. Davis, *Behind Barbed Wire,* 128; "The Constitution on Trial: The Internment of the Japanese During World War II," Document G, 20, The Huntington, http://www.huntington.org /uploadedFiles/Files/PDFs/LHTHinternment.pdf.

14. Okubo, *Citizen 13660,* 207; Park, "Facilitating Injustice," 471–472.

15. Smith, *Democracy on Trial,* 395; Okubo, *Citizen 13660,* 208, 209.

16. Smith, *Democracy on Trial,* 386, 395; Girdner and Loftis, *The Great Betrayal,* 424.

17. Jennifer Speidel, "After Internment: Seattle's Debate over Japanese Americans' Right to Return Home," Seattle Civil Rights and Labor History Project, www.depts.washington .edu/civilr/after_internment.htm; Kevin Allen Leonard, "'Is That What We Fought For?' Japanese Americans and Racism in California: The Impact of World War II," *Western Historical Quarterly,* 21, no. 4 (November 1990), 467.

18. Bosworth, *America's Concentration Camps,* 215.

19. Polenberg, "The Good War?," 319; David Neiwert, "'Scoop' and the Internment Camps," *Orcinus* (blog), http://dneiwert.blogspot.com/2006/06/scoop-and-internment-camps.html.

20. Leonard, "'Is That What We Fought For?,'" 468; Tateishi, *And Justice for All,* 255.

21. Takaki, *Hiroshima,* 80; Levine, *A Fence Away from Freedom,* 25. Pvt. James P. O'Neill, "The Nisei Problem," *Yank,* July 13, 1945, 22, www.unz.org/Pub/Yank-1945jul13-00022.

22. "Desegregation of the Armed Forces," Harry S. Truman Library and Museum, www.trumanlibrary.org/whistlestop/study_collections/desegregation/large/#1946.

23. Tateishi, *And Justice for All,* 259.

24. Crost, *Honor by Fire,* 153.

25. Eric J. Sundquist, "The Japanese-American Internment: A Reappraisal," *American Scholar,* 57, no. 4 (Autumn 1988), 534; Bosworth, *America's Concentration Camps,* 214.

26. Bosworth, *America's Concentration Camps,* 214; Maga, "Ronald Reagan and Redress for the Japanese-American Internment," 614.

27. Takaki, *Hiroshima,* 99.

28. Ibid., 100; Robinson, *By Order of the President,* 258.

29. "Nisei World War II Stamp Campaign," *NVC Newsletter,* 57, no. 10 (November 2007), NVC Foundation, www.nvcfoundation.org/newsletter/2007/II/nisei-world-war-ii-stamp -campaign/.

30. Leonard, "'Is That What We Fought For?,'" 148–149, 471, 478.

31. Levine, *A Fence Away from Freedom,* 177; Renteln, "A Psychohistorical Analysis of the Japanese American Internment," 626.

32. Tetsuden Kashima, "American Mistreatment of Internees During World War II: Enemy Alien Japanese," in Roger Daniels, Sandra C. Taylor, and Harry H. L. Kitano, eds., *Japanese Americans: From Relocation to Redress,* rev. ed. (Seattle: University of Washington Press, 1991), 110.

33. Judith Thurman, "Dressing Up: How Charles James Elevated American Fashion," At the Galleries, *New Yorker,* May 5, 2014, 80.

34. Don T. Nakanishi, "Surviving Democracy's 'Mistake': Japanese Americans and the Enduring Legacy of Executive Order 9066," *Amerasia Journal,* 35, no. 3 (2009), 61; Kashima, "American Mistreatment of Internees During World War II," 113.

35. Patricia J. Machmiller, "The Roar of Silence: Poems on the Legacy of the Japanese American Internment Experience," *JAMsj* (blog), https://jamsj.wordpress.com/2011/02/08/the-roar-of -silence-poems-on-the-legacy-of-the-japanese-american-internment-experience/; Cordelia Hebblethwaite, "Pain and Redemption of World War II Interned Japanese-Americans," BBC News, www.bbc.com/news/magazine-17080392.

36. Bill Hosokawa, *Nisei: The Quiet Americans* (New York: Morrow, 1969), 455.

37. Weglyn, *Years of Infamy,* 260; Hosokawa, *Nisei,* 432.

38. *"Loving v. Virginia,"* Cornell University Law School, www.law.cornell.edu/supremecourt /text/388/1.

39. Earl Warren, *The Memoirs of Chief Justice Earl Warren* (New York: Doubleday, 1977), 149.

40. Maga, "Ronald Reagan and Redress for the Japanese-American Internment," 608.

41. Levine, *A Fence Away from Freedom,* 196.

42. Ibid.

43. *Personal Justice Denied,* 18. Italics added.

44. Orville Schell, "Rounding Up Americans," Books, *New York Times,* January 1, 1984. For a very detailed explanation of the government's cover-up, see Peter Irons, *Justice at War* (New York: Oxford University Press, 1983), 202–218.

45. Donald K. Tamaki, "Foreword: Sixty Years After the Internment: Civil Rights, Identity Politics, and Racial Profiling," *Asian American Law Journal,* 11, no. 1 (January 2004), 149, http://scholarship.law.berkeley.edu/aalj/vol11/iss1/6.

46. Ibid.

47. Maga, "Ronald Reagan and Redress for the Japanese-American Internment," 611.

48. William J. Clinton, "Remarks on Presenting the Congressional Medal of Honor to Asian-American Heroes of World War II," June 21, 2000, American Presidency Project, www.presidency.ucsb.edu/ws/?pid=58671.

49. Ibid.

VII: REMEMBERING THE PAST

1. Middle East Media Research Institute, Jihad and Terrorism Studies Project, "Contemporary Islamist Ideology Authorizing Genocidal Murder," Special Report no. 25, January 27, 2004, MEMRI, www.memri.org/report/en/0/0/0/0/0/0/1049.htm; Jonathan D. Halevi, "Al-Qaeda's Intellectual Legacy: New Radical Islamic Thinking Justifying the Genocide of Infidels,"

Jerusalem Viewpoints no. 508, December 1, 2003, Jerusalem Center for Public Affairs, www.jcpa.org/jl/vp508.htm.

2. President George W. Bush, "Remarks to Airline Employees in Chicago, September 27, 2001," American Presidency Project, www.presidency.ocsb.edu/ws/?pid=65084.

3. Qur'an, 2:190, 2:256; Youssef H. Aboul-Enien and Sherifa Zuhur, *Islamic Rulings on Warfare* (Carlisle, PA: Strategic Studies Institute, U.S. Army War College, 2004), 22, www.strategicstudiesinstitute.army.mil/pdffiles/pub588.pdf.

4. Sheila Musaji, "Muslim Reactions to September 11th," http://crescentlife.com/heal%20 the%20world/muslim_reaction_to_sept_11.htm. See also Mohammad Abid Amiri, "Muslim Americans and the Media After 9/11," *Islam and Muslim Societies,* 5, no. 2 (2012), www .muslimsocieties.org/Vol_5_No_2_Muslim_Americans_and_the_Media_after_9_11.html.

5. Hilal Elver, "Racializing Islam Before and After 9/11: From Melting Pot to Islamophobia," *Transnational Law and Contemporary Problems,* 21 (Spring 2012), 145; Ann Coulter, "Future Widows of America: Write Your Congressman," *Jewish World Review,* September 28, 2001, www.jewish-worldreview.com/cols/coulter092801.asp.

6. Abdus Sattar Ghazali, "2010: Another Hard Year for American Muslims," CounterCurrents.org, December 26, 2010, www.countercurrents.org/ghazali261210.htm; Lena Kampf and Indra Sen, "History Does Not Repeat Itself, but Ignorance Does: Post-9/11 Treatment of Muslims and the Liberty-Security Dilemma," Humanity in Action, www.humanityinaction.org/knowledgebase/168-history-does-not-repeat-itself-but-ignorance -does-post-9-11-treatment-of-muslims-and-the-liberty-security-dilemma.

7. Elver, "Racializing Islam Before and After 9/11," 139; Ed Grabianowski, "How the Patriot Act Works," How Stuff Works, http://people.howstuffworks.com/patriot-act.

8. David Cole quoted in Eric L. Muller, "Influence or Impact? Racial Profiling and the Internment's True Legacy," *Ohio State Journal of Criminal Law,* 1, no. 1 (2003), 106, Social Science Research Network, http://ssrn.com/abstract=462522.

9. Maga, "Ronald Reagan and Redress for the Japanese-American Internment," 610.

10. Rob Verger, "*Newsweek* Rewind: How We Covered the Internment of Japanese-Americans During WWII," *Newsweek,* February 24, 2014, www.newsweek.com/newsweek-archives -how-we-covered-internment-japanese-americans-during-wwii-230048.

11. Maya Angelou's poem "On the Pulse of Morning" was written for the January 20, 1993, inauguration of President Bill Clinton. For the complete text, see http://poetry.eserver.org /angelou.html.

SOME MORE THINGS TO READ

Adams, Ansel. *Born Free and Equal: Photographs of the Loyal Japanese-Americans at Manzanar Relocation Center, Inyo County, California.* New York: U.S. Camera, 1944.

Ano, Masaharu. "Loyal Linguists: Nisei of World War II Learned Japanese in Minnesota." *Minnesota History,* 45, no. 7 (Fall 1977), 273–287.

Armor, John, and Peter Wright. *Manzanar.* New York: Times Books, 1988. A collection of photographs by Ansel Adams, with commentary by John Hersey.

Asahina, Robert. *Just Americans: How Japanese Americans Won a War at Home and Abroad.* New York: Gotham Books, 2006.

Biddle, Francis. *In Brief Authority.* Garden City, NY: Doubleday, 1962.

Blum, John Morton. *V Was for Victory: Politics and American Culture During World War II.* New York: Harcourt Brace Jovanovich, 1976.

Bosworth, Allan R. *America's Concentration Camps.* New York: Norton, 1967.

Brcak, Nancy, and John R. Pavia. "Racism in Japanese and U.S. Wartime Propaganda." *Historian,* 56, no. 2 (June 22, 1994), 671–684.

Broom, Leonard, and Ruth Reimer. *Removal and Return: The Socio-Economic Effects of the War on Japanese Americans.* Berkeley: University of California Press, 1973.

Commission on Wartime Relocation and Internment of Civilians. *Personal Justice Denied.* Washington, DC: Civil Liberties Public Education Fund; Seattle: University of Washington Press, 1997.

Connell, Thomas. *America's Japanese Hostages: The World War II Plans for a Japanese Free Latin America.* Westport, CT: Greenwood, 2002.

Cook, Haruko Taya, and Theodore F. Cook. *Japan at War: An Oral History.* New York: New Press, 1992.

Cooper, Michael L. *Fighting for Honor: Japanese Americans and World War II.* New York: Clarion Books, 2000.

Crost, Lyn. *Honor by Fire: Japanese Americans at War in Europe and the Pacific.* Novato, CA: Presidio Press, 1994.

Daniels, Roger. *Concentration Camps USA: Japanese Americans and World War II.* New York: Holt, Rinehart and Winston, 1971.

———. "The Japanese American Cases, 1942–2004: A Social History." *Law and Contemporary Problems,* 68 (Spring 2005), 159–171. http://scholarship.law.duke.edu/cgi/viewcontentcgi?article=1355&content=lcp.

———. *The Politics of Prejudice: The Anti-Japanese Movement in California and the Struggle for Japanese Exclusion.* 2nd ed. Berkeley: University of California Press, 1977.

————. "Words Do Matter: A Note on Inappropriate Terminology and the Incarceration of the Japanese Americans." In *Nikkei in the Pacific Northwest: Japanese Americans and Japanese Canadians in the Twentieth Century,* edited by Louis Fiset and Gail Nomura, 183–207. Seattle: University of Washington Press, 2005.

Daniels, Roger, Sandra C. Taylor, and Harry H. L. Kitano, eds. *Japanese Americans: From Relocation to Redress.* Rev. ed. Seattle: University of Washington Press, 1991.

Davidov, Judith Fryer. "'The Color of My Skin, the Shape of My Eyes': Photographs of the Japanese-American Internment by Dorothea Lange, Ansel Adams, and Toyo Miyatake." *Yale Journal of Criticism,* 9, no. 2 (Fall 1996), 223–244.

Davis, Daniel S. *Behind Barbed Wire: The Imprisonment of Japanese Americans During World War II.* New York: Dutton, 1982.

Donald, Ralph R. "Awakening a Sleeping Giant: The Pearl Harbor Attack on Film." *Film and History,* 27, nos. 1–4 (1997), 40–46.

Dower, John W. *War Without Mercy: Race and Power in the Pacific War.* New York: Pantheon Books, 1986.

Drinnon, Richard. *Keeper of the Concentration Camps: Dillon S. Myer and American Racism.* Berkeley: University of California Press, 1987.

Duus, Masayo Umezawa. *Unlikely Liberators: The Men of the 100th and 442nd.* Translated by Peter Duus. Honolulu: University of Honolulu Press, 1987.

Edgerton, Robert B. *Warriors of the Rising Sun: A History of the Japanese Military.* New York: Norton, 1997.

Ellis, John. *The Sharp End: The Fighting Man in World War II.* New York: Scribner, 1980.

Flamiano, Dolores. "Japanese American Internment in Popular Magazines: Race, Citizenship, and Gender in World War II Photojournalism." *Journalism History,* 36, no. 1 (Spring 2010), 23–35.

Friday, Karl F. "Bushido or Bull? A Medieval Historian's Perspective on the Imperial Army and the Japanese Warrior Tradition." *History Teacher,* 27, no. 3 (May 1994), 339–349.

Friedman, Max Paul. "The U.S. Internment of Families from Latin America in World War II." *DEP,* no. 9 (2008), 57–73. www.unive.it/media/allegato/dep/n9-2008/Saggi/Friedman-saggio.pdf.

Fujiyoshi, Ronald S. "The Nature of Japanese Racism." *Chinese American Forum,* 10, no. 4 (April 1995), 15–16.

Garrett, Greg. "It's Everybody's War: Racism and the World War II Documentary." *Journal of Popular Film,* 22 (April 1994), 70–78.

Gesensway, Deborah, and Mindy Roseman. *Beyond Words: Images from America's Concentration Camps.* Ithaca, NY: Cornell University Press, 1987.

Girdner, Audrie, and Anne Loftis. *The Great Betrayal: The Evacuation of the Japanese-Americans During World War II.* New York: Macmillan, 1969.

Gordon, Linda. *Dorothea Lange: A Life Beyond Limits.* New York: Norton, 2009.

Gordon, Linda, and Gary Y. Okihiro, eds. *Impounded: Dorothea Lange and the Censored Images of Japanese American Internment.* New York: Norton, 2006.

Grodzins, Morton. *Americans Betrayed: Politics and the Japanese Evacuation.* Chicago: University of Chicago Press, 1949.

Harries, Meirion, and Susie Harries. *Soldiers of the Sun: The Rise and Fall of the Imperial Japanese Army.* New York: Random House, 1991.

Harrington, Joseph D. *Yankee Samurai: The Secret Role of Nisei in America's Pacific Victory.* Detroit: Pettigrew Enterprises, 1979.

Hastings, Max. *Retribution: The Battle for Japan, 1944–45.* New York: Knopf, 2008.

Hatamiya, Leslie T. *Righting a Wrong: Japanese Americans and the Passage of the Civil Liberties Act of 1988.* Stanford, CA: Stanford University Press, 1993.

Havens, Thomas R. H. *Valley of Darkness: The Japanese People and World War Two.* New York: Norton, 1978.

Hibbert, Christopher. *The Dragon Wakes: China and the West, 1793–1911.* New York: Harper & Row, 1970.

Hodgson, Geoffrey. *The Colonel: The Life and Times of Henry Stimson, 1867–1950.* New York: Knopf, 1990.

Hohri, William Minoru. *Repairing America: An Account of the Movement for Japanese-American Redress.* Pullman: Washington State University Press, 1988.

Hosokawa, Bill. *Nisei: The Quiet Americans.* New York: Morrow, 1969.

Houston, Jeanne Wakatsuki, and James D. Houston. *Farewell to Manzanar: A True Story of Japanese American Experience During and After the World War II Internment.* Boston: Houghton Mifflin, 1973.

Howard, John. *Concentration Camps on the Home Front: Japanese Americans in the House of Jim Crow.* Chicago: University of Chicago Press, 2008.

Ichioka, Yuji. *The Issei: The World of the First Generation Japanese Immigrants.* New York: Free Press, 1988.

Ienaga, Saburo. *The Pacific War, 1931–1945: A Critical Perspective on Japan's Role in World War II.* New York: Pantheon Books, 1978.

Inada, Lawson Fusao, ed. *Only What We Could Carry: The Japanese American Internment Experience.* Berkeley, CA: Heyday Books, 2000.

Inouye, Daniel K. *Journey to Washington.* Englewood Cliffs, NJ: Prentice-Hall, 1967.

Irons, Peter. *Justice at War: The Story of the Japanese American Internment Cases.* New York: Oxford University Press, 1983.

———, ed. *Justice Delayed: The Record of the Japanese Internment Cases.* Middletown, CT: Wesleyan University Press, 1989.

Ito, Kazuo. *Issei: A History of Japanese Immigrants in North America.* Seattle: Japanese Community Service, 1973.

Japanese American Citizens League. *Power of Words Handbook: A Guide to Language About Japanese Americans in World War II.* https://jacl.org/wordpress/wp-content/uploads/2015/08/Power-of-Words-Rev.-Term.—Handbook.pdf.

Kennett, Lee. *For the Duration . . . : The United States Goes to War, Pearl Harbor—1942.* New York: Scribner, 1985.

Kumamoto, Bob. "The Search for Spies: American Counterintelligence and the Japanese-American Community, 1931–1941." *Amerasia Journal,* 6, no. 2 (1979), 45–75.

Leonard, Kevin Allen. "'Is That What We Fought For?' Japanese Americans and Racism in California: The Impact of World War II." *Western Historical Quarterly,* 21, no. 4 (November 1990), 463–482.

Levine, Ellen. *A Fence Away from Freedom: Japanese Americans and World War II.* New York: Putnam, 1995.

Lingeman, Richard R. *Don't You Know There's a War On? The American Home Front, 1941–1945.* New York: Putnam, 1970.

McCullough, David. *Truman.* New York: Simon & Schuster, 1992.

McNaughton, James C. *Nisei Linguists: Japanese Americans in the Military Intelligence Service During World War II.* Washington, DC: Department of the Army, 2006.

McWilliams, Carey. *Brothers Under the Skin.* Boston: Little, Brown, 1943.

———. *Prejudice: Japanese-Americans, Symbol of Racial Intolerance.* Boston: Little, Brown, 1945.

Miller, Stuart Creighton. *The Unwelcome Immigrant: The American Image of the Chinese, 1785–1882.* Berkeley: University of California Press, 1969.

Morgan, Ted. *FDR: A Biography.* New York: Simon & Schuster, 1985.

Morison, Elting E. *Turmoil and Tradition: A Study of the Life and Times of Henry L. Stimson.* Boston: Houghton Mifflin, 1960.

Morison, Samuel Eliot. *"Old Bruin": Commodore Matthew C. Perry, 1794–1858.* Boston: Little, Brown, 1967.

Muller, Eric L. *Free to Die for Their Country: The Story of the Japanese American Draft Resisters in World War II.* Chicago: University of Chicago Press, 2001.

Nakanishi, Don T. "Surviving Democracy's 'Mistake': Japanese Americans and the Enduring Legacy of Executive Order 9066." *Amerasia Journal,* 35, no. 3 (2009), 51–84.

National Park Service. *Manzanar Historic Research Study.* http://nps.gov/history/history/online _books/manz/hrs1/htm.

Neumann, William L. *America Encounters Japan: From Perry to MacArthur.* Baltimore: Johns Hopkins Press, 1963.

Niiya, Brian, ed. *Encyclopedia of Japanese American History.* Updated ed. New York: Facts on File, 2001.

Norman, Michael, and Elizabeth M. Norman. *Tears in the Darkness: The Story of the Bataan Death March and Its Aftermath.* New York: Farrar, Straus and Giroux, 2009.

Okada, John. *No-No Boy.* Seattle: University of Washington Press, 1981. First published 1957 by Charles E. Tuttle Company.

Okamura, Raymond Y. "The American Concentration Camps: A Cover-up Through Euphemistic Terminology." *Journal of Ethnic Studies,* 10, no. 3 (Fall 1982), 95–115.

Okihiro, Gary Y. *Cane Fires: The Anti-Japanese Movement in Hawaii, 1865–1945*. Philadelphia: Temple University Press, 1991.

———. *Whispered Silences: Japanese Americans and World War II*. Seattle: University of Washington Press, 1996.

Okubo, Miné. *Citizen 13660*. Seattle: University of Washington Press, 2014. First published 1946 by Columbia University Press.

Padover, Saul K. "Japanese Race Propaganda." *Public Opinion Quarterly,* 7, no. 2 (Summer 1943), 191–204.

Park, Yoosun. "Facilitating Injustice: Tracing the Role of Social Workers in the World War II Internment of Japanese Americans." *Social Service Review,* 82, no. 3 (September 2008), 447–483.

Perrett, Geoffrey. *Days of Sadness, Years of Triumph: The American People, 1939–1945*. New York: Coward, McCann & Geoghegan, 1973.

Polenberg, Richard. "The Good War? A Reappraisal of How World War II Affected American Society." *Virginia Magazine of History and Biography,* 100, no. 3 (July 1992), 295–322.

Ramadas, Sandhya. "How Earl Warren Previewed Today's Civil Liberties—and Got It Right in the End." *Asian American Law Journal,* 16 (2009), 73–130. http://scholarship.law.berkeley.edu/aalj/vol16/iss1/3.

Rees, Laurence. *Horror in the East: Japanese and the Atrocities of World War II*. New York: Da Capo Press, 2002.

Rehnquist, William H. *All the Laws but One: Civil Liberties in Wartime*. New York: Knopf, 1998.

Robinson, Gerald H. *Elusive Truth: Four Photographers at Manzanar: Ansel Adams, Clem Albers, Dorothea Lange, Toyo Miyatake*. Nevada City, CA: Carl Mautz Publishing, 2002.

Robinson, Greg. *By Order of the President: FDR and the Internment of Japanese Americans*. Cambridge, MA: Harvard University Press, 2001.

———. "Norman Thomas and the Struggle Against Internment." *Prospects: An Annual of American Cultural Studies,* 29 (October 2005), 419–434.

Sarasohn, Eileen Sunada, ed. *The Issei, Portrait of a Pioneer: An Oral History*. Palo Alto, CA: Pacific Books, 1983.

Schiffrin, André. *Dr. Seuss & Co. Go to War: The World War II Editorial Cartoons of America's Leading Comic Artists*. New York: New Press, 2009.

Sinkler, George. *The Racial Attitudes of American Presidents: From Abraham Lincoln to Theodore Roosevelt*. Garden City, NY: Doubleday, 1971.

Smith, Page. *Democracy on Trial: The Japanese American Evacuation and Relocation in World War II*. New York: Simon & Schuster, 1995.

Smithsonian Institution. "A More Perfect Union—Japanese Americans and the United States Constitution." http://amhistory.si.edu/perfectunion/transcript.html#process1.

Spector, Ronald H. *Eagle Against the Sun: The American War with Japan*. New York: Free Press, 1985.

Steiner, Stan. *Fusang: The Chinese Who Built America.* New York: Harper & Row, 1979.

Sung, Betty Lee. *Mountain of Gold: The Story of the Chinese in America.* New York: Macmillan, 1967.

Takaki, Ronald T. *A Different Mirror: A History of Multicultural America.* Boston: Little, Brown, 1993.

———. *Double Victory: A Multicultural History of America in World War II.* Boston: Little, Brown, 2000.

———. *Hiroshima: Why America Dropped the Atomic Bomb.* Boston: Little, Brown, 1995.

Tanaka, Chester. *Go for Broke: A Pictorial History of the Japanese American 100th Infantry Battalion and the 442nd Regimental Combat Team.* Richmond, CA: Go for Broke, 1982.

Tanaka, Yuki. *Hidden Horrors: Japanese War Crimes in World War II.* Boulder, CO: Westview Press, 1996.

Tateishi, John. *And Justice for All: An Oral History of the Japanese American Detention Camps.* New York: Random House, 1984.

TenBroek, Jacobus, Edward N. Barnhart, and Floyd W. Matson. *Prejudice, War and the Constitution.* Berkeley: University of California Press, 1975. First published 1954 by University of California Press.

Terkel, Studs. *"The Good War": An Oral History of World War Two.* New York: Pantheon Books, 1984.

Tomita, Mary Kimoto. *Dear Miye: Letters Home from Japan, 1939–1946.* Stanford, CA: Stanford University Press, 1995. Letters written by a Nisei living in Japan during World War II.

Uchida, Yoshiko. *Desert Exile: The Uprooting of a Japanese American Family.* Seattle: University of Washington Press, 1982.

Wagatsuma, Hiroshi. "The Social Perception of Skin Color in Japan." *Daedalus,* 96, no. 2 (Spring 1967), 407–443.

Ward, Jason Morgan. "'No Jap Crow': Japanese Americans Encounter the World War II South." *Journal of Southern History,* 73, no. 1 (February 2007), 75–104.

Warner, Denis, and Peggy Warner. *Sacred Warriors: Japan's Suicide Legions.* New York: Van Nostrand Reinhold, 1982.

Weglyn, Michi. *Years of Infamy: The Untold History of America's Concentration Camps.* New York: Morrow, 1976.

Wenger, Gina L. "Documentary Photography: Three Photographers' Standpoints on the Japanese-American Internment." *Art Education,* 60, no. 5 (September 2007), 33–38.

Wilson, Dick. *When Tigers Fight: The Story of the Sino-Japanese War, 1937–1945.* New York: Viking, 1982.

Wilson, Robert A., and Bill Hosokawa. *East to America: A History of the Japanese in the United States.* New York: Quill, 1982.

Wu, Hui. "Writing and Teaching Behind Barbed Wire: An Exiled Composition Class in a Japanese-American Internment Camp." *College Composition and Communication,* 59, no. 2 (December 2007), 237–262.

Yenne, Bill. *Rising Sons: The Japanese American GIs Who Fought for the United States in World War II.* New York: St. Martin's Press, 2007.

SOME USEFUL INTERNET SOURCES

"Ansel Adams's Photographs of Japanese-American Internment at Manzanar." Library of Congress. www.loc.gov/pictures/collection/manz.

Asia for Educators. http://afe.easia.columbia.edu/tps/topic_index.htm. A marvelous source for information, documents, and pictures on all aspects of Asian history.

"Children of the Camps: The Documentary." PBS. www.pbs.org/childofcamp/.

"Confinement and Ethnicity: An Overview of World War II Japanese American Relocation Sites." National Park Service. www.nps.gov/parkhistory/online_books/anthropology74/.

Denshō: The Japanese American Legacy Project. http://densho.org. This is a key site, containing hundreds of articles, photos, and interviews of those who underwent the camp experience. Not to be missed.

Japanese American National Museum. www.janm.org. A useful collection of documents, photos, and exhibits.

Japanese American Relocation Digital Archives. www.calisphere.universityofcalifornia.edu/jarda. This site contains thousands of photos, documents, and teaching materials on the uprooting.

"Manzanar: National Historic Site, California." National Park Service. www.nps.gov/manz/index.htm.

"Teaching with Documents: Documents and Photographs Related to Japanese Relocation During World War II." National Archives and Records Administration. www.archives.gov/education/lessons/japanese-relocation/index.html.

War Relocation Authority. *A Challenge to Democracy.* www.archive.org/details/Challeng1944.

"War Relocation Authority Photographs of Japanese-American Evacuation and Resettlement, 1942–1945." Online Archive of California. www.oac.cdlib.org/findaid/ark:/13030/tf596nb4h0/.

PICTURE CREDITS

Ansel Adams, Library of Congress: 117, 119, 132, 133

AP Photo: 189

California Historical Society: 134

California State Parks: 57

Corbis: 158

Densho Encyclopedia: 87

Dorothea Lange: 110

Dorothea Lange, U.S. National Archives and Records Administration: 98, 100, 101, 102, 103, 135 (bottom), 138

FDR Presidential Library and Museum: 4

Fred Clark, UC Berkeley, Bancroft Library: 113, 114

Courtesy of the Fred T. Korematsu Institute: 185

Gilman Collection, Purchase, Joseph M. Cohen Gift, 2005: 21 (left)

Gordon Hirabayashi: 183

Henri Meyer: 17 (bottom)

Hiromichi Matsuda: 163

Honoré Daumier: 17 (top)

Imperial War Museums: 165

Itou Kaneo: 35

Kobayashi Eitaku: 9

Leslie's Illustrated Weekly Newspaper: 28

Library of Congress: 43, 44, 53, 54, 80, 83, 90, 96, 127, 135 (top), 172, 175, 176

Los Angeles Times: 93

Los Angeles Times/American Stock Archive/Getty Images: 69

Masao Masuda and Susan Shoho Uyehara, Japanese American Living Legacy/Nikkei Writers Guild: 193

Miné Okubo: 107

Nagasaki Prefecture: 23

National Park Service: 105, 201

National Wide Pictorial Service: 182

Naval History & Heritage Command: 2

New York Police Department: 95

New York Times: 205

PD-US: 11, 15, 22, 26, 37, 39, 49, 63, 84, 150, 186, 206, 208

Ray Jerome Baker, courtesy of Bishop Museum: 51

Ringle Collection: 82

Roy D. Graves Pictorial Collection: 48

Ryosenji Treasure Museum: 21 (right)

Shinju Soto: 33

Special Collections & Archives, UC San Diego Library: 79

Time, Inc.: 151

Toyo Miyatake: 121

Uchida Kuichi: 24

UCLA, Library Special Collections, Charles E. Young Research Library: 74, 75

U.S. Air Force: 147, 161

U.S. Army: 149, 191

U.S. Army Center of Military History: 89, 195

U.S. Army Signal Corps: 152

U.S. Government: 202

U.S. Marine Corps: 164

U.S. National Archives and Records Administration: 3, 32, 70, 104, 116, 123, 148 (top), 148 (bottom), 156, 169

U.S. Navy: 76, 143

War Relocation Authority: 108

INDEX

Note: *Italic* page numbers refer to illustrations.